THE ECUMENICAL MOVEMENT

THE
ECUMENICAL MOVEMENT

WHAT IT IS AND WHAT IT DOES

NORMAN GOODALL

Second Edition

LONDON
OXFORD UNIVERSITY PRESS
NEW YORK TORONTO

Oxford University Press, Ely House, London W.1

Glasgow New York Toronto Melbourne Wellington
Bombay Calcutta Madras Karachi Lahore Dacca Kuala Lumpur Hong Kong
Cape Town Salisbury Ibadan Nairobi Lusaka Addis Ababa

First edition 1961
Second edition 1964
Reprinted 1966

73391

Set by W. & J. Mackay & Co. Ltd., Chatham, Kent
and reprinted lithographically by
Latimer Trend & Co. Ltd., Whitstable

PREFACE
to the Second Edition

This volume was first published shortly before the Third Assembly of the World Council of Churches at New Delhi. It was written in the light of the preparations for the Assembly and with knowledge of the action which the Assembly was likely to take in regard to the integration of the World Council of Churches and the International Missionary Council. The Assembly has since been held and the merging of these two expressions of the ecumenical movement has been ratified. Some of the material in the following chapters may therefore be read as descriptive of an organization now in being, not merely as an indication of what was proposed. In regard to the structure and working of the newly integrated organization no amendment to the descriptive part of this book is called for; only its tense need be changed.

It can also be said that, in a sense other than grammatical, the mood is now different. It is indicative, not conditional. Expectation, tinged only with a slight degree of uncertainty, has given place to realization. In so far as the World Council of Churches is a symbol and embodiment of the ecumenical movement, it can now be affirmed that in structure, purpose, and intention 'mission lies at the heart of the movement'.

The formal act of integration took place on the first day of the New Delhi Assembly and there was general recognition that it constituted a deeply impressive as well as significant moment. There was no dissentient voice or vote and the more formal constitutional proceedings led into an act of worship in which thanksgiving was offered 'for every fresh realization that to stay together in Christ means to go forth together with him'. The following prayer, taken from the order of service used, reflects something of the spirit in which the long discussions about this proposal were concluded in a decisive act:

O Thou who art the author and perfecter of our faith, to

whose grace we owe every good resolve, accept, we beseech Thee,to the praise of Thy glory, this offering of our obedience. Let the best which past years have held be carried into days of new and greater achievement for Thy name's sake. May the mind of Christ and the compassion of Christ so animate the life of this Council that in all its new relationships and undertakings He may have the pre-eminence. As we have been allowed of Thee to be put in trust with the Gospel, so keep us faithful to the trust, witnesses in all the world to the saving power of Christ, constrained by his love to live not unto ourselves. May the unity of Thy Church be deepened by obedience to her mission and her mission be furthered in the unity that is of Thy giving. So may the new resolves of this day be perfected in Thy holy and blessed will, until all the ends of the earth shall see Thy salvation and Thy Kingdom shall come, through Jesus Christ our Lord, to whom, with Thee and the Holy Spirit, belongeth all power, love, magnificence and mercy, now and for ever.

Only time can tell the outcome of all this. One strong impression carried from New Delhi by many participants was of an Assembly which—even more than its predecessors—was looking out upon the world and moving in thought and planning into the world; it was not turning in upon itself. It would be wrong to claim this solely as a first-fruit of the act of integration: it was something which had characterized the long preparations for the Assembly and which had for years been increasingly felt in all the Council's activities, as most of the chapters in this book indicate. In this respect the merging of the International Missionary Council with the World Council of Churches was the natural expression and culmination of something always inherent in the movement. Yet to a new degree the Assembly was pervaded by this sense of obligation to move out into the great areas of human need, to challenge unbelief and to meet at greater depth religious systems—old and new—which lack the saving name and power of Christ.

With the Third Assembly the Council became much more fully representative of the non-Roman churches than hitherto.

Twenty-three new member churches were admitted, bringing the total to 197;[1] at Amsterdam it was 147. Understandably, attention was specially focused on the coming of the Russian Orthodox Church into membership. On behalf of the Patriarch of Moscow and All Russia, the leader of the Russian delegation, Archbishop Nikodim, read a message to the Assembly in which the Patriarch said:

The Russian Orthodox Church is aware of the difficulties along the road towards the oneness of all Christians in the Church, and she is grateful to the Almighty for the mercy he has revealed in helping disunited Christendom to realize the sinfulness of this division and the duty incumbent upon it to achieve unity. She sees in the joint activities of the Churches an effective manifestation of that consciousness, which is directed towards finding ways of restoring the lost unity of all Christians.

The Russian Orthodox Church is prepared to strengthen the Orthodox witness of her Sister-Churches, members of the World Council of Churches in the Commission and Department of Faith and Order. She is prepared to take part in the work of the other commissions, sections, and departments of the Council, with the aim of furthering the development of Christian work, and doing everything in her power to serve mankind to establish brotherly kindness on earth (2 Peter 1.7), as well as equity (Psalm 99.4) and peace (Ephesians 6.15) among all peoples.

This was an historic turning-point, both in relation to the Russian Church's attitude to the ecumenical movement and in respect of the position of Orthodoxy *vis-à-vis* the rest of the non-Roman churches. In some of the earliest days in the ecumenical movement there were outstanding individuals who brought into its discussions and fellowship the distinctive contribution of the Eastern churches. On occasion, notable initiatives affecting the subsequent course of the movement came from highly placed leaders of the Orthodox world.

[1] Since the Third Assembly 7 more churches (listed in Appendix III (D)) have been admitted by the Central Committee in August 1962.

Since Amsterdam the responsibilities of membership in the World Council have been powerfully exercised by those Orthodox churches which became foundation members of the Council. But the action at New Delhi (which also brought the Orthodox Churches of Bulgaria, Roumania and Poland into membership) means that practically the whole of the Orthodox world is now fully committed to the ecumenical movement. Some of the great potentialities of this are obvious. There is a new accession of strength to the whole life of the World Council. There are new ties, between churches as well as individuals, across the east-west political frontiers. There are new possibilities of understanding and reconciliation at various points of tension in the contemporary scene. But perhaps the most important consideration arises from something which may be less immediately noticeable and of which there is as yet less awareness. For the Christian Church a new era is opening in the relationships between the Eastern and Western traditions. To a far wider and deeper extent than hitherto, there can and should be fruitful encounter in theological discourse, in liturgical perception, in such great issues as the relation between the Church and the world and the meaning of the Christian mission. It is of immense importance in regard to all this that other member-churches of the World Council should not only think of the New Delhi accessions as adding strength to an existing fellowship; they should be seen as the opening of a path into fields where there will be much to explore, to learn, to re-think and to experience, for the sake of growth in that full catholicity into which the ecumenical movement is leading us.

Two other features of New Delhi bear on this demand. For the first time observers from the Roman Catholic Church were present at a World Council meeting as, to some extent, official representatives of their Church. Individual Roman Catholics had attended earlier gatherings but in a personal capacity only. This new step is one result of that 'change of climate' which is referred to elsewhere in this volume. While the biggest questions concerning the implications of this change must as yet remain unanswered, every step of this kind is to be welcomed. There is no doubt that at New Delhi the presence of these observers was interpreted as both challenge and opportunity to reflect on the full meaning of 'ecumenical'.

From a very different angle the same challenge was posed by the coming of two Pentecostal churches into membership. While elements congenial to the movement which these churches represent are present in some of the older member-churches of the World Council, these two churches from Chile constitute the first of their kind to identify themselves fully with the Council. Their action was welcomed because of their significance spiritually and also because they are part of that most potent Latin American evangelicalism which needs to be better known and understood elsewhere.

The increase in the numerical membership of the Council, together with evidence that many more churches in Asia and Africa may be seeking membership, has reopened the question whether the *size* of a church should affect its eligibility for membership. The Constitution of the Council simply provides that 'the question of size must also be taken into consideration'. It is recognized that there are situations in which this factor must be outweighed by other considerations —for example, in regard to a very small Christian church set within a strongly Muslim context. While safeguarding this freedom to recognize exceptions, the Third Assembly instructed the Central Committee 'to interpret the criteria concerning size in such a way that, as a rule, no church with an inclusive membership of less than ten thousand be admitted to membership during the period between the Third and Fourth Assemblies'. In the discussion of this in the Central Committee, one of the Russian Orthodox members of the committee made a contribution which is worth recording here. 'The first Christian community in Jerusalem', he said,

was very small but it was a true Church representing the fullness of Christian truth. Many small churches today have this sense of possessing the fullness of the Gospel. Further, we do not know what the future will bring. Some small churches may become large and some large churches may become small. Small and large together must be included in our quest for unity.

More fundamental to the question of membership in the World Council was the discussion on the Basis, when the change anticipated in this volume[1] was effected. One or two hesitancies were expressed. A representative of the Mennonite Society feared that even the brief additions proposed implied that the Council was embarking on the process of creed-making. He was anxious lest any step of this kind might begin to exclude from membership 'groups whose members accept Jesus Christ as Lord without explicitly formulating the dogmatic implications thereof'. He was supported in this by a delegate from the Remonstrant Brotherhood or Arminian Church of the Netherlands. A similar view was voiced by a speaker from the Seventh Day Baptist General Conference in the United States. A Society of Friends delegate feared that 'in the basis of membership the major emphasis would tend to be on belief in Christ rather than on living in the light of Christ'. A leading American Presbyterian, who admitted that he had shared some of these hesitancies, said that he now recognized the desirability of making the proposed change 'in order to make clear to some churches outside our fellowship that it is not "mere togetherness" which is the foundation of the ecumenical movement but an authentic Christian confession based upon the Scriptures'. This whole discussion was of a high order and while there were a few abstentions from voting the new Basis was adopted by an overwhelmingly favourable decision.

Did the Third Assembly bring nearer the possibility of greater visible unity among the churches? In relation to this question many delegates left New Delhi with a sense of disappointment, or at least uncertainty if not bewilderment.

[1] See pp. 68–69.

On the one hand, the more comprehensive character of the gathering, with its undoubted richness of fellowship and sense of spiritual unity, was an experience moving in itself and as a foretaste of what might yet be. On the other hand, there was no sense of a new break-through at the points where progress towards formal unity continues to be impeded. The Archbishop of Canterbury (Dr. A. M. Ramsey) voiced, most persuasively, the reminder that, according to the Scriptures, holiness and unity are terms which must always be kept together. A truly Christian unity—he urged—cannot be won at a faster pace than our growth in Christian holiness. Another notable contribution came from an American Lutheran (Professor Joseph Sittler) who discussed the problem of ecclesiastical unity in the setting of 'cosmic unity'— that undefeatable purpose of God which is to sum up all things in Christ, 'in whom all things cohere'. Each of these very different utterances helped to lift the whole question out of the realm of purely ecclesiastical concepts and procedures. In the same way the whole plan of the Assembly, with its insistence on the inter-relation of unity, witness and service, helped to put the unity question within its proper, and more liberating, perspectives. Yet there was no single, leading and liberating word in this matter which the Assembly could then and there make its own, no new action which—as an Assembly—it could take with immediate and observable effect on the problem.

In part, this is no more than a reminder that responsibility for decisive action in many great realms of Christian obedience, including that of Christian unity, cannot be delegated to, or appropriated by, a world assembly. The point of responsibility, like the centre of authority, still lies with the member churches. In this respect the Third Assembly did, in fact, take action *vis-à-vis* the churches which may yet prove to be the beginning of a new and more fruitful period in the long quest for unity. As this book records,[1] prior to New Delhi the Central Committee had submitted to the churches a

[1] See pp. 144f.

tentative description of the nature of the unity to which experience within the ecumenical movement appears to be
leading us. The unity discussion at New Delhi focused clearly
on this statement, with the result that in an expanded and
slightly amended form[1] it has now been put before the
churches, in the name of the Assembly, and with the plea that
its many searching and radical implications will be wrestled
with. More especially, since this statement implies that the
crucial issue is whether Christian unity can be made visible
by 'all in each place' joining in 'fully committed fellowship'
and 'reaching out in witness and service', the challenge is
pre-eminently a challenge to every local congregation and
parish. Once again, unity is seen to be inseparable from
mission. This was the first and last and constantly recurrent
note of the Third Assembly. It was sounded in the opening
sessions when the delegates accepted the challenging symbol
of an integrated World Council–Missionary Council. It was
voiced again and again by the Asian and African delegations,
larger in number and more powerful in speech than at any
previous Assemblies. It rang out in the challenge of the
representatives of Youth with their impatience at every sign
of lethargy in relation to evangelism and disunity in witness.
It lay at the heart of the Assembly's repeated emphasis on
the responsibility of the Christian layman as the spearhead of
the Christian impact on society. And it was present in that
reshaping of the Basis of the Council in an additional phrase
no less important than any other of the amendments— '. . .
and therefore seek to fulfil together their common calling'.

The real answer to the question: 'Was New Delhi a
"success"?' waits on the response to this challenge by 'all in
each place'.

At a meeting of the Central Committee of the Council held
in the year following New Delhi one of the officers expressed

[1] See Appendix II (8); pp. 218–33

the view that 'New Delhi already seems to be a very long way off'. This did not imply that all for which the Third Assembly stood had become antiquated. It was an acknowledgement that the speed of history always seems to be gathering momentum and that great movements must move. Even as the second edition of this book goes to press the fourth World Conference on Faith and Order adds its Montreal chapter to the story written at Lausanne, Edinburgh and Lund: another meeting of the Central Committee takes place in Rochester, New York, and the Commission on World Mission and Evangelism (in line with the historic Assemblies of the International Missionary Council) prepares for a further world meeting at Mexico in December 1963. This book, with its supplementary information, is therefore still in the nature of an interim report, as every such document must be if the movement which it seeks to describe and interpret is true to itself.

Geneva   NORMAN GOODALL
1963

PREFACE

(1960)

When Mr. Nicodemus Boffin engaged Mr. Silas Wegg—a
literary man *with* a wooden leg—to initiate him into the
mysteries of Print, he produced for the first reading (as
Dickens reminds us) a sumptuous edition of *The Decline-and-
Fall-Off-The-Rooshan-Empire.* It was in 'Eight-wollumes. Red
and Gold. Purple ribbon in every wollume.' Before the
exercise began Boffin, it will be remembered, asked Wegg if he
was familiar with this great work; to which Wegg modestly
replied: 'I haven't been not to say right slap through him very
lately, having been otherwise employed.'

This book is written mainly for the otherwise employed,
who lack the opportunity—possibly the inclination—to go
right slap through all the historical and descriptive material
now available about the ecumenical movement. The official
history of the movement—*The History of the Ecumenical
Movement,* edited by Ruth Rouse and Stephen Neill—is a
superb achievement of eight hundred pages, though it lacks
the purple ribbon. The official report of the Edinburgh 1910
Conference, the most famous landmark in the movement,
occupies nine volumes (red and gold); the report of Jerusalem
1928 is in eight volumes, that of Tambaram 1938 in seven.
The records of most of the later meetings, including the
reports of Assemblies of the World Council of Churches, have
been compressed to more compassable dimensions, but the
reference shelf still grows and few but the most assiduous
students have been slap through its contents.

This book is not an epitome of all this material but it is
concerned with the story to which the kind of volume just
named provides the official key. I have depended on these
sources, drawn directly from them at some points and used
them, with other records, in the light of a personal involvement in the movement now covering nearly twenty-five years.
Sixteen of these have been spent as a whole-time staff member

of one or other of the organizations referred to in the volume.

I have tried to write, not for my colleagues in the movement—they can do this, and better, for themselves; nor for those who have already made a study of it. I have wanted to be of service to the growing number of men and women who have heard a little about these things and want to know more; and for those who may have had some contact with one part of the movement but would like to see the part within the whole. The book may possibly be of service, also, to some teachers who find in the Agreed Syllabus to which they are working that the story of the ecumenical movement's twentieth century phase appears as a significant period in Christian history.

Throughout this book I have repeatedly stressed the distinction between the ecumenical movement and the organizations which express or serve it. The distinction is important, but movement and organization are inseparable, and I hope that in its account of the two organizations which have played so great a part in these events this book will help its readers to appreciate the significance of the movement as a whole.

Although I cannot entirely separate myself as author from myself as a staff member of the International Missionary Council and the World Council of Churches, I must make it clear that this book is a personal exercise, not an official publication.

Responsibility for any judgements, opinions or speculations which these pages contain or reflect is mine alone. The volume has nevertheless been written with a sense of indebtedness to these two Councils and to my colleagues in their service greater than I can express.

NORMAN GOODALL

Benson
Oxford
1960

CONTENTS

Chapter I

ORIGINS

————◦◉◦————

What is 'Ecumenical'?

It was January 1945. For more than four years I had been familiar with black-out conditions in England. Then there came a night when I landed from the air on a brilliantly lighted airfield and drove through the shopping centre of a city at peace. For an hour or two I forgot the purpose of my visit as I gazed at shop-windows in a dazzle of lighting and looked at luxuries that seemed to belong to a world of long ago.

This was my first assignment as a whole-time servant of the ecumenical movement. It was one which took me from the nightly blitz in London to the peace-time conditions of Stockholm, a neutral capital. The British Foreign Office made the visit possible and the Royal Air Force provided the transport for a journey which took me over enemy occupied territory; we flew in a blacked-out plane at a height which made it necessary to wear oxygen masks.

There were no strings attached to the travel authorization of the Foreign Office. Yet I was visiting a neutral country to confer with people who were in and out of Germany. I received reports about conditions in Germany from friends who had been in Berlin the week before I met them, and I still recall the strange unreality of a moment at lunch when my host was interrupted by a long-distance telephone call from Germany. My assignment was not a Government one. It had to do solely with the world-wide work of the Church and the well-being of those engaged in it. In particular, I went to confer with leaders of the Swedish missionary societies and with colleagues from Norway and Denmark about ways and means of maintaining in war-time the missionary work of the continental churches—the Scandinavian, Dutch, and French. But not these alone; my mission was equally concerned with the missionary work of the German churches.

It was no small thing that even in time of war facilities should be given for this kind of mission. More will be said in a later chapter about the undertaking in which this visit was only an episode. The point to be noted here is that this kind of work was possible because there existed an international Christian organization whose standing and integrity were recognized by governments. I could cross difficult frontiers because of the organization I represented. Moreover, while I happen to be an English Congregationalist, I was travelling as the emissary of an organization whose membership was interdenominational as well as international. I was the servant of American Episcopalians, Methodists, Lutherans, Presbyterians, and Baptists; of German and Scandinavian Lutherans; of Anglicans and British Free Churchmen, and a host of other Christian agencies of differing nations and denominations. I was acting in the name of Christians in the East as well as in the West.

The movement which made possible this kind of thing has come to be known as the Ecumenical Movement. This word *ecumenical* does not trip lightly from English lips. Has it too many syllables for us? It is no longer than the word *economical*. It is shorter than *episcopalian* and much briefer and less clumsy than *undenominational* or *interdenominational*. Yet in spite of some resistance to its use, the word seems gradually to be finding its place in the vernacular of Christians. It is, in fact, not a new word, and there are some people who have been long familiar with it. When Pope John XXIII announced in 1959 his intention to convene an Ecumenical Council, the term appeared as one that had been current in certain ecclesiastical circles for centuries. On the continent of Europe and in the United States of America it has for a long time been in commoner use than in England amongst Protestants as well as Roman Catholics. In scores of different languages it now appears in the same spelling and without translation. The fact is that at a very early stage in Christian history a word was needed to express the range of the Church's fellowship. As so often happened, the Greeks had a word for it, and this Greek word passed into the language of the whole world.

It was appropriate that it should do so, for the Greek word *oikoumene* simply means 'the whole inhabited world'. In its earliest use it described that portion of the earth which had been brought within the orbit of Greek civilization as opposed to barbarian lands. Then, with the rise of Rome, the Greeks hailed the Romans as the masters of the *oikoumene*. The Roman Emperor Marcus Aurelius was eulogized as 'the Benefactor and Saviour of the whole *Oikoumene*'. In this Greek and Roman usage the geographical breadth of the word carried with it an awareness of a society or civilization held together under common loyalties and standards. There is an interesting and significant use of the word in this sense in Acts xvii.6, where Paul and Silas are described as 'These that have turned the *oikoumene* upside down'. Turning the *oikoumene* upside down meant disturbing the stability of the imperial rule; it threatened the cohesion of society. As the next verse in the Book of Acts puts it: 'These all do contrary to the decrees of Caesar, saying that there is another king, one Jesus'.

It is worth noting here two other uses of the Greek word *oikoumene* in the New Testament. In Matthew xxiv.14 there is the declaration that 'This Gospel of the Kingdom shall be preached in all the world (. . . in all the *oikoumene*) for a witness unto all nations'. Again, in Hebrews ii.5 there is a reference to 'the *oikoumene* to come'—the world to come: this future *oikumene* is the redeemed and perfected society of the Kingdom of God.

The word ecumenical, then, is deeply rooted in the centuries and has played its part in Greek, Roman, and Christian civilizations. Such a word has potentialities which belong to a living thing; it has to be defined and defined again. Some of its contemporary meanings in relation to the Ecumenical Movement will be illustrated as this book describes the growth of

this modern movement, but something of its origins should be
remembered whenever we use it in reference to the world-
wide scope of the Church's fellowship and the world-wide
range of its task.

The Ecumenical Movement of today is a movement, not a
single organization. Many different agencies give expression
to the movement or contribute to it. No one organization is
its exclusive instrument or holds monopoly rights in it. This
book is chiefly concerned with two world-wide councils which
are playing a distinctive part in the movement—the World
Council of Churches and the International Missionary Council;
but both of these spring from a source which has created and
used (and still uses) other agencies for its own great purpose.
This original source lies in the Christian Faith itself; it is that
spiritual power which draws men together in Christ and then
sends them out in his name to claim the whole *oikoumene* for
him. The tragic contradiction in Christian history is that
even while men have been drawn together in Christ, the
unity of Christians with one another has been a precarious
unity. St Paul's Epistles are eloquent on this theme. All are
one in Christ. Christ is not divided. There should be no
schism in the body. And yet much of Paul's writing is directed
towards the healing of divisions. This paradox reappears in
the later history of the Church, with its major crises of
disunion in the great schism of the eleventh century between
Eastern and Western (or Byzantine and Roman) Catholicism,
and in the European Reformation of the sixteenth century.
Yet, even across such great divides as these, there were
always men and women who never lost sight of the fact that
Christians constitute a distinctive, world-wide community—a
single *oikoumene* of Christ. And on either side of these dividing
lines there have been those who have sought to make more
manifest this given, world-wide unity in Christ.

Prominent amongst them, in modern history, have been the
missionaries and the evangelists. The 'father of modern
missions', William Carey, proposed in 1806 that there should

be convened 'a meeting of all denominations of Christians at
The Cape of Good Hope somewhere about 1810', to be
followed by a similar gathering once every ten years. Carey
made this suggestion in a letter to his friend Andrew Fuller,
secretary of the Baptist Missionary Society, but Fuller was not
enthusiastic. 'I consider this as one of bro' Carey's pleasing
dreams', he wrote.

If Carey's pleasing dream was not realized on a world
scale, it found partial but significant fulfilment on a national
or regional basis. From Carey's day onwards there were held
in India, Japan, China, and Latin America gatherings of
missionaries of various nationalities and denominational
allegiances. They were convened for mutual conference
regarding the needs and problems of the missionary enterprise and they did much to foster as well as express a unity
which over-arched denominational differences. 'No shadow of
bigotry falls on us here', wrote Carey, concerning one of
these gatherings. 'It would have done your heart good to have
joined us. . . . In these meetings the utmost harmony
prevails and a union of hearts unknown between persons of
different denominations in England.'

As a matter of fact, 'persons of different denominations in
England' were not altogether denied this enriching experience. More than ten years before Carey suggested the Cape
of Good Hope meeting, missionary zeal had brought together
in London a group of Anglicans, Presbyterians, Methodists,
and Independents in the formation of the London Missionary
Society. At the inaugural meeting of this Society in 1795 an
Anglican preacher declared that 'The petty distinctions among
us, of names and forms, the diversities of administrations and
modes of Church Order, we agree, shall this day be merged
in the greater, nobler and characteristic name of Christians.'
This was a signal illustration—but not the only one—of a
movement in fellowship across the denominations. Until a few
years ago (when its place was taken by more comprehensive
organizations) there continued to meet in London an interdenominational group which had an unbroken history going

back to 1819. It bore the unexciting name of the London Secretaries Association. Its membership was composed of secretaries of missionary societies, Anglican and Free Church, and meetings were convened for the original stated purpose of 'mutual counsel and fellowship'. A hundred and forty years ago relationships between missionary societies in England had already transcended the denominational.

It was not only concern for missionary work abroad which helped men to realize the nature of the *oikoumene* to which they belonged as Christians. Evangelical zeal in England and Scotland, on the European continent and in the U.S.A., brought representatives of many denominations together in experiences comparable to those which Carey and his friends and their successors enjoyed in India. In 1842 a German pastor toured England, France, Belgium, and Switzerland, pleading for an organization which would constitute 'a spiritual union amongst all those in all lands who are fighting for God's holy cause and for the pure Gospel.' In the same year, at a meeting of the Congregational Union in London, John Angell James urged the formation of an Evangelical Union of Protestants, while similar pleas were being voiced in Scotland by such men as Thomas Chalmers. These were some of the steps which resulted in the creation of the Evangelical Alliance which was launched in London in 1846. Eight hundred delegates from more than fifty denominations attended this inaugural meeting; they came from most of the European countries, including Scandinavia, and from the U.S.A. and Canada. More will be said in a later chapter about the present work of the Evangelical Alliance and its links with the World Evangelical Fellowship; here it should be noted for its part in the ecumenical movement from the earlier decades of the nineteenth century onwards. More than a hundred years ago the word ecumenical was frequently used within the Alliance to denote the fact that it transcended national and denominational divisions.

There were other areas of Christian activity within which this same sense of unity in fellowship and purpose was being experienced. Notable amongst these were the Bible Societies.

Their primary purpose was the translation and circulation of the Scriptures but in this task they drew together representatives of a great diversity of nations and denominations. The British and Foreign Bible Society came into existence in 1804 with a committee composed equally of Anglicans and Dissenters. It had an Anglican and Free Church secretary and a 'foreign secretary' drawn from the European continent. This British society was, in fact, the outcome of Continental (German) evangelical influence as well as of British zeal. Even within its first ten years it formed branch societies in many other countries and established contacts not only with 'evangelical' churchmen but with representatives of the Orthodox Churches in Russia and Greece, with Copts and Armenians and with the Syrian Church in Malabar, South India. The great American Bible Society was formed twelve years after the launching of the British Society; other national societies with the same aims followed, and when these were federated in an organization called the United Bible Societies in 1947 sixteen of these interdenominational agencies were represented in the new body. Closely linked with the work and purpose of the British and Foreign Bible Society was the Religious Tract Society which was formed even earlier—in 1799. This again worked through, and for, all denominations, and under its present title of the United Society for Christian Literature it continues to express the united concern and action of the churches in the promotion of Christian literature.

In some respects the most fruitful of these areas within which Christian unity in experience and action was being furthered was the student world. Here the chief ecumenical agencies were the Y.M.C.A., the Y.W.C.A. and the Student Christian Movement. The Y.M.C.A. began in England (with an English Congregational layman—George Williams—as its foremost figure). It soon spread to the United States where it achieved spectacular success in colleges and universities. Prominent in the American Y.M.C.A. was D. L. Moody whose influence on Henry Drummond in Edinburgh was amongst the creative forces which shaped the Student Christian

Movement. There was inter-play between these movements and countries; there were similar stirrings in continental Europe, and as an outcome of these many manifestations of the same spirit the World's Student Christian Federation was born in 1895. For several decades before this and through all the succeeding years the Student Christian Movement has helped generations of students, of every nationality, to understand and experience a quality of Christian discipleship which has given them a profound awareness of an *oikoumene* in Christ. They have been members of denominations; but they have known that they belong to a world-wide Christian society, with a single, central loyalty and a common purpose.

*   *   *

Edinburgh 1910

While all this was happening, William Carey's pleasing dream of a world-wide gathering of Christian leaders, inter-denominational in its scope and missionary in its purpose, was nearing realization. Here the great landmark was an event which was commemorated in 1960 by special Jubilee services in Westminster Abbey and St. Giles Cathedral, Edinburgh, in New York, Toronto, and elsewhere. These services were acts of thanksgiving for the fiftieth anniversary of what has come to be known as 'Edinburgh 1910'.

Edinburgh 1910 was called a World Missionary Conference. It was not the first time that a missionary gathering international in its membership had been held. London had been the scene in 1888 of a meeting attended by more than fifteen hundred people from many different countries and churches; distinguished churchmen and missionary leaders from Germany, Norway, and the United States added lustre to a gathering which included such men as Henry Drummond, and Hudson Taylor of the China Inland Mission. A still larger conference of this kind was held in New York in 1900; characteristically, perhaps, it was described as 'the largest missionary conference ever held'. This included the blessed word *ecumenical* in its title, for it was called an Ecumenical

Missionary Conference. The word was used—so it was explained—'because the plan of campaign which it proposes covers the whole area of the inhabited globe'. The speakers included outstanding Asians, with several Indian women amongst them, and such notable westerners as Timothy Richard, Wardlaw Thompson, Robert E. Speer, and a young chairman of the youth committee of the Conference named John R. Mott.

John R. Mott is one of the key names in the whole story of this modern ecumenical movement and he really marks the turning point between all the earlier international meetings and Edinburgh 1910. Mott was an American layman—a Methodist—born to lead, with a presence, an utterance, a will, and a mind all beautifully tempered for the tasks to which he gave himself. The turning point of his career was in 1886 when he attended a student conference. Moody was leader; Sankey was singing 'Tell it out among the nations'; and William Ashmore, as one summoning men to a war of conquest, was rallying youth to world missionary service. From this point onwards Mott was determined—as he put it—'to lay siege to the student world'. He became one of the architects of the Y.M.C.A. and the principal founder of the World's Student Christian Federation and for years he was the foremost evangelist amongst students the world over. A picture from Egypt can be taken as typical of hundreds of such occasions:

He came to Cairo and addressed a meeting of Egyptian students in one of the leading theatres. Although he spoke by interpretation, he swept those students off their feet and his impassioned words were applauded again and again by men who usually are difficult to stir.

For years Mott was the central figure in at least four major world movements: he was President of the World's Alliance of the Y.M.C.A.s, General Secretary and later Chairman of the World's Student Christian Federation, Chairman of the International Missionary Council, and the first Honorary President of the World Council of Churches. An American Free

Churchman, he was so much at home in the world of Eastern Orthodoxy that he was awarded a D.D. by the Russian Orthodox Theological Seminary in Paris. A brilliant organizer, he was a man of deep spirituality. 'Organize as though there were no such thing as prayer', he used to say, 'and pray as though there were no such thing as organization.' Honours were lavished upon him as the years passed—university degrees, decorations from governments—oriental and occidental—and the Nobel Peace Prize. 'The world's most useful man', was the description of him given by President Woodrow Wilson who tried in vain to secure his services as American Ambassador to China. But Mott's central and abiding characteristics were his intense personal devotion to the living Christ and a passion to win others to the same experience and loyalty. A year or so before his death I asked him the unoriginal question: 'If you had your time over again what would you do?' The answer was quick and eager: 'The same, God willing; but I would start with school-children and not wait until they reached student-age.'

Mott, then in his early forties, was chairman of the World Missionary Conference of Edinburgh 1910. For the preceding two years he had given his best thought to its preparation and it could be said that he spent the rest of his life in the follow-up work of this meeting. In itself the gathering was remarkable enough. Christian conferences, national and international, have become such a commonplace since that it is not easy to recapture the uniqueness of this assembly. But in its range of representation, the nature of its preparations, and the organization set up to carry on its work, it broke new ground. It had commanded the support of many of the most responsible leaders in the churches and in the missionary movement. Anglicans of the stature of Archbishops Randall Davidson and Cosmo Gordon Lang, Bishop Gore and Bishop Montgomery (father of Field-Marshal Montgomery) were involved in it. Free Church leaders such as R. F. Horton, Richard Glover, J. H. Ritson, F. W. Macdonald, George Robson, and D. S. Cairns were delegates. Great names from the European continent appear in its reports—Julius Richter of Germany and Alfred Boegner of France; and the American delegation included Robert E. Speer, Douglas Mackenzie, Logan Roots and Charles H. Brent. Amongst the twelve hundred members of the conference were such laymen as Sir Robert Laidlaw, Professor Michael Sadler, and Sir Albert Spicer from Britain; Count Moltke from Denmark; Silas McBee, Seth Low, and William Jennings Bryan from the U.S.A. Missionaries whose names had long been household words in Europe and America, with the principal officers of the great missionary societies of the West, brought their distinctive contribution; and— though their number was small—the most significant portent in the membership was to be seen in the Asian and African delegates. Among these were two men who, for many years to come, were to enrich the Churches East and West through their outstanding qualities—Cheng Ching Yi of China and V. S. Azariah of India. Even the youths who served as ushers were a significant team, for they included William Temple, later Archbishop of Canterbury, John Baillie, later a President of the World Council of Churches, and John McLeod Campbell, later Master of the Charterhouse and, like Baillie, among the senior statesmen of the Church in 1960, when the fiftieth anniversary of Edinburgh 1910 was celebrated.

Edinburgh 1910 did not end with the inspiration of its own sessions. One of the new things about it was the provision it made for carrying on its work. It closed with the formation of a Continuation Committee. Amidst today's plethora of committees it would be easy to regard this action as an anti-climax. It was, however, very far from being this. The con-ference itself, with all its inspiration, had a severely business-like quality in it. As one of its recorders said, it did not consist of 'an elaborate programme of addresses performed before admiring crowds'. Most of its participants had been involved in hard preparatory work, writing and reading papers on questions of missionary policy, and for the greater part of the sessions speeches were limited to seven minutes. (As another observer wrote: 'Some showed that it was

possible to make a great speech in seven minutes; some
showed, equally, that even after seventy-times-seven minutes
the speech would still have been a small one.') Most of these
business discussions proved that still more solid work was
needed if those who cared about winning the world for Christ
were to fashion policies adequate to a new day. It was in this
conviction that the Continuation Committee was appointed
and launched upon its task. What then followed became of
lasting significance largely because the committee had as its
whole-time secretary the man who, as one of Mott's lieu-
tenants, had also been the principal secretary of the conference.
This was another layman—a Scot—who, today well into his
eighties, still exercises one of the most penetrating and ardent
minds with which any movement has been blessed in modern
times. His name is J. H. Oldham.

Edinburgh 1910 and the subsequent course of the ecumenical movement are inseparable from John R. Mott's leadership.
They are similarly inseparable from the wisdom and tenacious
devotion of J. H. Oldham. His was the searching, reflective
mind which complemented Mott's gifts and set the stamp of
thoroughness upon all the preparatory work and the proceedings of the Edinburgh conference. Depth and clarity of
thought, a swift and unerring discrimination between the
relevant and irrelevant, a capacity for constraining others to
give of their best and think harder than ever before, these are
some of the characteristics which Oldham has displayed since
early manhood. Coupled with these powers there has always
been in him an acute sensitiveness to the significance of
contemporary events. This could be called political acumen:
it is truer to call it prophetic insight—a capacity to appraise
the passing scene in the light of those fundamental truths
which have their origin in Christ and derive their living quality
from him.

Oldham, like Mott, subsequently shared in a succession of
enterprises which were all part of the ecumenical movement.
He was the first and most distinguished secretary of the
International Missionary Council. He carried chief res-

ponsibility for the Oxford Conference of 1937 on Church, Community, and State. During the Second World War he launched and edited the *Christian News-Letter* and created the Christian Frontier Movement. He was one of the most influential advisers in the formation of the British Council of Churches, the World Council of Churches, and the Commission of the Churches on International Affairs. It was in line with his vision and conviction that much of his best work was done outside the explicitly Christian organizations of churches and missions. It was, for example, due to Oldham more than to any other single person, that in 1925 a group of experts on African questions decided to create an International Bureau of African Languages and Literature. With its headquarters in London, it secured the participation, from other countries besides Britain, of government administrators, scientific and educational workers, representatives of commerce as well as missions. Oldham charted its course, secured the necessary financial help from such sources as the Rockefeller Foundation and, while still serving the International Missionary Council, was for some years honorary Director of the Bureau. Men of the calibre of Lionel Curtis, Lord Lothian, Lord Lugard, and Lord Hailey co-operated closely with him in an enterprise which eventually became the International Institute of African Affairs.

This was one illustration of the way in which Oldham's conception of Christian responsibility in public affairs found characteristic expression. Many years later and beyond his eightieth birthday, he was giving himself afresh to the needs of Africa—especially to the problems of a multi-racial society —with a thoroughness and acumen which made his home a rendezvous for men of all races who were carrying the daily burden of political, legislative, and administrative responsibility. With all this, it is significant that amongst his many published works the most widely-known and used is a little book for the pocket called *A Devotional Diary*.

Later chapters of this book will touch on some of these movements which Oldham influenced. Here the point to be emphasized is that Edinburgh 1910 became momentous largely because it enjoyed the partnership of Mott and Oldham. It was this same partnership which set to work to make the Edinburgh Continuation Committee something much more than 'just another committee'.

A little more than a decade after its formation the Edinburgh Continuation Committee changed its name and became the International Missionary Council. In this intervening decade much had happened. In the first place, the movement of which this small committee was an expression had become still further known and respected for the solidity of its work. It was a focal point for serious study and fresh thinking concerning the world mission of the Church. One of the earliest undertakings of the Continuation Committee was the launching of a quarterly journal, the *International Review of Missions*, which quickly took a leading place amongst the scholarly quarterlies. It was international in its contributors, its editorial board, and in the range of its concerns. It reflected and served the interests of all denominations and combined a high standard of thought and writing with a lively attention to the most immediate tasks and problems of the missionary enterprise. Its two hundredth number will appear in October 1961—no small achievement for a quarterly journal. What matters more is that through all these years it has been acknowledged throughout the world for the importance of its contributions to a proper understanding of the world situation and the meaning of the Christian mission.

The *International Review of Missions* is one illustration of the way in which the Edinburgh Continuation Committee set about its task. The Committee did more, however, than promote a literary discussion of the frontier tasks of the churches. Just as in the Edinburgh conference there had been a fruitful meeting of minds from different nations and denominations, so this process of personal meeting continued; and it was deepened by developments which ensured that people acquired the habit of thinking and working together, across their denominational and national boundaries, as a regular part of their job. One example of this may be taken from the work

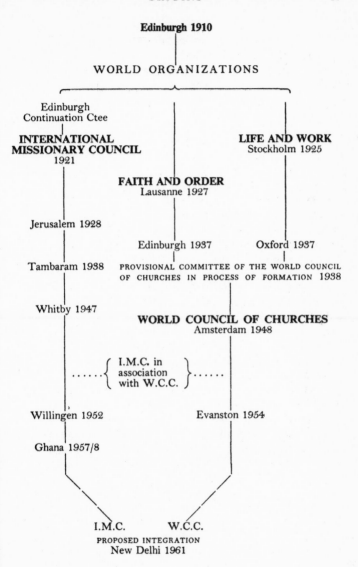

Edinburgh 1910

WORLD ORGANIZATIONS

Edinburgh
Continuation Ctee
**INTERNATIONAL
MISSIONARY COUNCIL**
1921

LIFE AND WORK
Stockholm 1925

FAITH AND ORDER
Lausanne 1927

Jerusalem 1928

Edinburgh 1937   Oxford 1937

Tambaram 1938   PROVISIONAL COMMITTEE OF THE WORLD COUNCIL
OF CHURCHES IN PROCESS OF FORMATION 1938

Whitby 1947

WORLD COUNCIL OF CHURCHES
Amsterdam 1948

...... { I.M.C. in
        association
        with W.C.C. } ......

Willingen 1952   Evanston 1954

Ghana 1957/8

I.M.C.   W.C.C.
PROPOSED INTEGRATION
New Delhi 1961

of the Conference of Missionary Societies in Great Britain and Ireland, commonly known as the Conference of British Missionary Societies. This is the member-unit in Britain of the International Missionary Council. It expresses on the national plane the purposes and character of the international organization.

*   *   *

The Conference of British Missionary Societies

There is a building in London (near Sloane Square) called Edinburgh House. The name was adopted to commemorate Edinburgh 1910. The London office of the International Missionary Council is there, but the principal tenant of the house is the Conference of British Missionary Societies. J. H. Oldham inevitably had a hand in the launching of this, as did his co-secretary at the 1910 conference, Kenneth Maclennan. Maclennan was another layman whose fine business competence was one of the great gifts to this whole movement. He had qualities which specially appealed to Oldham—a clear, precise mind and a swift efficiency. 'I have often asked myself,' said Oldham in a conversation about Maclennan, 'what significance God attaches to efficiency. While it may not be a moral value, it has a spiritual quality.' Maclennan—formerly a practising lawyer—possessed this in abundance. Several years before Edinburgh 1910 he had played a leading part in creating what became known as the United Council for Missionary Education. This brought together a group of British missionary societies for the purpose of jointly promoting missionary study on the basis of textbooks specially prepared and published by the Council. After an unpretentious beginning it soon won widespread confidence and support and thirty years later it could boast of having published six million copies of missionary books and pamphlets. Maclennan's work with this Council and his share in the secretarial work of the Edinburgh conference led to his becoming the first whole-time secretary of the Conference of British Missionary Societies which was formally launched in 1912. There was inevitable overlapping between this British organization and the Continuation Committee of Edinburgh, but the British Conference became the main instrument within the British scene for giving effect to the ideals and policies formulated at Edinburgh. In its inception about forty British societies became members. These included the principal Anglican and Free Church missions. About sixty missionary societies and other agencies are now within its membership. The range of co-operation can be seen in the fact that amongst the members are: the Church Missionary Society and the Society for the Propagation of the Gospel, the Society for the Promotion of Christian Knowledge, and the United Society for Christian Literature; the missionary agencies of the Presbyterian, Methodist, and Baptist Churches; interdenominational bodies such as the London Missionary Society, the British and Foreign Bible Society, and the Mission to Lepers; the Salvation Army, the Friends Service Council, the Assemblies of God, and the Regions Beyond Missionary Union. The majority of these contribute to the work of the Conference on an agreed percentage of their own income. The annual budget of the Conference is approximately £16,000[1]; additional funds are also raised for special purposes.

Like other expressions of the ecumenical movement the Conference of British Missionary Societies is primarily consultative in character; it is not a centralized agency administering the work of its member societies. Its most characteristic and useful service lies in the fact that a week seldom passes without a group of missionary leaders, representing different denominations, meeting at Edinburgh House for the purpose of sharing information and discussing some aspect of missionary policy. These meetings either take the form of 'area committees' or committees concerned with some general function of the missions. The former deal with problems in particular

---

[1] In illustration of the regular support which the Conference receives on the agreed basis, the following amounts were contributed for the year 1959: Methodist Missionary Society £3,298; Church Missionary Society £2,420; Society for the Propagation of the Gospel £1,340; London Missionary Society £1,095; Salvation Army £100; Friends Service Council £165; Assemblies of God £95.

reg ions—Africa, the Middle East, Asia, and the Far East. The latter may be concerned with Medical Mission policy, the promotion of Christian literature, the training of missionary candidates, or missionary education in the home churches. Special groups are convened as special needs arise—in regard, for example, to developments in China or new opportunities in Tibet or the latest crisis in Africa or the Middle East. Although responsibility for decision and administration remains with the missionary societies, this process of regular consultation frequently leads to the adoption of common policies. Further, when financial support is needed for united undertakings overseas— as in some of the united colleges or hospitals or in literature programmes—it is within these committees at Edinburgh House that agreements are made as to the proportionate help which the societies shall give to the common undertaking. On this basis of continuous contact in the sharing of information, convictions and plans there has been built up within the Conference of British Missionary Societies a degree of understanding and confidence which gives considerable weight to any representations which the Conference may make. This was evident, for example, through the work of its India Committee during the years of greatest tension between India and Britain prior to the granting of political independence. There was constant consultation between missionary leaders with special knowledge of India; there was a frank sharing of views with friends in India—Christian and non-Christian; there were delegations to Delhi and to the India Office in London; and although it is impossible to assess the result of activity of this kind, there is no doubt that it was a worth-while contribution to the ministry of reconciliation. Even more significant has been the service rendered by the British Conference to African affairs. Following the expert contribution of Oldham[1] to the study of African problems, the Conference enjoyed a succession of secretaries greatly respected in

[1] Oldham was for some years concurrently a secretary of the Conference of British Missionary Societies and of the International Missionary Council.

Government as well as mission circles for their knowledge and judgement in African affairs. Conference representatives have shared in the work of various Government commissions on educational policy, and the present Advisory Committee (to the Secretary of State) on Education in the Colonies is the result of an initiative taken by the Conference in 1924.

In times of emergency—especially those arising during war-time—the existence of a well-established united agency such as the British Conference has proved invaluable. Raising funds for the victims of floods in China or famine in India, negotiating with the Bank of England and the Treasury during currency restrictions, handling visa problems for missionary societies during the limitations on war-time travel—these and countless similar services have been made possible by the existence of a place called Edinburgh House. And all such services have been part of that central purpose of the original Edinburgh conference—the furtherance of the world mission of the Church.

Chapter II

CO-OPERATION IN MISSION

The International Missionary Council

The Conference of British Missionary Societies is by no means the only agency of its kind within which Christian leaders, for many decades, have been habitually working together for the furtherance of the world mission of the Church. This British organization has its counterparts in other countries. Indeed, some of these other associations are older than the British Conference and even antedated Edinburgh 1910. As early as 1885 a group of twelve German missionary societies formed a Committee of the German Evangelical Missions primarily in order that dealings with the German Colonial Office might be on a united basis. This practical need led to growing fellowship between the German missions. The successor body to this earlier committee—the German Missionary Council—is now a focal point for the interdenominational study of missionary policy. Like the British Conference, it is also a valuable clearing-house and a centre from which much united activity is planned. In the years immediately following Edinburgh 1910 similar missionary conferences, drawing their membership from various denominations, were established in other continental countries—Sweden, Denmark, Norway, Finland, Switzerland, and the Netherlands.

In 1893—again some years before Edinburgh 1910—the largest of these national conferences of missions was launched in the United States of America, with a membership which crossed the Canadian border and included missionary agencies in that country. This organization was called the Foreign Missions Conference of North America. Its membership grew rapidly from that of twenty-three mission boards to nearly eighty. Much of the preparatory work for Edinburgh 1910 was done within this North American Conference whose activities were largely in fields comparable to those touched on in the preceding description of the British Conference. It developed strong specialist agencies concerned with the policy of medical missions and rural or agricultural missions, and one of its lasting contributions to missionary research and study was its creation of a Missionary Research Library in New York. This now contains one of the most complete collections of missionary literature in the world and is a place of pilgrimage for students—of all nationalities—of the history and policy of missions. Just as the British Conference brought together Christian leaders with special competence in African, Indian, and Middle Eastern affairs, so this North American Conference on the basis of its numerous and close ties with Japan and China, Korea, Formosa, and Thailand, has made its own distinctive contribution to the Christian understanding of the Far East as well as to the discussion of missionary policies in these regions. In 1950 this Foreign Missions Conference of North America became an integral part of the National Council of the Churches of Christ in the United States of America and now functions within that Council as the Division of Foreign Missions. As with the British Conference its main support comes from its member missions. Its normal budget in recent years has been approximately $700,000 (£250,000). Still larger amounts have been raised annually for special purposes.

There were from the beginning close contacts between these various national or regional federations of missionary agencies. For natural reasons the ties were specially close between the North American and British Conferences. The Edinburgh Conference of 1910, although exercising no directive authority over the churches and missions represented in its membership, had proved to be a point where general agreement on broad issues of missionary policy and strategy had been reached. In particular, the Conference challenged Christians in the West to reckon with the astonishing opportunities provided by events in Asia. The year 1910 marked one of the greatest revolutions in China's history—the end of the Manchu Dynasty and the birth of that modern China which has since moved from revolution to revolution. A few years previously Japan had leaped into prominence as a modern power. In India the National Congress was taking shape and events were already in train which found their inevitable culmination in 1947 in the independence of India. Fifty years ago one of the most obvious implications of this widespread ferment in Asia was the challenge it presented to the Christian west—for service (especially in the fields of education and medicine), for sympathetic understanding, and Christian witness. This summons was presented in force to the Edinburgh Conference and through it to the churches of the West. Despite the coming of war four years later—a cataclysm which did not seem even to be a possibility in 1910—the period between 1910 and about 1928 was one which saw the steady expansion of western missions into the orient, especially from the United States. Many of the great Christian medical and educational institutions in Asia were established or greatly strengthened during this period and in much of this expansion there was consultation and planning between the national missionary conferences of North America and Britain and their opposite numbers on the European continent. In this growth of international and interdenominational missionary policy-making the Edinburgh Continuation Committee, with Mott as its chairman and Oldham as secretary, played a natural part; but these leaders soon recognized that if there was to be a fully responsible international centre for this kind of collaboration, it needed to be more than a committee which existed in 'continuation' of a particular conference. In 1921, therefore, the Edinburgh Continuation Committee gave place to a new organization which assumed the name of the International Missionary Council. The principal functions of the Council were:

to stimulate thinking and investigation on missionary questions;

to make the results available for all missionary societies and missions;

to help co-ordinate the activities of the national missionary
organizations of the different countries and of the societies
they represent;

to bring about united action where necessary in missionary
matters;

to help unite Christian public opinion in support of freedom
of conscience and religion and of missionary liberty;

to help unite the Christian forces of the world in seeking
justice in international and inter-racial relations.

Seventeen national organizations became members of this
International Missionary Council. They were predominantly
missionary councils, that is, federations on a national basis of
missionary societies. Of these seventeen, thirteen were in the
lands of what are sometimes called the 'older churches'—
churches rooted in the life of Europe and the U.S.A., of
Australia, New Zealand, or South Africa. The remaining four
were in Asia or the Middle East; they were in countries
commonly referred to as 'mission fields'. These four councils
had a special significance for the future of the International
Missionary Council. They contained within their membership
representatives of missionary societies working in these fields;
they were also beginning to include delegates from what were
then being called 'younger churches'. These were the indigenous or national churches which were emerging in Asia and
Africa. The missionary councils in these lands were thus not
only councils of missionaries; they were bodies which were
becoming representative of the indigenous Christian forces in
the country. As this representative character increased, most
of these councils changed their name from 'missionary councils'
to 'Christian councils' or 'councils of churches'. Thus in India
the National Missionary Council became in 1921 the National
Christian Council; in Indonesia a National Council of Churches,
formed in 1950, took over functions previously performed by
the Missions Consulate of the Netherlands Indies. This kind
of development has recently been accompanied by a further
significant symptom. In some of these national councils the
missionary societies are no longer directly represented as

voting members. Membership is wholly composed of the indigenous churches. If a 'foreign' missionary finds himself elected as a voting member, it is not by virtue of his status as a missionary; he is there as a delegate appointed by the indigenous church.

During recent years national councils of the kind just illustrated have assumed increasing prominence within the membership of the International Missionary Council. The original membership of the Council has grown from seventeen to thirty-eight councils. Of these thirty-eight, only fourteen are missionary councils in the lands of the older churches; the remaining twenty-four are Christian councils in Asia, Africa, the Middle East, Latin America, and the Caribbean.

Structurally, then, the International Missionary Council is a world-wide federation of national councils. It works through an Assembly, held every four years, at which all the national councils are represented by delegations proportionate to their size. Between these large assemblies, a small Administrative Committee carries responsibility and special committees are convened for particular purposes. The Council has offices in London and New York. Since 1951 it has also shared responsibility with the World Council of Churches for the maintenance of an East Asia secretariat with its principal office in Burma. The present Chairman of the Council is an African and there are eight vice-chairmen drawn from different countries and representing various denominations.[1]

What does the Council do? The statement of its original functions, quoted above, indicates that the main emphasis is on study, counsel, and co-ordination. It is not an international missionary society conducting operations; nor is its structure mainly that of an administrative body. There have, however, been many occasions on which the existence of an international

---

[1] In 1960 the Chairman was Dr. C. G. Baeta of Ghana. The Vice-chairmen were: The Rt. Rev. W. D. L. Greer (Bishop of Manchester); Dr. Irene Jones (U.S.A.); Dr. Helen Kim (Korea); Dr. D. G. Moses (India); the Rt. Rev. Chandu Ray (Pakistan); Dr. Alfonso Rodriguez (Cuba); Dr. B. G. M. Sundkler (Sweden). The General Secretary is Bishop Lesslie Newbigin.

agency of this kind has made possible administrative action of special significance and timeliness. Here is one of the most notable of them.

The Treaty of Versailles, which followed the First World War and inaugurated an uneasy peace, has often been a subject of debate and bitter criticism. There is, however, at least one of its clauses which reflects something different from the atmosphere of war and recrimination. It is a little clause which exempted certain enemy properties from sequestration by the allied powers. Amongst other things, the Treaty provided that German property in Allied hands at the end of the war should be expropriated towards the payment of German reparations. It was due to Dr. J. H. Oldham and some of his colleagues on the Edinburgh Continuation Committee that the authors of the Versailles Treaty were prevailed upon to exempt German mission property from this proviso. As an alternative to sequestration the Treaty provided that certain properties should be transferred to 'boards of trustees appointed by or approved by the Governments and composed of persons holding the faith of the mission whose property is involved'. At first, and for some years afterwards, this action of Oldham and his colleagues was sadly misunderstood in Germany; it was regarded as an Anglo-Saxon device to secure control of German missionary work. This misinterpretation was part of the grievous tangle of suspicion and bitterness which, in the immediate aftermath of war, affected church as well as national relationships. In time, however, the real significance of the step was appreciated in Germany no less than elsewhere. For, thanks to this Treaty provision, property worth between three and four million pounds sterling was saved for purposes in line with the objects for which the German missions had originally acquired them.

Even before the framing of the Treaty of Versailles, action had been taken, in at least one remarkable instance, which anticipated this kind of trusteeship. Amongst the property which, during the First World War, came under the control of the Custodian of Enemy Property, there were large undertakings in South India and West Africa which were owned by the Basel Missionary Society. The Basel Mission is one of the greatest of those European missions which made the nineteenth century what Professor Latourette has called the 'Great Century' in the expansion of Christianity. The headquarters of the Mission are in Switzerland but throughout its history the society has drawn support and recruited missionaries from other European countries, especially Germany. For many years Germany was ably represented also in its direction. It was one of the first missions to undertake, on a large scale, industrial and commercial activity, for the purpose of improving the economic and social conditions of the people amongst whom it worked.

Probably very few people realize that khaki-coloured cloth, now so universally used for uniforms, was first manufactured by the Basel Mission at Mangalore, South India. As the Oxford English Dictionary points out, the Urdu word for dusty or dust-coloured, first became an adopted English word in 1857. Six years before this date, a master-weaver named Haller went to Mangalore as a missionary of the Basel Mission, set up a few hand-looms and built a little dye house. It was Haller who first produced cloth of a colour which suggested borrowing the word *khaki*. Almost as world-wide in its distribution was another product of these Basel Mission industries —the Malabar tiles. In Ghana—then the Gold Coast—the mission also ran a large trading concern which dealt in cocoa, copra, ivory, and rubber. When the First World War broke out some of these industrial properties in South India and West Africa were under German management and were therefore treated as enemy holdings. They were sequestrated by the British Government and the trading operations were suspended. Meantime, responsibility for maintaining the evangelistic and church-building work of the Mission was taken care of through the International Missionary Council. Towards the end of the war it was learned that the British Government was proposing to sell the industrial properties; at this point J. H. Oldham and Kenneth Maclennan intervened and succeeded in persuading the Government to safeguard these resources for philanthropic purposes in keeping with their original design. The result was the creation of two bodies, the Commonwealth Trading Company and the Commonwealth Education and Welfare Trust. The Company was authorized to continue, on a limited profit basis, the trading operations in India and West Africa; the Trust was to be responsible for applying any profits—beyond those permitted to the Company —to charitable purposes specified by the Act and in keeping with the original missionary purpose of the undertakings. One half of the membership of the Trust was to be nominated by the Conference of British Missionary Societies. Since its formation in 1919 the Trust has received and disbursed grants from the Company amounting to approximately £120,000. These have been applied to such purposes as medical and educational work, orphanages, and other social services.[1]

The action taken in connexion with the Treaty of Versailles was part of a wider operation made possible by the growth of international missionary co-operation. Within a few weeks of the outbreak of war in 1914 John R. Mott (America then being neutral) had visited Britain and Germany, Holland and Switzerland to see how far international co-operation could guard the missionary enterprise from some of the disruptions of war. During the following years much was done to secure the continuance of work in places where missionaries had become interned or where funds were no longer available. At the end of the war, in addition to the safeguarding of missionary property, the International Missionary Council, either through its own officers or through the national councils which made up its membership, secured the gradual resumption of some of their former work by the German missionary societies. As part of the same watchfulness, the Council's officers also

---

[1] At the time of writing, the Government of Ghana has signified its intention to nationalize these trading operations in Ghana. It proposes to set aside a capital sum in compensation, to be applied by the Government to purposes in Ghana which the Commonwealth Trust is invited to approve.

secured explicit guarantees of religious liberty and missionary freedom within the terms of the Mandates entrusted to various Governments by the League of Nations. Years later, when it was clear that war was once again imminent, this earlier experience was made the basis of quick action. Only a few weeks before the storm broke in September 1939 John R. Mott, as chairman of the International Missionary Council, once again visited Britain, together with the American secretary of the Council—A. L. Warnshuis. On their return it was resolved in the Committee of the Council to pursue four lines of policy. Communications would be kept open as far as this could be secured with Government help; missionary work cut off from its supporting base would be temporarily taken over by arrangement with the national Christian council in the country concerned; efforts would be made internationally to meet the financial needs of missionaries no longer in contact with their homeland; similar attempts would be made to safeguard mission property. This was the beginning of an enterprise which lasted for more than a decade and which constituted the biggest administrative task undertaken by the International Missionary Council. During these years missions of one country were taken over by those of another on a trusteeship basis. American, British, and Commonwealth missionaries, Swedish and Swiss, took care of German work in Africa, India, the Middle East, and the Pacific. Money for the support of what were called 'Orphaned Missions' was raised in almost all the countries that were free to do so and much of it was contributed without any restriction as to the denominational needs to which it could be applied. Free Churchmen helped Episcopalians, Episcopalians helped non-episcopal missions, Lutherans came to the rescue of missions associated with Reformed churches. British, American, and Swiss missionaries did 'locums' for Germans; and at one stage in the war Germans who were still free to work in Palestine came to the assistance of Danish missionaries in Syria. Contact was maintained with interned missionaries and negotiations were conducted with governments on various aspects of the total problem. During the years immediately after the end of the War delicate and often difficult negotiations were carried on with various authorities, ecclesiastical and civil, and between younger churches and older, until at last this great international trusteeship was fulfilled and its account honourably rendered. The International Missionary Council was not the only agency in this field. In particular, it worked in close association with the Lutheran World Convention (later the Lutheran World Federation) which took responsibility on a large scale for most of the missionary work of the Lutheran churches. Others of the main historic denominations undertook parallel responsibility for particular pieces of work; but the point of co-ordination of this world-wide task, as well as the administration of a large part of it on an interdenominational basis, lay with the International Missionary Council.

Reference has already been made to the fact that one of the first ventures of the Edinburgh Continuation Committee was the publication (in 1912) of the *International Review of Missions*. When the Continuation Committee gave place to the International Missionary Council the first function of the new Council was defined as being 'to stimulate thinking and investigation on missionary questions'. This business of scholarly research into the nature of the missionary task was maintained as an essential part of the Council's work. In addition to the publication of the *Review* and of brochures on sundry subjects, this process of study and research has been applied from time to time to special areas of concern. Some of the most fruitful of these endeavours were made within a Department of Social and Industrial Research which for some years was part of the Council's organization.

Between Edinburgh 1910 and the next world missionary conference convened by the International Missionary Council there was a long interval of eighteen years. War and its sequel largely accounted for this. When the meeting was eventually held at Jerusalem in 1928 the world of 1910 seemed generations distant. Amongst the new emphases of this conference were, first, its contention that the spread of secularism, East and West, was now the most serious factor with which the Christian mission had to reckon; secondly, its assertion that the propagation of the Gospel must involve the Christian in a mission of social redemption as well as individual conversion. 'The Gospel of Christ', declared the Council's official report, 'contains a message, not only for the individual soul, but for the world of social organization and economic relations in which individuals live'. The Council recognized that, from this standpoint, Western society, no less than the East and Africa, needed a new, redeeming impact of the Gospel, but special attention was given to the implications for the Christian mission of the growth of industrialism in Asia and Africa. Amongst the most active participants in these discussions were R. H. Tawney, author of *Religion and the Rise of Capitalism*, and Harold Grimshaw of the International Labour Office.

As an outcome of all this the International Missionary Council set up in 1930 its Department of Social and Industrial Research, with an office in Geneva. Its principal officer was a former secretary of the Institute of Pacific Relations—J. Merle Davis, who brought a wide experience and a scholar's integrity to his task. Amongst the many social problems which came within the purview of the department were the trade in narcotics, forced labour, migrant labour, and child welfare. In 1932, with the help of the Carnegie Corporation, Merle Davis led a commission of inquiry into the problems arising from the opening up of copper mines in Northern Rhodesia. The commission's published report *Modern Industry and the African* was taken seriously by those responsible for the policies of Government as well as by the missions. One consequence was the formation of the United Missions in the Copperbelt in which five British missionary societies joined their resources in a common programme. Later undertakings in line with this research work of the Council involved a large-scale study of African marriage problems, conducted by a team which included a jurist and an anthropologist as well as a missionary. There was also collaboration in this study with Roman Catholic scholars and missionaries.

More recently, the Council's activity in 'stimulating think-ing and investigation on missionary questions' has been focused sharply on the training of an indigenous Christian ministry, especially in Asia and Africa. Ten years after the meeting in Jerusalem, another world-gathering was convened at Tambaram, Madras, in 1938. Amongst the needs to which this meeting drew special attention was the critical dependence of the younger churches on an adequately trained ministry. So far as international action was concerned, the Second World War postponed the formulation of plans, but in the years after the end of the War a series of detailed surveys of the needs of the churches and missions was made in India, Africa, and Madagascar. Eventually the generous interest of Mr. John D. Rockefeller, Junior, was enlisted in this cause and a munificent gift of two million dollars (over £700,000) was offered on condition that an equal amount was raised for the same purpose by missionary societies. With speed as well as generosity eight of the larger American mission boards met this challenge, and in 1958 there was established, under the authority of the International Missionary Council, a Theological Education Fund which is responsible for administering this money. A large part of the fund is earmarked for the improvement of theological college libraries and for the translation and produc-tion of theological textbooks; the remainder is being allocated on lines which will strengthen existing colleges or help in the creation of new ones, at points where the world-wide witness of the Church can best be furthered.

* * *

The Christian Message in a Non-Christian World

It will be seen that in this process of 'stimulating thinking and investigation', practical ends as well as fundamental questions are kept constantly in view. There is a persistent endeavour to keep scholarship related to life, study to action. This is more than a matter of applying to practical situations theories which have been arrived at elsewhere. It is an endeavour to work on the basis that in life itself thought and action interpenetrate one another. The starting point of the undertaking is in the knowledge that in Christ and his Gospel we see, in one and the same moment, the Way and the Life as well as the Truth. From this standpoint the Council pursues its current programme of studies. A glance at one or two of them will illustrate further the principle just emphasized.

One of the most obvious areas of attention for the missionary movement lies in the fact of the non-Christian religions, especially those historic organized systems of belief which have held the religious allegiance of great communities—Islam, Hinduism, Buddhism. Fifty years ago and even less a great deal was said about the collapse of these religions. There were discerning missionaries who felt that the day of the ancient 'paganisms' and 'idolatries' was done. At the beginning of the present century one of the very great missionaries to India wrote:

There are undoubted signs that the ancient stronghold of Hinduism is beginning to crumble. . . . The time of victory draws near.

Again, writing from a high-caste area of India, another missionary said:

The people are enquiring, not with the old spirit of prejudice and self-satisfaction, but with the new spirit of unrest and expectancy which the decay of the power of caste has produced. . . . Our difficulty soon will be one of harvesting the fields that are so rapidly ripening.

This comment came from an area in which it has since proved almost impossible to pick a handful of corn, still less harvest ripening fields. Both these writers were wise men, not fools, and they were serious students of Hinduism and of prevailing trends in Hindu society.

Here is a word written only thirty years ago by one of the greatest missionaries in the Middle East—Canon Temple Gairdner of Cairo:

Since the war [the First World War] breaches have been
appearing in the solid front of Islam. To a great extent these
point to agnosticism and irreligion rather than to a truer
religious experience. . . . But it is proof of dissatisfaction
and gives promise of the acceptance of a better way . . . It
shows the collapse of Islamic pride and assurance.

What has happened since these words were written illustrates the precariousness of all such fore-telling. Islam now
displays a pride and assurance which, thirty years ago, seemed
to be going for ever. It is expanding in Africa, especially as a
religion without a colour-bar. It is enjoying new prestige and
confidence in the lands of its origin in the Middle East; and it
is extending its missionary outreach in some surprising direc-
tions in Europe. A few years ago a Moslem missionary from
Pakistan settled in Denmark, confidently asserting that he was
the vanguard of a movement to win Scandinavia for Islam
'through literature, through the preached word and the activity
of a missionizing congregation'. In 1956 there was concluded
in Burma a conference which had lasted two years and which
constituted a World Buddhist Council—the sixth of such
gatherings in 2,500 years. In many respects this was a symptom
of a renaissance within Buddhism, but not the least startling of
its actions was the launching of a Buddhist world mission
inaugurated in the conviction that the time was ripe to speak a
saving word from Buddhism to a Christian West which had
been responsible for two world wars and the first use of atomic
weapons against an Asian people.

At the Jerusalem meeting of the International Missionary
Council in 1928 the main emphasis—as already recalled—was
on the world-wide spread of secularism and its challenge to the
Christian mission. This was felt to be more serious than any
lingering power within the non-Christian religions. When the
Council met again ten years later in Tambaram (Madras) a
different note was sounded. Renewed attention was given to the
non-Christian religions, especially under the provocative
leadership of Professor Hendrik Kraemer of Holland, a former
missionary in Indonesia and one of those highly competent lay-

theologians which Holland has a genius for producing. A now famous book by Dr. Kraemer—*The Christian Message in a non-Christian World*—was written for this meeting in Madras at the request of the International Missionary Council in recognition that the Christian mission needed to reckon with these religions with a new seriousness.

Although war hindered the immediate and adequate follow-up of most of the findings of Tambaram this debate on the relation between Christianity and the non-Christian religions was by no means evanescent, and since the war fresh steps have been taken towards working out a new Christian approach to these other faiths. Working through the Christian councils which compose its membership, the International Missionary Council has shared in the setting-up of a number of study-centres. There is one on Islam in India; another with its base of operations in Jordan which conducts 'extension courses' in other Arab countries. There are two which concentrate on Buddhism, one in Ceylon and the other in Burma. In South India there is a centre for the study of 'Religion and Society' which gives special attention to modern developments within Hinduism. In all these, work gathers round a director who is a specialist in the study of the religion concerned; courses are held for short periods, attended by pastors, teachers, and evangelists—both nationals and missionaries, and there is regular contact with leading Moslems, Buddhists, and Hindus, on a basis which facilitates fruitful theological and personal discussion.

Amongst the great historic religions designated 'non-Christian' a unique place belongs to Judaism. It was the faith in which Jesus was nurtured; it constituted that central line of Revelation which passed into the Incarnation. The scriptures of Judaism form the Old Testament of Christians; synagogue and temple have left their mark on the Church. There is continuity between the new People of God redeemed in Christ and that ancient People of God which received the Law and the Prophets and looked for the coming of the Messiah. The New Covenant presupposes the Old. Yet the rift between Synagogue and Church continues and the 'mystery of Israel', sharpened by modern politics and a new return of exiles to a promised land, constitutes a most searching challenge to the Church's understanding of its mission. In recognition of the significance of all this there is, within the International Missionary Council, a special committee on the Christian Approach to the Jews. Some of its leading members were themselves nurtured in Judaism; some are Christian theologians with special competence in Jewish studies; some are front-line workers in presenting the Gospel to Jews. Different nationalities and denominations are represented in the membership of the committee and there is a constant endeavour to show the bearing of this work on the whole missionary task of the Church—that mission which, while gathering the Gentiles into its saving grace, was historically 'to the Jew first'.

★   ★   ★

Partners in Obedience

Another of the current studies within the International Missionary Council has as its object a better understanding of what is happening in some of the 'younger' churches. One of the great features of the missionary movement today—indeed, its most significant feature—lies in the emergence of indigenous churches in Asia and Africa. These now constitute a front line in the Church's witness to the world; they must more and more be the spear-head of its mission. Their importance cannot be exaggerated. It is possible, nevertheless, to speak in too easy, too complacent terms about the younger churches, and to assume—especially when life seems to be at a low ebb in churches which are not only old but weary—that the younger churches are leaping ahead, free from the hindrances and weaknesses which beset their older partners in the West. This is far from being generally true. A year or two ago some searching investigations were made into the condition of certain younger churches in East Africa. They are churches with a relatively brief but heroic history, part of a Christian movement which in its broad features constitutes a great chapter in the 'expansion of Christianity'. But they have now grown beyond the period of first-generation Christians and their short history has included the involvement of their country in modern war. Some of the results now brought to light are deeply disturbing. In one village, out of sixty-four Christians all but four or five are in the habit of consulting the tribal spirit-diviner. In another parish, out of thirty-eight confirmed members of the Church not more than six are in regular attendance. In another area, out of fifty-three married men (Christians) only fourteen have remained monogamous. What are the African Christian leaders and pastors doing about this? Of course, they are disturbed, though often bewildered, and they are exercising their teaching and pastoral ministry. But the investigation which has drawn attention to these sobering facts includes some comments which provoke awkward reflections. 'Committees devour the time of the best leaders of the Church', says the report. 'Pastorate committees followed by deanery committees occupy nine days three times a year. A pastor who is also a member of a diocesan committee may spend two months out of twelve in committee work.' The pastor also has other responsibilities besides teaching, preaching, visiting his flock, and attending committees. He is much concerned about the church collections and the balance sheet. As an African ruefully put it: 'Our pastors have no time to go after the lost sheep; they're too busy looking for the lost coin.'

This is not the whole story of the younger churches of today. Here is another picture also drawn from an East African territory:

Here were some of the African clergy and teachers. . . . They have forsworn the use of arms and go out to the churches and schools each day, marked men, to carry out their work. . . . There were empty chairs in the room, for casualties have been heavy. The priest on my right had been seized and slashed repeatedly—this by well-dressed young men talking English—and asked at each cut to deny his faith and say that Christ was a European. Six others were killed nearby and he was left for dead. . . . Opposite me sat another man, weak and limping for torture. Yet all looked calm, confident, even happy.

This was written by a *Times* correspondent soon after the grievous Mau-Mau tumult. It matters to the whole Church, not only to a particular village or country, that the truth of things—good or bad—should be known, and that its lessons should be taken to heart. Whether through light or shade, these authentic accounts of what is happening in the younger churches carry consequences for the training of the ministry, the organization of the church, the relations between the older and younger churches, and many other aspects of missionary policy. This is why the International Missionary Council initiated the investigation referred to above, in the course of its present younger church studies. Comparable studies have been carried out in Northern Rhodesia (by a team which included an Anglican missionary, a German Lutheran, an African educationist, and African pastors) and they are in process in other parts of the world.

The International Missionary Council is not a 'super-missionary society': it does not itself administer any direct missionary work, nor does it in any sense control the missionary movement. Nevertheless, its deliberations have made their own contribution to the policy and strategy of the world mission of the Church. The Edinburgh Conference of 1910 drew attention to a new era in Asia and its consequent opportunity and challenge. The Jerusalem meeting in 1928 warned against the menace of a world-wide secularism. From Madras in 1938 there came a searching word concerning Christianity and the non-Christian religions. Alongside main emphases of this kind these world-gatherings have provided information and guidance on such matters as medical missionary policy, educational policy, relations between missions and governments and so on. Since the Second World War there have been three major meetings of the International Missionary Council at Whitby, Ontario, in 1947, at Willingen, Germany, in 1952, and in Ghana in 1957. Each of these has contributed, through discussion and reports, to the framing and revision of missionary policy. In particular, these post-war meetings have been greatly concerned with changes in emphasis which the emergence of the younger churches involve. The Whitby meeting gave world-wide currency to the phrase 'partners in obedience'. The partnership envisaged was that of younger and older churches jointly pursuing the task of world-wide evangelization. The importance and urgency of continued western participation in this world-wide responsibility were not under-rated; but more forcefully than hitherto it was made plain that the missionary enterprise was no longer to be regarded chiefly in terms of the work of 'missions', with younger churches viewed either as the 'results' of missions or as junior agents. The churches in India, China, and elsewhere were to be regarded as partners with the Western churches in a common obedience. This carries with it radical consequences for the work of the older missionary agencies, and especially the attitude of their supporters. The Willingen meeting carried this kind of thinking further and made considerable play with the phrase 'mission in unity'. At Edinburgh 1910 (as the next chapter indicates) the questions which bear most directly on the unity of the Church—those of Faith and Order—were excluded from the agenda. Throughout its subsequent history the International Missionary Council has maintained the position that such questions are not directly within its purview. But expressions of concern and hope regarding Christian unity which were nevertheless voiced in 1910 have become more insistent in later meetings of the International Missionary Council. Not surprisingly, they have found strong utterance through the voice of younger church representatives. At the Willingen meeting in 1952 the younger church delegates presented a statement which included the following:

We believe that the unity of the churches is an essential condition of effective witness and advance. In the lands of the younger churches divided witness is a crippling handicap. We of the younger churches feel this very keenly. While unity may be desirable in the lands of the older churches it is *imperative* in those of the younger churches.

After discussion of this question in the full meeting the following statement was adopted and stands on record as the conviction and concern of a Council which was formed not, in the first instance, to deal with the question of the Church's unity but with the furtherance of its mission to the world :

The calling of the Church to mission and unity issues from the nature of God Himself, made known to us in the whole Biblical revelation of the work and purpose of God in Christ. God has made of one blood all nations of men. In Christ we see God's redemptive action; in Christ God is still at work reconciling all things to Himself in one restored humanity. Christ called His apostles that they might be one with Him and with one another, and that He might send them forth, to share with Him His mission for the redemption of the world. The calling of the Church is to be one family in Him and to make known to the whole world, in word and deed, His Gospel of the Kingdom. Christ prayed for His disciples that they might be one in Him, as He and the Father are one, that the world might believe that the Father had sent Him.

The love of God in Christ calls for the threefold response of worship, unity and mission. These three aspects of the Church's response are interdependent; they become corrupted when isolated from each other. Division in the Church distorts its witness, frustrates its mission, and contradicts its own nature. If the Church is to demonstrate the Gospel in its life as well as in its preaching, it must manifest to the world the power of God to break down all barriers and to establish the Church's unity in Christ. *Christ is not divided.*

It is true that there are differences among us due to the various gifts and workings of the Holy Spirit within the one fellowship. But there are also differences among us which disrupt the Body of Christ, and separate us from one another. They spring from trusting in something other than the Cross of Christ.

We believe that through the ecumenical movement God is drawing His people together in order that He may enable us to discern yet more clearly the contradictions in our message and the barriers to unity which are also hindrances to effective witness in a divided world. We can no longer be content to accept our divisions as normal. We believe that in the ecumenical movement God has provided a way of co-operation in witness and service, and also a means for the removal of much that mars such witness and service.

We therefore recommend that National Christian Councils should consider afresh their responsibility in relation to the cause of Christian unity within their own areas. It is not the purpose of the ecumenical movement to set up an ecclesiastical superstructure, and action in matters of faith and order must remain the responsibility of the churches. Nevertheless, within the co-operative activity of such bodies as Christian Councils the disunity of the churches continues to hinder the fulfilment of the Church's mission.

We further recommend that the member Councils of the International Missionary Council should consider fresh ways of relating their experience and concern for unity to the deliberations and actions of the churches within their membership, and to the Commission on Faith and Order of the World Council of Churches.

We further believe that God is calling us to seek every opportunity of fellowship with those Christians who are not members of the International Missionary Council and its constituent bodies. It is our earnest prayer that God will bring us together in mutual love and understanding and that we may serve as fellow-labourers in making Christ known as the Saviour of the world.

This expression of the plea for mission-in-unity concentrates on the need for the Church to demonstrate more faithfully that reconciling and unifying grace which is part of its Gospel. But at Willingen the phrase mission-in-unity had another emphasis also. The emphasis was upon the first word—*mission*. It was a return to the Whitby call for partners-in-obedience, obedience to the mission of the Church. The emergence of the 'younger' churches does not only carry with it implications for the attitude and policy of western missions in relation to the Christian communities in Asia and Africa. It is—or ought to be—a fact of enormous significance and potentiality for the furtherance of Christ's mission to the world. The Churches, West and East, old or young, should be united-in-mission, one in their missionary obedience. A familiar term in the story of missions is 'the Home Base'. This signifies the sending church, the base from which the missionaries go out. It is the place where the vision of a world won for Christ is kept fresh and clear; where successive generations of the world's best manhood and womanhood perceive the grandeur of the missionary vocation and respond to it: it is the place of sacrificial giving and sustained prayer for the world-wide task of the Church. But where is this Home Base today? Since the end of the eighteenth century it has been most obviously located in the West, amongst the churches of Europe and America or in the extensions of the Western churches in Australia and New Zealand. But today it can be rightly said that 'the Home Base is everywhere'. It is—or should be—wherever the Church exists; in the great metropolitan centres and the scattered villages of Asia, amongst the copper mines of Northern Rhodesia, in Indian communities on the High Andes, in the Papuan bush, or on the 'astonishing clusters' of South Sea islands. For generations some of these churches have constituted noble embodiments of the world mission's Home Base. In the chapel of a small theological college in Papua there is a memorial window commemorating the service of many missionaries who laid down their lives in a 'foreign' land. The names are not western ones. They are the names of 'natives' of South Sea islands—Samoa, the Cook Islands and so on—who heard and responded to the call to missionary service. Some of them were colleagues of the pioneer missionaries from the West and there are island churches in the South Pacific which now have nearly a century of missionary service to their credit. In 1959, when the Churches in East Asia came together in Malaya to inaugurate the East Asia Christian Conference, it was learned that there were more than two hundred of their members—Indians, Indonesians, Japanese, Filipinos—on missionary service in other lands. This fact was reported, not to induce complacency but to stimulate others to follow the example, on a scale commensurate with the needs of the world and the nature and calling of the Church.

The missionary enterprise—the very words *mission* and *missionary*—still suggest to most people an exclusively Western undertaking. This springs from a too limited, too parochial conception of the Home Base. How can the churches in the West be made more challengingly aware that they are part of a world-wide Church, every section of which is called into missionary service? How can the churches of Asia and Africa be quickened to greater missionary endeavours within a world-wide partnership in obedience? Answers to questions of this kind have not been provided when they have found agreement in a group discussion and been formulated in findings or resolutions. They have to be worked out, and lived out in the worship and activity of churches differing enormously from one another in their history, cultural situation, political context, and resources. The International Missionary Council cannot itself do what can only be accomplished in these thousand different local situations. But it seeks to use its resources, in consultation, knowledge, experience, and organization, in ways which will help churches and missions throughout the world to see their own path more clearly and to advance along it in a unity which furthers mission and on a mission which deepens unity.

Chapter III

CHURCHES IN COUNCIL

Faith and Order

The Edinburgh Conference of 1910 was mainly composed of delegates chosen by missionary societies. It was not, strictly speaking, a representative gathering of the churches. It is true that some of these missionary societies—especially in the U.S.A.—were organically part of the churches: they were mission 'boards' reponsible to church assemblies and to this extent they reflected the convictions and policies of their churches. Even in the more independent missionary 'societies' leadership generally lay in the hands of men who were prominent in the councils of their respective denominations. The Edinburgh Conference, therefore, reflected in its composition important elements in the life of the churches. Yet it was not an authoritative and representative meeting of the churches as such. Moreover, some of the greatest issues affecting the life of the churches and giving them their distinctive character were explicitly ruled out of the purview of the Conference. This exclusion covered questions of Faith—the doctrinal bases of the churches and their differences from one another; it also involved questions of Order—matters pertaining to the ministry and the sacraments, to the exercise of authority, and the right ordering of the Church's life. Yet these questions of doctrine and order are just the questions on which the unity of the churches turn. Members of the 1910 Conference might, as individuals, feel deeply about the disunity of the Church; the Conference itself could not begin to discuss the deepest issues underlying this disunity.

This limitation was to some extent a necessity arising from

the main purpose of the Conference. It had quite enough on its agenda apart from this great matter. The limitation was also self-imposed, in deference to the situation in which the meeting was convened. Some of its most valued participants, especially representatives of the Anglican Communion, could not—at that date—have agreed to share in the gathering if this limiting condition had not been accepted. Archbishop Lang, Bishop Gore, Bishop Montgomery and others felt bound to insist that these questions of Faith and Order could only be responsibly discussed by the accredited representatives and theologians of the churches themselves.

This does not mean that the word unity was never mentioned at Edinburgh. Far from it. One of the eight volumes constituting the report of the Conference bears the title 'Cooperation and the Promotion of Unity'. In view of the composition of the conference it is significant that this report adopted as its starting point, with 'wholehearted agreement', the assertion of a meeting held three years earlier in Shanghai, namely, that 'the ideal object of missionary work is to plant in each non-Christian nation one undivided Church of Christ'. This—the report stated—is 'the ideal which is present to the minds of the great majority of missionaries'. In mingled warning and hope the report also anticipated that 'in some mission fields at any rate, the problem of unity may, before long, be settled, or at any rate taken in hand, by the indigenous churches independently of the views and wishes of western missionaries'. Further, the experience of the Conference itself—the depth of its fellowship and the moving quality of its shared inspiration—inevitably quickened in many of its participants the hope as well as the longing that a more manifest Christian unity was attainable. The chairman of the group responsible for the report on Co-operation and the Promotion of Unity (Sir Andrew Fraser, a former Governor of Bengal) declared that 'We have had before us the vision of unity, a vision fair and beautiful, far better and far higher than anything we have dreamed of before. . . . We know some of the difficulties . . . we do not see how these differences are to be reconciled . . .

but we do say this, that disunion is lamentable and disastrous'.
A Presbyterian speaker (Dr. J. Campbell Gibson) said:

While I rejoice in cooperation, I do not believe that the
minds of Christian men can ultimately rest in less than that
highest level of all, the unity of the Church of God, of which
we have robbed ourselves too long and which it may cause us
weary years to restore; but it will be restored by our Lord
Himself, if we seek it in humility; with infinite patience, and
with an endless consideration for the difficulties of our
brethren.

A leading Congregationalist (Dr. J. Wardlaw Thompson)
sounded a similar note:

I look forward now with greater hopefulness than ever to a
day when we shall be able to meet to consider questions which
have been tabooed at this Conference—and very properly
tabooed—and shall be able to talk frankly to each other about
the things on which we differ as well as the things on which
we agree, recognizing that we are members of the Body of
Christ. . . . I long for the time when we shall see another
conference and when men of the Greek Church and the Roman
Church shall talk things over with us in the service of Christ.

To this we may add the word of an Anglican delegate (Bishop
Montgomery):

One day we shall be one, but it will be effected by a higher
union than is in sight at present when our deepest convictions
and needs are met and satisfied, not whittled away.

A later chapter in this volume will return to this problem of
unity and to the search for that 'higher unity' of which Bishop
Montgomery spoke fifty years ago. At this point we recall
some of the steps by which, following Edinburgh 1910, the
churches officially began to take counsel with one another on the
great questions of Faith and Order which lie at the heart of
the unity problem.

'Whenever God gives a vision He also points to some new
responsibility, and you and I, when we leave this Assembly,
will go away with some fresh duties to perform.' These were

the words of an American delegate to the Edinburgh Conference—Bishop Charles H. Brent of the Episcopal Church of the United States. Charles Brent was another of the remarkable men who have been powerfully influenced by the ecumenical movement and who in turn have left their mark upon it. A Canadian by birth and later an American citizen, from the time of his ordination he took the world as his parish. After ministries in Canada and the U.S.A. he became Bishop of the Philippines and proved to be one of the great missionary-bishops of his generation. Many great tasks claimed him; he was President of the International Opium Conferences of 1909 and 1911 and during the First World War was senior chaplain to the American expeditionary force. He was an indefatigable worker and in his closing years it was clear that he was over-driving himself against illness and physical weakness. Yet this was not just restlessness and impatience. He had acquired, said one of his friends, 'the triple secret of wisdom, enthusiasm and serenity'. When he died it was said of him 'that he had more friends than any man of his time . . . warriors and ecclesiastics, pagans and Christians, lovers and little children'.

This was the man who went away from Edinburgh in 1910 knowing that God was 'pointing to some new responsibility'. Before leaving, he had told a friend that one of the fresh duties laid upon him was to initiate another world conference, this time explicitly dealing with those questions of Faith and Order which had been 'tabooed' at Edinburgh.

'Most of us', as Brent said some years later, 'are, in our hearts, devotees of the cult of the incomplete—that is, sectarianism'. From 1910 onwards, amidst all his other responsibilities, Brent lived for this purpose of liberating Christians from their contentment with the incomplete in their conception of what it means to be a member of the Church of Christ. His first initiative was with his own Church in the United States. Here he was strongly supported by such stalwarts as W. T. (later Bishop) Manning and by another of those gifted laymen who have proved to be key figures in the ecumenical movement—Robert H. Gardiner, an American lawyer and a member of the Episcopal Church. Within a few months of the Edinburgh Conference the following resolution was unanimously passed by both Houses of Convention of the Protestant Episcopal Church of America:

That a Joint Commission be appointed to bring about a Conference for the consideration of questions touching Faith and Order, and that all Christian Communions throughout the world which confess Our Lord Jesus Christ as God and Saviour be asked to unite with us in arranging for and conducting such a Conference.

Seventeen years were to pass before the first fully constituted World Conference on Faith and Order could be held. This period included the First World War and the restless years of peace-making when the enmities and sorrows of war intensified the problems of reconciliation amongst churches as well as nations. It was a long time, for instance, before many German church leaders after 1918 could feel at home in the ecumenical movement and in the countries which had been at war with Germany there were also Christians who found the task of reconciliation far from easy. But this seventeen-year interval also had other causes, most of them arising from the difficult and delicate character of the task which Brent and his friends had set themselves.

It is some measure of the progress of this whole movement that today we can scarcely enter into the fears, suspicions and misconceptions which had to be dealt with before the churches could be brought together, through their recognized leaders, to discuss the thorny but inescapable questions of Faith and Order. Moreover, the vision of unity cherished by the pioneers at this time was of a comprehensiveness which created its own vast problems. The resolution of the American Episcopal Church had been addressed to 'all Christian Communions throughout the world which confess Our Lord Jesus Christ as God and Saviour'. This could not exclude either the Roman Catholic Church or the Orthodox Churches of Russia and the East; and within the rest of the Christian world there were innumerable diversities—historical, cultural, doctrinal, and liturgical as well as linguistic. Except, therefore, for the war years the period between 1910 and 1927 was occupied in correspondence and consultations, in the writing and discussion of documents reflecting the characteristics and the nature of the total problem. During this time of confidence-winning and clarification, the number of participants in the venture steadily increased and from many countries leading church-men and theologians became identified with the cause. Many of these continued to play a great part in the ecumenical movement as a whole as well as in this Faith and Order process. To name them all would produce a long and impressive catalogue. Representative figures included Professor William Adams Brown, Dr. Parkes Cadman and Bishop Francis J. McConnell of the U.S.A.; Professor Adolf Deissmann and Dr. Siegmund-Schultze of Germany; Professor Wilfred Monod of France; Dr. A. E. Garvie, Professor J. Vernon Bartlet, Bishop Charles Gore, Bishop A. C. Headlam, Bishop (later Archbishop) William Temple, Dr. H. B. Workman, and Dr. G. F. Barbour from Great Britain; Archbishop Nathan Söderblom of Sweden and Bishop E. J. Palmer of Bombay. In some respects the most significant fact about this growing-together of leading churchmen was its inclusion of representatives of the Eastern Orthodox churches, notably Dr. Stefan Zankov of Bulgaria, Archbishop Chrysostom of Greece and Archbishop Germanos Strenopoulos of Thyateira. This last-named was henceforth to become one of the best-known and best-loved figures in the whole movement. From this period until his death in 1951 (when he was still serving as one of the first co-Presidents of the World Council of Churches) he made the movement one of his chief concerns and contributed immeasurably to its strength.

The response, during these years between 1910 and 1927, to the invitation 'to all Christian Communions' thus included a significant part of the Orthodox Church. What of the Roman Catholic Church? It was included in the invitation, and amongst the many comings and goings at this time there were approaches to Rome. The original appeal to give consideration to the holding of a world conference on Faith and Order had, in fact, been sent (in Latin) to all the cardinals and bishops of the Roman Church. It was not, however, until 1919 that a North American delegation, visiting Europe and the East for the purpose of promoting the conference, discussed the proposal in person with Pope Benedict XV and with Cardinal Gaspari. 'Discussed' is perhaps too strong a word, for the audience with His Holiness, though cordial throughout, was not what is sometimes called an 'ecumenical conversation'. To borrow a classical 'Irishism', 'the reciprocity was all on one side'. As the members of the deputation subsequently reported :

the contrast between the Pope's personal attitude towards us and his official attitude towards the Conference was very sharp. One was irresistibly benevolent, the other irresistibly rigid. The genuineness of the Pope's personal friendliness towards us was as outstanding as the positiveness of his official declination of our invitation.

On leaving the audience-room there was handed to the visitors a written statement which remains important for its unambiguous assertion of the Roman conception of 'reunion'. The statement reads :

The Holy Father, after having thanked them for their visit, stated that as successor of St Peter and Vicar of Christ he had no greater desire than that there should be one fold and one Shepherd. His Holiness added that the teaching and practice of the Roman Catholic Church regarding the unity of the visible Church of Christ was well known to everybody and therefore it would not be possible for the Catholic Church to take part in such a Congress as the one proposed. His Holiness, however, by no means wishes to disapprove of the Congress in question for those who are not in union with the Chair of Peter, on the contrary, he earnestly desires and prays that, if the Congress is practicable, those who take part in it may, by the Grace of God, see the light and become reunited to the visible Head of the Church, by whom they will be received with open arms.

Since this historic interview there has been no official participation of the Roman Catholic Church in the regular conferences or meetings of the Faith and Order Movement or its
successor body, the World Council of Churches. There have,
however, been many informal contacts, personal exchanges of
information and views, and attendances of Roman Catholic
visitors or observers at the major assemblies of the ecumenical
movement. Fuller reference to these and to the position of the
World Council of Churches and International Missionary
Council in relation to Roman Catholics is made elsewhere in
this book.

When, at last, the first World Conference on Faith and
Order was convened at Lausanne in 1927, there came into
being an international organization which was to become one
of the main strands in the World Council of Churches. It took
the name of the Faith and Order Movement and existed as an
independent body until the launching of the World Council in
1948. Incidentally, one of the remarkable things about it as an
organization was the amount of work it accomplished on
slender resources. Except for a very brief period—soon
terminated through lack of funds—it had no whole-time officer
until 1948 but was dependent on the voluntary service of men
already carrying heavy professional responsibilities. For this
achievement credit was due, first, to the American layman
already named—Robert L. Gardiner, and subsequently to
Canon Leonard Hodgson of Oxford, Dr. Floyd Tomkins of
the U.S.A., and Canon Tissington Tatlow whose name is
inseparably linked with the Student Christian Movement and
who was also one of the key figures in the ecumenical movement
generally.

Only two fully constituted world conferences of the Faith
and Order Movement were held prior to the creation of the
World Council of Churches. The Lausanne conference of 1927
was followed ten years later by a similar gathering at Edinburgh in 1937. But in the intervening years the Movement had
moved considerably by means of smaller consultations and the
production of written material. In this process a growing

number of churchmen of all nationalities and communions
embarked on the serious business of learning to know one
another's minds, of entering with deeper knowledge and
sympathy into traditions other than their own. This involved,
also, hard and sometimes new work in stating and explaining
one's own inheritance and convictions for a deeper purpose
than that of propaganda or controversy—a salutary discipline.
Sometimes the studies and discussions dealt with similarities
between the traditions and practices of the various churches;
more often they were concerned with the differences and the
theological assumptions which underlay them. Not least, this
whole process led, consciously and unconsciously, to new
approaches to one another on the part of representatives of
different denominations and different nationalities. A deeper
sympathy and considerateness were nurtured; this, perhaps
more than anything else, has contributed to that change of
atmosphere in the relation between the churches which is so
marked a feature of the present time.

The process was not without its frustrations and pitfalls.
Differences arising from national characteristics as well as
theology can affect the pace of mutual understanding in matters
of Faith and Order, as in other matters. During one of these
meetings, when the swift-moving mind of William Temple
wished for speedier progress, Temple wrote to his brother:

All goes happily but . . . we have moved very slowly. The
Germans can never discuss what to do tomorrow without
showing how their view depends on the divine purpose in
creation—the existence of which must therefore be first
established. None the less, we do get on.[1]

There were plenty of opportunities, also, for participants to
discover that the impression they made on others was rather
different from what they assumed to be the case. For example,
most Protestant delegates to these gatherings took it for
granted that the last word in conservatism and immobility was
to be found in the representatives of Eastern Orthodoxy. It

[1] F. A. Iremonger: *William Temple*, p. 403.

was surprising and refreshing to hear Professor H. S. Alivisatos of Greece (still today attending World Council meetings as the doyen amongst the lay theologians of the Orthodox Church) say in 1937:

I should like to confess to you what my long experience with the Faith and Order movement has taught me from the beginning. The close contact I have had with brethren and friends of other denominations has convinced me that the Greek Church, being regarded as a very old, traditional, and, to a certain extent, a petrified body, is by far more liberal than some even extreme Protestant Churches of considerably younger age. I assure you that I have learned at home what tradition and tenacity means, but I have never been able to understand it better and more fully than since I had the privilege of sitting near to some very good Protestants, and to see with what tenacity they defend their traditions.

The great thing in all this is the enlargement of sympathy and understanding which such 'encounter' nourishes—one of the richest by-products (or, maybe, primary products) of all these movements. As Archbishop Garbett once recorded in his diary, after attending a meeting of the Conference of British Missionary Societies:

These meetings are changing my outlook in regard to the Free Churches: I forget we belong to different Churches, and I am conscious only of our common Christianity.[1]

A minor bracketed note in the same diary illustrates the process working at another level. Writing at Jordans ('the Mecca—or, perhaps rather, the Assisi—of the Society of Friends') the Archbishop recorded:

We are *very* well fed, I had feared we should live on Quaker Oats and Cadbury's Cocoa. . . .[2]

More seriously, it was yet another illustration of what growing together means when this High Churchman could write:

[1] Charles Smyth: *Cyril Forster Garbett*, p. 460.
[2] op. cit., p. 463.

Jordans is a delightful place. . . . Close by is the Quaker Meeting house, very plain, with wooden pews: there was something very beautiful in its simplicity. No symbol of the Divine, but the absence of any material focus of devotion may help many to realize the better the Unseen Presence which is with them in their gatherings.[1]

From the initiative of Bishop Brent and his colleagues in 1910 until the outbreak of the Second World War in 1939 this process of study and understanding went on, gathering more and more men and women within it across the national and denominational frontiers. The process was continuous, though the peak moments came in the world conferences of 1927 and 1937. During the decade between these larger gatherings a good deal of published work was produced on four main themes: the Doctrine of Grace; the Ministry and the Sacraments; the Church of Christ and the Word of God; and the Church's Unity in Life and Worship. The work done on these themes after the Lausanne Conference in 1927 became the basis of the discussions at Edinburgh in 1937. Writing of the contrast between these two events, Canon Hodgson said:

At Lausanne most of the delegates met as strangers and had to make their main aim the statement of their own convictions; at Edinburgh they met as friends who, though loyal to their divided Churches, trusted one another as brothers in Christ, could take for granted general familiarity with what they stood for, and could concentrate on trying to see whether deeper mutual understanding might not diminish the area of disagreement.

It is not the main purpose of these world gatherings to issue public declarations or messages to the world at large; the delegates come together to *confer*, to perceive more clearly what they and their churches should say and do. Nevertheless, alongside the more important detailed reporting of the conferences, two public statements came out of Lausanne and Edinburgh. Their different titles have some significance. Lausanne found agreement in a 'Message', Edinburgh in an

[1]op. cit., p. 463.

'Affirmation'. The Message of Lausanne concerned the Gospel; the Affirmation of Edinburgh spoke of the unity of those who confess allegiance to Christ as Head of the Church. This sequence was right—for the deepest reasons. But it was also true that those who gathered at Lausanne were not yet ready to make an agreed affirmation about the nature of the unity which they were beginning to experience, as representing different churches. They were more likely to achieve this by starting with the Gospel—'the joyful message of redemption, the gift of God to sinful man', as the Message put it.

Progress towards agreement on any major subject was far from easy at Lausanne: indeed, some of the delegates came away far more conscious of differences than when they went. But the Message won unanimous assent and part of its wording was incorporated in the Message issued the following year by the Jerusalem meeting of the International Missionary Council. It was also used by the Church of Christ in China when this united Church formulated its statement of Faith.

Ten years later the Affirmation of the Edinburgh Conference could refer, with a new confidence, to the unity already given to the 'several communions' and to which the churches were seeking to give fuller expression. There is a ringing note about the opening paragraphs of this Affimation:

We are one in faith in our Lord Jesus Christ, the incarnate Word of God. We are one in allegiance to him as Head of the Church, and as King of kings and Lord of lords. We are one in acknowledging that this allegiance takes precedence of any other allegiance that may make claims upon us.

This unity does not consist in the agreement of our minds or the consent of our wills. It is founded in Jesus Christ himself, who lived, died, and rose again to bring us to the Father, and who through the Holy Spirit dwells in his Church. We are one because we are all the objects of the love and grace of God, and called by him to witness in all the world to his glorious Gospel.

In this conviction and experience of a given unity in Christ, the Edinburgh meeting of 1937 moved much nearer agreement on the great themes which had been studied since Lausanne. It is noteworthy that the deepest consensus was reached in the discussion on 'The Grace of our Lord Jesus Christ'. It was even possible for the delegates to assert in this report: 'There is in connexion with this subject no ground for maintaining division between Churches'. Nevertheless, on the crucial question of the Ministry and the Sacraments agreement on the nature of grace could not be matched by a common mind on the means of grace and their right ordering. This remains the central area of unresolved differences. The further studies put in hand at Edinburgh therefore moved more closely into this realm and in subsequent years important documents were issued on *The Church*, *Ways of Worship*, and *Intercommunion*. These documents, again, were the outcome of years of discussion, study and growth in personal understanding of the kind already described. Once more the process culminated in another World Conference on Faith and Order, held at Lund in 1952.

It is important here to recognize the limitations as well as the possibilities of this process of growing together. For the personal participants there is almost always real growth in the process and great gain in undertanding and agreement. Nevertheless, although delegates to Faith and Order conferences are representatives of Churches, the real point of progress and of decisive action lies with the Churches, not with a world conference. The present constitution of the Faith and Order Commission contains these clauses:

Its main work is to draw Churches out of isolation into conference, in which none is to be asked to be disloyal to or to compromise its convictions, but to seek to explain them to others while seeking to understand their points of view. Irreconcilable differences are to be recorded as honestly as agreements.

Only Churches themselves are competent to take actual steps towards reunion by entering into negotiations with one another. The work of the Movement is not to formulate schemes and tell the Churches what they ought to do, but to act as the handmaid of the Churches in the preparatory work of clearing away misunderstandings, discussing obstacles to reunion, and issuing reports which are submitted to the Churches for their consideration.

Other chapters of this book touch on some of the actions taken by the churches in the movement towards unity and on the implications of this principle by which the ecumenical movement operates.[1] At no point is it more important to stress the difference between the functions and authority of a world conference and the authority and responsibility of the churches than in regard to these questions of Faith and Order. The difference not only limits the power of a world conference. It underlines the obligation resting on the churches. Something of this appears in the 'Word to the Churches' which prefaces the report of the Lund conference of 1952. In the course of this message the Conference said:

We have now reached a crucial point in our ecumenical discussions. As we have come to know one another better our eyes have been opened to the depth and pain of our separations and also to our fundamental unity. The measure of unity which it has been given to the Churches to experience together must now find clearer manifestation. A faith in the one Church of Christ which is not implemented by acts of obedience is dead. There are truths about the nature of God and His Church which will remain for ever closed to us unless we act together in obedience to the unity which is already ours. We would, therefore, earnestly request our Churches to consider whether they are doing all they ought to do to manifest the oneness of the people of God. Should not our Churches ask themselves whether they are showing sufficient eagerness to enter into conversation with other Churches and whether they should not act together in all matters except those in which deep differences of conviction compel them to act separately?

When the Lund conference was held in 1952 the Faith and Order Movement had become incorporated within the World Council of Churches. Before recounting this part of the story

[1] See especially Chapter V ('Towards Unity') and Chapter VI ('Trends and Prospects'), pp. 101–145

it is necessary to recall yet another world movement which also became part of the World Council in 1948. This was called the Life and Work Movement.

*   *   *

Life and Work

The title of the movement reflects its main concern—the implications of the Gospel for the daily life and work of men. It dealt especially with those social and international relationships which remind us that no man is an island. 'Man' is 'man-in-society'. Our redemption, while going to the heart of man as an individual, also goes to the heart of the matter by touching that corporate entity, human society.

The pioneer in the ecumenical movement most signally associated with the Life and Work Movement bore the engaging name of 'Flower of the South'. This sounds as though ecumenical leadership had already passed to Japan or China. In fact, the name is better known in its Swedish equivalent where Flower of the South is spelt Söderblom. Nathan Söderblom, Lutheran Archbishop of Uppsala and Primate of Sweden, left his gracious mark upon the ecumenical movement generally and on the Life and Work Movement in particular.

Nathan Söderblom died in 1931. More than forty years earlier, while still a student, he had written in his diary: 'Lord, give me humility and wisdom to serve the great cause of the free unity of Thy Church'. Christian unity was in his heart throughout a many-sided ministry and what, for him, gave special urgency to the matter was the need of a divided world for authentic witness to the unifying power of Christ. The broken and warring society of nations needed to see the reconciling work of Christ reflected in the Church universal. The years equipped Söderblom well for the international leadership which he gave. He served as pastor to the Swedish Church in Paris and as a Professor in Germany. The diary-entry of the student had been written in America and he was at home in England. Speech came easily to him in French, German, English, and the

Scandinavian tongues. He had been reared in a Swedish parsonage where the world mission of the Church was a ruling passion and before becoming Primate of Sweden he had been a Professor of Comparative Religion. Scholarship and homeliness were combined in his bearing; wit and wisdom were his in plenty. Always he displayed an unfailing interest in people and a passionate concern for those in greatest need. He once said that he was struck with the order of the confessions in the General Confession. 'We have left undone those things which we ought to have done' precedes 'and we have done those things which we ought not to have done'. This is true to the New Testament, said Söderblom, and the great burden upon his heart lay in the omissions of the Church in its witness to the world, especially in the realms of international justice and peace. Söderblom's great mission in life was to repair the omissions.

One of Söderblom's students[1] has said that nothing quickened Söderblom's indignation more deeply than 'the spiritual treacheries and disasters involved in a war between professedly Christian nations'. Söderblom was not the only Christian leader to feel this burden but as a citizen of a neutral country as well as a churchman he made persistent endeavours during the First World War to assert the supra-national role of the Church and to voice its call to reconciliation. Soon after the outbreak of war he tried—unsuccessfully—to secure the signatures of leading churchmen in the countries at war to an appeal for peace; as the war dragged on he made further endeavours to achieve some form of Christian conference across the dividing lines of war. One of these attempts, in 1917, won the support of a number of Christian leaders in England whose chief spokesman was William Temple. While disclaiming competence to prescribe the political course which should be followed, Temple shared Söderblom's conviction that the Churches had a part to play in affirming the principles on which peace might be re-established; he hoped, therefore, that even while the war was on, it might be possible to convene an

[1] Nils Karlström in *A History of the Ecumenical Movement*, p. 546.

international Christian conference in the service of reconciliation and peace.

None of these efforts achieved their aim but even the attempts gave evidence of a Christian standpoint which was not merely neutral but supra-national. They helped also to give expression to, and remind the world of, Christian realities in friendship and calling which were stronger than the enmities and divisions of war.

These activities of Temple, Söderblom and others were part of their profound conviction that while the Kingdom of God can never be equated with any pattern of human society, Christ's Gospel of the Kingdom carries with it guidance and power for the better ordering of men's relationships with one another. This was the starting point of various movements, in different countries, which contributed to the formation of the Life and Work Movement. In Great Britain a notable gathering was held in 1924 under the title 'Conference on Christian Politics, Economics and Citizenship', commonly known as 'Copec'. This is described in the *History of the Ecumenical Movement* as 'the most considerable effort made up to that date anywhere in the world to focus Christian thought and action on the urgent problems of the day'.[1] The key figure in 'Copec' was its chairman, William Temple, but much had depended on long preparatory work for which credit was greatly due to Lucy Gardner and C. E. Raven (Anglicans), Hugh Martin (Baptist) and Malcolm Spencer (Congregationalist). While this was a British initiative, eighty of the delegates were from countries outside Britain, including China and Japan.

In the United States, from the early years of the new century, there had been a diversity of Christian movements, interdenominational in their membership, giving expression to what came to be known as 'the Social Gospel'. As early as 1908 the Federal Council of the Churches had, at its inaugural assembly, adopted a pronouncement bearing the title 'The Social Creed of the Churches'. Closely akin to this

[1] op. cit., p. 540.

social concern there emerged also a series of movements with their emphasis on international affairs and on the part which the churches might play in fostering right relationships between the nations. The most widely influential of these was the World Alliance for Promoting International Friendship through the Churches. This was chiefly the outcome of the vision and devotion of an English layman—Willoughby Dickinson, later Lord Dickinson, strongly supported by many of the leaders of the churches in Europe and America. National groups federated in the Alliance at one time existed in approximately thirty-six different countries.

Out of such tributary streams as these, reinforced by the concern for peace and social justice which had been quickened by the tragedy of war, there came the larger international movement which culminated in 1925 in the 'Universal Christian Conference on Life and Work'. This was held at Stockholm and Archbishop Söderblom was its chairman. It is noteworthy that amongst its members were representatives of the Orthodox Church, including the Patriarchs of Alexandria and Jerusalem. The presence of these leading Orthodox churchmen was of great significance for the future of the ecumenical movement; it was also in line with an historic initiative taken a few years earlier by the Ecumenical Patriarchate of Constantinople. In 1920 an Encyclical Letter was issued from the Patriarchate and addressed 'to all the Churches of Christ, wherever they may be'. This Encyclical expressed the conviction 'that a closer intercourse with each other and a mutual understanding between the several Christian Churches is not prevented by the doctrinal differences existing between them and that such an understanding is highly desirable and necessary'. Amongst other aims, the Encyclical pleaded for a move of this kind in order that the Churches might develop an organ of common expression and action.

The declared purpose of this Universal Christian Conference on Life and Work was:
to concentrate the mind of Christendom on the mind of Christ as revealed in the Gospels towards those great social,

industrial and international questions which are so acutely urgent in our civilization.

The Stockholm Conference did not solve problems which have baffled more than one generation; but in its day this international gathering constituted a landmark in the recognition by the churches of their social responsibility. It was also a new thing that churches reflecting such great differences in tradition, outlook and national background, should try to reach agreement on the nature and main direction of Christian responsibility in the national and international order. Stockholm followed the precedent of Edinburgh 1910 in setting up a Continuation Committee to work further at these problems and five years later this gave place to a more permanent organization called the Universal Christian Council for Life and Work. The declared objective of the Council was 'to perpetuate and strengthen the fellowship between the Churches in the application of Christian ethics to the social problems of modern life'.

At this time—1930—the 'social problems of modern life' were legion, but one area of anxiety was already beginning to loom larger than any other. Its background was the dispeace which had followed the Treaty of Versailles. Instead of a brave new world, with proof that the strife of 1914–18 had been the war-to-end-war, the world seemed for many to have become a shabbier and harsher place. Financial disasters, economic regression, unemployment and general disaffection were becoming characteristic of the time, and in this setting there began to appear an ominous threat to justice, freedom and peace in the emergence of a new conception of the State—or the resurgence of an old conception of tyranny. Germany and Italy provided the most obvious and forbidding signs of this new era; but something more widespread was happening to the minds of men all over the world.

It was this situation which gave main direction to the activities of the Universal Christian Council on Life and Work during the nineteen-thirties. Many great names in Europe and America, representing various schools of churchmanship, were associated with this period, but it is significant that the most distinctive contribution came from one who was regarded primarily as a representative of the missionary movement— Dr. J. H. Oldham, who was still at this time secretary of the International Missionary Council. Oldham was convinced that secularism—the widespread abandonment of belief in a living God and the tacit assumption that man has the last word on things—was the most serious contemporary threat to the Christian mission. This had been the main concern of the Jerusalem meeting of the International Missionary Council. This secularism constituted a twofold menace to the Christian revelation as the way, the truth and the life. On the one hand, the new totalitarian governments were exercising over the wills of men an absolute authority which denied any prior responsibility to God; on the other hand, scientific humanism was capturing their minds. Both the State in its new paganism and the Community in its loss of religious faith were now standing over against Christian belief and the Christian way of life. Here was a radical gulf which threatened every year to grow wider. This was the crucial point of Christian mission- ary witness. It was made more urgent because of the attempts being made, especially in Germany, to make religious insti- tutions and doctrines subservient to a conception of life which was essentially pagan and secular. The 'community' or *Volk* was replacing any conception of a divine society; the Church would only be tolerated if it became docile to the will of the new Caesar and the national community over which he exercised his sway.

It was thus that the subject of Church, Community, and State became the theme of the next world conference of the Universal Christian Council of Life and Work. It took place in Oxford in 1937 with Oldham as the chief architect of its work and a Presidium which included Dr. William Adams Brown of the U.S.A., the Archbishop of Canterbury (Cosmo Gordon Lang), the Primate of Sweden (Archbishop Erling Eidem), the Orthodox Archbishop Germanos, and Bishop V. S.

Azariah of South India. Lay members distinguished for their competence in many of the technical fields relevant to the main theme included Professor Max Huber from Switzerland (President of the Permanent Court of International Justice at the Hague and President of the International Committee of Red Cross), Lord Lothian, Sir Alfred Zimmern, Sir Walter Moberley, (Sir) John Maud, and John MacMurray from Great Britain; Francis B. Sayre, John Foster Dulles, and Charles P. Taft from the U.S.A. A long process of study and research preceded the conference. Long before it met, the menace of totalitarianism and of the new paganisms had become plain for all to see. Indeed, the darkness that was falling over Germany had already cast its cloud over the work of the Life and Work Council three years before the Oxford meeting. In 1934 a committee of the Council had publicly allied the movement with the Confessing and resisting Church in Germany. This action precipitated a rift between the main membership of the Council and those German participants in the movement who were identified with the 'German Christian' Church in its subjection to the State. By 1937 no delegation from the German Evangelical Church could leave Germany for England.

The published report of the Oxford Conference remains one of the most impressive productions in the large library of ecumenical publications. Churches and many other agencies drew heavily on its findings and individuals prominent in public affairs profited by its wisdom as they made their own witness to the Lordship of Christ over the kingdoms of men.

*　　*　　*

The World Council of Churches

The Oxford Conference on Church, Community and State was the second world meeting of the Life and Work Movement. Within a few days of this gathering there was held in Edinburgh the second world meeting of the Faith and Order Movement. This conjunction was deliberate, for at the close of each of these conferences actions were taken which meant that henceforth the work of these two movements would be incorporated in a single and new organization, the World Council of Churches.

The possibility of creating such a Council had been mooted by various people at various times. The previous international and inter-denominational gatherings had concentrated on particular aspects of the Church's nature and task. While they had included in their membership representatives of many churches, none of them constituted a standing-council of the churches, concerned to see the work of the Church in its wholeness and providing an instrument through which, in acknowledgement of a common calling and loyalty, there would be a growing together in Christian experience and obedience. 'What I advocate', Archbishop Söderblom had written in 1919, 'is an Ecumenical Council of Churches. This should not be given external authority but would make its influence felt in so far as it can act with spiritual authority. It would not speak *ex cathedra*, but from the depth of the Christian conscience.' The minds of other Christian leaders, including the Orthodox Ecumenical Patriarch of Constantinople, were moving in a similar direction at this time.

Experience in such movements as the Faith and Order Movement and the Universal Christian Council for Life and Work quickened the desire for this further step and provided the ground from which to move forward. Before the meetings of the two earlier movements in 1937 closed, each of them passed a resolution favouring the creation of a Council of Churches and expressing a willingness that the new Council should take over and continue the tasks of the Faith and Order and Life and Work organizations. Much careful work had been necessary before this step was reached and many men outstanding in their generation contributed to the result; but at this most formative stage a special debt was due to four men— William Temple and J. H. Oldham of Great Britain, and William Adams Brown and Samuel McCrea Cavert of the U.S.A. It was Dr. Cavert—then General Secretary of the Federal Council of Churches in America—who first suggested the name World Council of Churches.

Although the decisive step was taken in 1937 eleven years

were to pass before the new Council could be formally constituted. The main reason for this was the outbreak of war in
1939, coupled with the strains of the preceding years and the
inability of the German churches to take part in international
conferences. Meantime a Provisional Committee, set up in
1937, took responsibility for shaping the Council-to-be during
a period in which it became known as 'The World Council of
Churches in process of formation'. Few international organizations have enjoyed a more lively and effective ante-natal
existence. Again, this was due to more people than can be
enumerated but a few names inevitably stand out with special
lustre. The first Chairman of the Provisional Committee was
William Temple. The Vice-Chairmen were John R. Mott, Dr.
Marc Boegner, and Archbishop Germanos. The General
Secretary was Dr. W. A. Visser't Hooft and he was assisted by
two Associate General Secretaries—Dr. William Paton, a
Presbyterian (at that time Secretary of the International
Missionary Council), and Dr. Henry Smith Leiper. Dr. Leiper,
an American Congregationalist, brought immense vitality and
resourcefulness to the formative years of the Council. It is
doubtful if any one could fully measure the extent to which
the subsequent strength of the Council was due to his champion-
ship of it, especially in America. William Paton's untimely
death in 1943 robbed the movement of one of its strongest
leaders and one who was esteemed throughout the world for
the clarity of his missionary vision and his integrity of purpose.
'If he had been an Anglican he would have been one of the
Archbishops', wrote the Archbishop of York (Dr. Garbett).
'He seemed to be indispensable,' continued the Archbishop,
'and it is impossible to see how we can do without him. A most
capable, wise, warm-hearted man.' Dr. Visser 't Hooft—a
Dutchman and a Reformed Churchman—brought an astonishing range of gifts and immense reserves of energy to the task.
As he is still serving, I record here no more than an interim
salute to one of the most remarkable and single-minded
servants of the Church in modern times. It is impossible now to
think of the World Council of Churches and many other phases

of the ecumenical movement apart from Dr. Visser 't Hooft's brilliant and distinctive leadership.

The next chapter will recall in more detail some aspects of the work of the World Council of Churches during its process of formation. The war inevitably coloured and even determined its main course: chaplaincy service, work amongst prisoners of war, preparation for Christian reconstruction after the war and the forging and maintaining of such links as were possible across the frontiers of war, constituted a noble contribution to the supra-national witness of the Church. Even though complete meetings of the Provisional Committee were impossible, ways and means were found for keeping its members in touch with one another, and the Geneva office of the Committee became a point of reference for Christian leaders throughout the world, especially for some of those valiant men and women who were involved in the Christian resistance movements in Scandinavia, Germany, Holland, and France. Men who played a critical part in public affairs as well as in their churches identified themselves with the aims and fellowship of this emerging Council. One of these was a Vice-Chairman of the Committee—Pastor Marc Boegner, the doyen of French Protestant ministers. Another was Bishop Eivind Berggrav, Primate of Norway, whose name became a household word speaking of courage and hope during the darkest years of the war. Bishop Berggrav, who combined a most acute mind with a childlike simplicity and great courage with gentleness, often recounted an experience during his detention by the Germans, when:

a peasant's wife had the idea to bring me every day a bottle of milk. The guards were accustomed to her coming but she was, of course, only allowed to go as far as to the fence, where the guard then took over the bottle. This day she didn't walk the path but came through the forest, jumped the fence and was before my kitchen window before the guards observed it. She whispered to me in a hurry: 'My husband listened to London yesterday evening, and he heard the Archbishop of Canterbury pray for you, bishop!' Then the guards arrived and took her away, but what a difference with me! No longer left alone but taken into the fellowship of Christian brethren, even in Great Britain. This moment is my deepest experience of 'Ecumenism' as a reality.

It was my privilege to visit Bishop Berggrav in his house in Oslo not long before his death. I had not seen him for several years and in the meantime he had been seriously ill. 'How are you?', I asked. 'Well,' he replied, 'I'm no better and no worse than when we met last.' 'That means you're still wonderful,' I said. 'No,' he answered in a flash, 'only still *wondering.*' 'Still wondering' is the confession of all who can look back in remembrance to what God wrought for the universal Christian cause through the frail instrument of a World Council of Churches 'in process of formation'.

In 1948 the qualifying phrase disappeared and the Council took formal shape at a memorable gathering in Amsterdam. Some of those who had led the work of the Provisional Committee during its significant decade continued their service as officers of the new Council. John R. Mott, who embodied in himself so many aspects of the whole movement, was appointed Honorary President. A Presidium of six was also created, the first holders of this office being Pastor Marc Boegner of France, the Archbishop of Canterbury (Dr. Fisher), Dr. T. C. Chao of China, Bishop G. Bromley Oxnam of the U.S.A., the (Orthodox) Archbishop of Thyateira (Dr. S. Germanos), and the (Lutheran) Archbishop of Uppsala (Dr. Erling Eidem). Dr. W. A. Visser 't Hooft was appointed General Secretary. The first Chairman of the Central Committee was Bishop G. K. A. Bell (subsequently appointed Honorary President) and the Vice-Chairman was Dr. Franklin C. Fry.[1]

[1] The officers in 1960 were *Presidents.* Dr. John Baillie of the Church of Scotland, Bishop Santo Uberto Barbieri of South America (Methodist), Bishop Otto Dibelius of Berlin (Lutheran), Archbishop Iakovus (Orthodox), Metropolitan Juhanon Mar Thoma of South India, Bishop Henry Knox Sherrill of the Protestant Episcopal Church of the U.S.A.; *Chairman of Central Committee:* Dr. Franklin Clark Fry (President of the United Lutheran Church in America and President of the Lutheran World Federation); *Vice-Chairman of Central Committee:* Dr. Ernest A. Payne (General Secretary of the Baptist Union of Great Britain and Ireland).

One hundred and forty seven churches became members of the Council at its inaugural Assembly. Some of the oldest Churches in the world were represented in the Assembly—the Church of Ethiopia and the Orthodox Syrian Church of Malabar. Some of the youngest were also present, such as the Presbyterian Church in Korea. Anglicans, Baptists, Old Catholics, Congregationalists, Calvinists and Lutherans, Methodists, Quakers, the Salvation Army, and the Orthodox Church all had their delegates. Few who were present are likely to forget the moment when the whole company gave assent to the 'Amsterdam Message', with its moving affirmation:

Here at Amsterdam we have committed ourselves afresh to Him, and have covenanted with one another in constituting this World Council of Churches. We intend to stay together.

On what basis was this done? The full answer to this lies in the many years of growing-together which preceded Amsterdam. The strength of this new beginning was in the realization, already tested in experience, that churches separated by history and tradition were being held and brought together by the one Lord. It lay in the deep awareness that their common foundation was Jesus Christ and his saving work. The Basis of the Council, as formulated in words, therefore read:

The World Council of Churches is a fellowship of churches which accept our Lord Jesus Christ as God and Saviour.

From time to time it has been contended that this formal Basis is inadequate in that it does not encompass the full range of Christian belief; it makes no specific reference to the Trinity, to the authority of the Scripture, to the coming again of Christ, or to other fundamental elements in the Christian faith. Partly in response to criticisms of this kind the Third Assembly of the Council in 1961 is being asked to adopt a slight expansion of the present Basis by making it read:

The World Council of Churches is a fellowship of churches which confess the Lord Jesus Christ as God and Saviour according to the Scriptures and therefore seek to fulfill together their common calling to the glory of the one God, Father, Son and Holy Spirit.

In appraising the significance of the World Council's Basis, whether in its present form or in its proposed revision, it must always be remembered that the Basis was never intended to serve the purpose of Creed or Confession. It was an affirmation concerning the central point around which the churches' coming-together gathers. It was an indication of the main ground on which the fellowship of the Council is established. It is for the churches as such to define the full scope of their beliefs in terms, credal or otherwise, according to their traditions and practice. A *Council* of Churches cannot usurp this function: it is not a 'super-Church' with its own credal statement. It is a fellowship of churches engaged—amongst other things—in a mutual sharing of conviction and experience and in a common desire to bear faithful witness to Christ. The Basis declares the starting-point from which this growing together proceeds. The churches begin with their common testimony to the divinity and saving work of Christ.

This character of the Council's Basis was re-affirmed at the Second Assembly at Evanston in 1954 in a statement which includes the following:

The World Council of Churches is an instrument at the service of the churches which enables them to enter into fraternal conversation with each other, to co-operate in various fields, and to render witness together to the world. It is not a new church (even less a super-church) and does not perform ecclesiastical functions.

Since the Council desires to make clear to the churches and to the world what it is, what it does, and who are its members it has adopted a *basis*. . . . This Basis performs three functions:

(1) It indicates the nature of the fellowship which the churches in the Council seek to establish among themselves.

For that fellowship, as a fellowship of churches, has its own unique character. It has a specific source and a specific dynamic. The churches enter into relation with each other, because there is a unity given once for all in the person and work of their common Lord and because the Living Lord gathers His people together.

(2) It provides the *orientation point* for the work which the World Council itself undertakes. The ecumenical conversations which take place in the World Council must have a point of reference. Similarly the activities of the Council must be submitted to an ultimate norm and standard. The Basis provides that standard.

(3) It indicates the *range* of the fellowship which the churches in the Council seek to establish.

The acceptance of the Basis is the fundamental criterion which must be met by a church which desires to join the Council. . . .

While the Basis is therefore less than a confession, it is much more than a mere formula of agreement. It is truly a basis in that the life and activity of the World Council are based upon it. And the World Council must constantly ask itself whether it is faithful to its Basis.

Each church which joins the World Council must therefore seriously consider whether it desires to participate in a fellowship with this particular Basis. On the other hand the World Council would overstep the limits it has set itself if it should seek to pronounce judgement as to whether any particular church is in fact taking the Basis seriously. It remains the responsibility of each church to decide itself whether it can sincerely accept the Basis of the Council.

The Council works through an Assembly composed of delegates appointed by the member-churches and through a series of committees. Only two meetings of the Assembly have so far been held—the inaugural meeting at Amsterdam in 1948 and a second one at Evanston, Illinois, in 1954. A third Assembly is being planned for December 1961, to be held in New Delhi. These great assemblies are formidable affairs. They involve a membership of from 500 to 600 voting delegates, with consultants, observers, and other categories of visitors. At Evanston there was a total attendance of 1,450. The numbers at New Delhi are expected to be close on a thousand of whom approximately 600 will be entitled to vote. A great meeting can be inspirational and both at Amsterdam and Evanston there were high moments when public speaking and public listening combined to further great ends. Moreover, when a gathering of this character is international in its composition, its impressiveness and kindling power can be all the greater. There is the colourful sight of delegates from all nations. There is the sound of a multitude of languages. This may sometimes resemble confusion of tongues more than close harmony, and the mechanics of working in the three official languages of the Council—English, French, and German— with occasional excursions into unofficial ones, may at times seem to darken counsel. Yet such difficulties only spring from the rich diversities of the fellowship, and this awareness of a wide-embracing membership, with differences transcended in great unities, becomes part of a memorable experience. So large an assembly can seldom be deliberative in the real meaning of the term; but by balancing sectional meetings or group discussions with the plenary sessions some real achievement in corporate thinking becomes possible.

The Assemblies are held too infrequently to suffice for the year-to-year needs of the Council. (Constitutionally an Assembly ordinarily meets every five years but so far the intervals have been of six and seven years.) A Central Committee, elected by the Assembly and meeting annually, therefore carries more detailed responsibility, and there is a further delegation of tasks to a small Executive Committee which meets twice yearly.[1] The Central Committee has a membership of ninety and the Executive twelve, plus *ex officio* members. In both cases, within the limits of numbers, care is taken to secure a balanced representation of denominations, geographical areas, and of the major interests of the Council. Writing of his experience between the first and second Assemblies

[1] On the organization of the World Council's committees, Divisions and Departments, see the Note on pp. 184 ff.

Bishop G. K. A. Bell, in his *Kingship of Christ*, testified warmly to the way in which the Central Committee had become 'a strong, cohesive body of Christian brethren, nearly all of them men and women holding posts of responsibility in their own churches. . . . They have come to know one another more and more intimately, and to appreciate the different points of view of the churches and countries from which their colleagues come'.[1] This is even more true of the more intimate fellowship of the Executive Committee with its more frequent meetings. These are some of the points at which the 'given' unity of Christians is experienced, with its compulsion to share and express the gift more fully. It has been my privilege, as a staff member, to attend nearly every meeting of the Central and Executive Committee since Amsterdam, as well as those of the Provisional Committee from 1946 onwards. Time after time, the business has included items of a kind which inevitably illustrated the widest possible divergences between people of different nations, races, cultures, and convictions. Public controversies such as those associated with affairs in Korea, Suez, Cyprus, Jordan, North Africa, and South Africa, have inevitably been reflected—often sharply—in these committee discussions. East-West relationships, with special reference to Russia or China, the tensions between the Communist and non-Communist world, the issue of colonialism and national independence, the racial problem, questions of war, disarmament and peace, have all in some form or another been reflected in these meetings, in discussion involving men and women with their roots and their day-to-day responsibilities in the areas of dispute. The same thing is true of matters more central to the life and witness of the Church. The great historic divergences of doctrine, outlook, and practice which have characterized Christian history have inevitably found a focal point in the fellowship and discussions of these bodies. There have been moments of difficulty; long and arduous sessions, including one occasion when a newly appointed Central Committee reached such an impasse that the closure on

[1] G. K. A. Bell: *The Kingship of Christ*, p. 82.

discussion was temporarily applied and the members adjourned to the chapel in the hope (not disappointed) of discovering how to begin again. There have been late-night and early morning endeavours in twos and threes to get near the truth of things about persons as well as principles. And through all this there has been a fulfilment of the Amsterdam pledge 'We intend to stay together', in experiences which have deepened the resolution and brought fresh testimony to the grace of our Lord Jesus Christ.

While these Central and Executive committees have their special place in the life of the Council, they are not the only occasions when comparable experiences become possible. The day-to-day work of the Council is organized within three main Divisions. The Division of Inter-Church Aid and Service to Refugees is responsible for the far-flung operations of relief and service to the needy and of that practical assistance between the churches which is an expression of their solidarity. Within the Division of Studies there are departments of Evangelism, Church and Society, Missionary Studies, and Faith and Order. In view of the earlier history and special significance of the Faith and Order Movement the department now bearing this name also works in conjunction with a Commission on Faith and Order which is responsible for convening (normally every three years) a world conference on some major aspect of the unity question. The third Division within this organizational pattern is named the Division of Ecumenical Action. A diversity of tasks comes within its purview: it has departments dealing with youth, the co-operation of men and women in Church and society, and the witness of the laity. This is also the Division through which the policy of the Ecumenical Institute at Bossey is related to the work of the World Council as a whole.

The next chapter will be concerned in more detail with the work of some of these Divisions and Departments. None of them is simply, or even primarily, a headquarters affair. In keeping with a central principle of the ecumenical movement, this headquarters structure—mainly located in Geneva—

exists to serve the churches and especially to assist and stimulate them in their own work and witness. These Departments and Divisions are clearing-houses, points of consultation, information and suggestion. Pre-eminently, their function is to help the churches to see and fulfil their own responsibilities within an ecumenical context. The help given from Geneva is only possible because it is guided and served by divisional and departmental committees on which the various member-churches are represented. Amongst other things, this means that every year several hundred people, of all nationalities and denominations, share responsibility for some aspect of the Council's work and do so in relationships which make possible some experience of that staying-together which is also a growing together.

To what extent does the World Council of Churches represent the churches in action or speak for them in its deliberations or public statements? Here it is necessary to emphasize again the self-imposed limitation on the Council, required by the nature of the ecumenical movement. In the words of the Evanston statement on the Basis, the Council is 'an instrument at the service of the churches. . . . It is not a new church (even less a super-church) and does not perform ecclesiastical functions'. This is made still more explicit in a section of the Council's constitution dealing with the question of authority. This reads:

The World Council shall offer counsel and provide opportunity of united action in matters of common interest.

It may take action on behalf of constituent Churches in such matters as one or more of them may commit to it.

The World Council shall not legislate for the Churches; nor shall it act for them except as indicated above or as may hereafter be specified by the constituent churches.

The constant point of reference and authority is the churches themselves. This, again, is made clear in that part of the constitution which refers to the making of public statements in the name of the Council:

In the performance of its functions, the Council through its Assembly or through its Central Committee may publish statements upon any situation or issue with which the Council or its constituent Churches may be confronted.

While such statements may have great significance and influence as the expression of the judgement or concern of so widely representative a Christian body, yet their authority will consist only in the weight which they carry by their own truth and wisdom and the publishing of such statements shall not be held to imply that the World Council as such has, or can have any constitutional authority over the constituent Churches or right to speak for them.

There are times when it is not easy to be content with the power of public statements whose authority consists 'only in the weight which they carry by their own truth and wisdom'. When feelings are running high on some public issue there are those who would wish a World Council to possess a more coercive authority, with the right to discipline and dismiss recalcitrant members. This would, however, mean a radical alteration in the whole nature of the Council and would be a departure from the main course and genius of the ecumenical movement. The Council is not a court of appeal or discipline; it can have no legislative power. It is worlds apart from being 'a Geneva counterpart of the Vatican'. It is a fellowship of churches which are prepared, on one condition only—acceptance of Christ as God and Saviour—to stay together and grow together, bringing their differences as well as agreements to the Lordship of Christ, the discipline of the Word and the guidance of the Spirit. In this process or pilgrimage there is no glossing-over of differences; no reluctance to challenge one another's assumptions and convictions and to work and pray for clearer light and fuller agreement. But one of the grounds on which there is hope of attaining this fuller unity in truth is the determination, subject to the one crucial condition, to stay together and learn together Christ's will for his Church.

Chapter IV

CROSSING THE FRONTIERS

Unity in Witness and Service

It was no accident that some of the earliest incentives which resulted in such organizations as the International Missionary Council and World Council of Churches came either from the foreign missionary movement or from groups whose chief concern was evangelical—the furtherance of the 'glorious Gospel of the blessed God'. These evangelical and missionary movements were essentially frontier-crossing movements. They moved in obedience to the Great Commission: 'Go ye therefore and teach all nations'. They thrust across the frontier between the Church and the world. They crossed cultural, linguistic, and geographical boundaries. They made their witness under the mandate: 'As the Father hath sent me so send I you'. The calling to Christian unity—another of the great driving forces of the ecumenical movement—has other accents besides that of witnessing to the world. It has its deepest springs in experience of Christ's reconciling work and in beliefs concerning his will for his disciples. But this also has its close and profound connexion with Christian responsibility towards the world: 'That they may be one; as thou, Father, art in me and I in thee, that they also may be one in us: that the world may believe that thou hast sent me'.

'Foreign' missionary activity and 'direct' evangelism will always be central to this frontier-crossing obedience. But the frontiers are many and witnessing to Christ requires from his disciples many forms of evangelical obedience. The 'direct' evangelism of the foreign missionary lands him in the business of language study, of reducing languages and dialects to writing, translating Scripture, teaching people to read, producing and distributing books. Here are all sorts of technical frontiers to cross. In many countries the beginnings of modern education, modern medicine and a host of other social services, have been due to missionary initiative. Christian missions still carry a large volume of this work and most of it has proved inseparable from the central purpose of evangelism.

Operations of this kind are sometimes classified as 'subsidiary activities' or 'auxiliary agencies'. In the sense that they are not direct proclamations of the Gospel through the spoken word there is justification for this way of regarding them. But there is more to it than this. One of William Carey's colleagues in Bengal was a printer. His days were spent in the mechanical business of dealing with paper, ink, printing presses, the employment of workers and so on. Subsidiary activities. But on a certain day in the year 1800 this printer-missionary wrote in his diary:

On this memorable day the first page of the New Testament was composed for printing in Bengali. Now, O Lord, let the day break and the sun arise!

And then the diarist (William Ward) added his adaptation of St. Paul's wondering testimony in Ephesians iii.8:

Unto me, who am less than the least of all saints, is this grace given, that I should *print* among the heathen the unsearchable riches of Christ.

The subsidiary activity had become the primary one of proclaiming the Gospel.

It is not difficult to appreciate this in relation to an occupation so closely related to evangelism as printing and publishing the Scriptures. It is less commonly recognized that there is something here which has profound implications for all kinds of work. At a memorable service in Beirut in 1956 thanksgiving was being offered by an international gathering for the work of the World Council of Church's Division of Inter-Church Aid and Service to Refugees. In the course of the service a bishop of the Eastern Orthodox Church recalled the significance for his own Communion of the practical assistance which many Orthodox priests and church members had received over the years through the work of this Division—food for the hungry, homes for the homeless and, in some instances, the means to start life again. This ministry had begun many years before, at a time when the Orthodox churches and the other member-churches of the World Council knew much less of one another than was the case later on. For this reason, there was also, at that time, less confidence and more hesitancy in these relationships. 'Even when we spoke to one another in the same verbal language,' said the Bishop, 'we did not yet understand. But when you came and served us in our need, you used a language of manual signs, the sign-language of brotherly love in Christ'. The prosaic business of dispatching food and clothing, or securing building supplies, or struggling with visas and endless documents, all become in these circumstances an articulation of the Word—a word of unity as well as succour and both used by grace. Such ministries are not merely subsidiary or auxiliary; they are integral to Christian testimony concerning Christ and his kingdom. As Dr. Visser 't Hooft said in that same service in Beirut, they derive their meaning from the 'philanthropy of God': and this is not just alms-giving. It is that self-giving which lies behind all God's other gifts and which finds its profoundest description in the words of John iii.16.

It is not always easy to keep this faith strong and this vision clear amidst the chores of the kingdom. But this is the standpoint from which a wide range of activity into which the World Council of Churches has been drawn needs to be understood and tested. For ten years prior to its formal inauguration in 1948 the World Council of Churches was 'in process of formation'. This process was much more than the constitutional one of framing an organization. It was not even confined to the process of growing together in understanding, through personal contact and discussion. It was a period of *doing*—most of all, a process of serving together at the places of greatest human need.

One of the most moving of these undertakings was the work carried on, under the aegis of the Provisional Committee of the World Council, amongst prisoners of war. Like other activities of the World Council, this ministry antedated even the formation of the Provisional Committee. The World YMCA operating in close relationship with the International Red Cross, had done valiant work amongst prisoners during the First World War. This work was, of course, resumed with the outbreak of war in 1939, and in policy and leadership there were close ties between these organizations and the emerging World Council of Churches. What chiefly concerned the Provisional Committee of the World Council was the provision of a regular chaplaincy service amongst the prisoners and one which would know itself to be part of a supra-national ministry, sustained by the prayers and the resources of churches throughout the world. In 1939, therefore, the Provisional Committee set up an Ecumenical Commission for Chaplaincy Service to Prisoners of War. Wherever possible it secured access to the camps on both sides of the main battle-lines. It gave regular help—Bibles, service books, church equipment etc.—to imprisoned pastors; it carried through all the difficult negotiations with Governments and military and prison authorities, in order to ensure that prisoners might receive pastoral help in their own language and through priests and ministers of their own denomination. There were endless difficulties and frustrations in the work. There were camps in Germany, Russia and elsewhere into which access was not allowed. Yet remarkable things were achieved, even including the gathering of imprisoned theological students of various denominations and nationalities into special camps where theological studies could be resumed under a 'Faculty' composed of captive professors. 'In spite of all its difficulties,' wrote one who saw much of this work at close quarters, 'the Church in Captivity is a reality. One of its characteristic features is its real and conscious feeling of belonging to a community which goes beyond its own.'

Akin to this ministry amongst military prisoners of war was a service rendered, often under more poignant and terrible conditions, to civilians who became both refugees and prisoners, deprived—in many instances—of national status, home and fortune, health and friends. These were the uprooted and deported peoples, driven into exile on grounds of race or politics, the impoverished—sometimes demented—survivors of massacres and unspeakable brutalities such as those which fell with appalling heaviness upon the Jewish people.

In exercising a ministry of compassion and succour to these, the saddest victims of man's inhumanity to man, the work of the World Council of Churches owed much to the inspiration and initiative of a remarkable movement which still works under the name CIMADE. The name is one of the more euphonious and permissible of those words which are made up of the initial letters of a longer title. In this instance the title is a French one —the *Comité Inter-Mouvements auprès des Evacués*. It had a peace-time predecessor in the *Conseil Protestant de la Jeunesse* which was initiated by the French YMCA, YWCA, the Girl Guides, the Boy Scouts and the Student Christian Movement. Many of the members of this movement themselves became displaced persons when they were forced to leave their homes in Alsace at the beginning of the Second World War. With the fall of France in 1940 they were involved in the agonizing internal conflict in France and most of them became members of the resistance movement. They set their faces against all anti-Semitic measures and directed their main activities as an organization to the helping of Jewish refugees. Amongst a great diversity of services—most of them conceived with astonishing ingenuity and carried through with great courage— they concentrated on two main activities. First, they assisted condemned Jews—through a Christian underground move- ment—to escape from the death-trains or to elude capture; secondly, they gave personal service in the great camps in the south of France where deported or escaped Jews from other parts of Europe were interned. The first of these activities involved the kind of hazards portrayed so poignantly in Charles Morgan's *The River Line*; Cimade was the source of innumer- able River Lines. The second type of ministry could often only be accomplished on condition that the Cimade workers themselves accepted the conditions of captivity—prison food, prison discipline, and sometimes prison punishment. In some instances these workers with the status of prisoners also operated through a River Line—or at any rate a subway between the camp and the outside world. Exciting and physically heroic as was this service, its most significant characteristic was its spiritual certainty and its unwavering recognition that in his greatest physical sufferings and extremities man needs not only bread, shelter, and healing for his broken body, but an authentic word in answer to the cry of a tortured mind and beaten life: 'Why?... Is there a God?... Does he care?' Few ministries of compassion and heroic activity have maintained, with greater discernment and conviction, this inseparable connexion between daily bread and the Bread of Life, water and the Living Water. After the war Cimade widened its membership and became more international as well as inter-denominational. It has recruited Swiss, Dutch, Scandinavian, American, English, Canadian, and Russian workers and has continued to concentrate on emergency needs such as those which have arisen in recent years in Algiers and Morocco.

Cimade, as will be seen, had its origin independently of the World Council of Churches; but within its young pre-war leadership, as in its later crusades, there were men and women already participating in the processes which led to the formation of the World Council of Churches. (The principal leader and for many years the guiding genius of Cimade was a French woman—theologically trained and also with experience in the diplomatic service—Dr. Madeleine Barot, who is now on the staff of the World Council of Churches.) There were also close working relationships between this organization and the wartime chaplaincy and relief service of the Provisional Committee of the World Council. Moreover, the human need to which Cimade gave itself in one part of Europe was appearing during these years in many other lands and on a vast scale. This growing and widespread need claimed much of the time and resources of the Provisional Committee of the World Council from the outbreak of war until the formal launching of the Council at Amsterdam in 1948. During this period Cimade was by no means the only organization with which the Provisional Committee was in touch. As with the chaplaincy service to prisoners of war, so with work amongst refugees, the World Council of Churches 'in process of formation' built on earlier pioneer service and, indeed, took some of this older work into its own structure and operations.

Outstanding amongst these earlier ventures was an organization known as the European Central Bureau for Inter-Church Aid which began to take shape in 1919 under the direction of a devoted Swiss Protestant, Dr. Adolf Keller. Its title of *European* Bureau signified its original main area of concern, though from 1922, when it was formally constituted, it was sponsored by the Federal Council of Churches in America as well as by the Federation of Protestant Churches in Switzerland. As the phrase *Inter-Church Aid* indicates, the earliest operations of this organization were in the form of help from one church to another in times of special need; refugee work came later. When churches in Central Europe and Germany began to suffer deprivations under totalitarian governments, this Central office organized international help for them. It soon extended its beneficent ministry to Armenian, Assyrian, and other Orthodox Christian communities. It also looked as far afield as Asia where Chinese famine victims came within its care. Then, when political and racial policies during the decade before the Second World War led to the uprooting of peoples, Dr. Keller's organization was one of the most effective channels through which aid was made available on an international and interdenominational basis.

In 1942 responsibility for the work of the European Central Bureau for Inter-Church Aid was taken over by the Provisional Committee of the World Council of Churches, which then created a Department of Reconstruction and Inter-Church Aid. The word *Reconstruction* is important here. The immediate and emergency needs were vast enough; no single organization could hope to cope with them. Yet, while continuing and expanding its immediate service on behalf of ruined churches, stricken pastors, and dispersed peoples, this new undertaking (in operation, it should be remembered, years before the inaugural Assembly of the World Council) was now thinking in terms of the vast post-war task of rebuilding churches and rehabilitating Christian communities. There could, of course, be little in the way of representative international meetings while the war raged, but a surprising amount was accomplished in maintaining contact between the members of the World Council's Provisional Committee; transatlantic crossings, or journeys to and from neutral Switzerland and Sweden, supplemented other communications, and national committees were formed in a number of countries to raise money, to educate public opinion, to influence government policies, and especially to keep this growing need of the refugees and the dispossessed upon the consciences and in the prayers and service of Christian people.

Such events as World Refugee Year, or the Christian Aid Weeks initiated in Britain by the British Council of Churches, or great generosity campaigns in the United States under the slogan 'One Great Hour of Sharing', have made this relief and refugee service perhaps the best-known activity of the World Council of Churches. It is not primarily an operation centralized in a Geneva administration. The main contributions in money, food and clothing and personal service have come through the work of independent national organizations such as Church World Service in the United States or the Inter-Church Aid and Refugee Service of the British Council of Churches. In the areas of need it is the responsibility of local or national committees (such as Japan Church World Service or Korea Church World Service) to formulate the programme of aid, scrutinize requests, and administer the resources as they become available. But these national agencies are kept in close touch with one another through the Geneva office of the Division of Inter-Church Aid and Service to Refugees of the World Council of Churches. At this central point there is co-ordination and clearing of appeals for help and of the response of the national committees. The Geneva office also works in direct contact with the member churches of the World Council in regard to the whole enterprise.

Although the main central responsibility of the World Council is one of clearance and co-ordination there are aspects of this work which can best be handled—sometimes only be handled—by initiatives taken at an international centre and to some extent followed through by more central action. This applies to parts of the refugee operation—dealing with the United Nations Relief and Works Agency for Palestine, or with the United Nations High Commissioner for Refugees (whose chief responsibility is for European refugees), or with the Inter-Governmental Committee for European Migration or with the United States Escapee Program. There is continuous collaboration with these agencies, and the World Council of Churches has undertaken tasks at the request of, and with resources provided by United Nations or inter-governmental agencies. Further, as its name indicates, the Division of Inter-Church Aid and Service to Refugees of the World Council of Churches is concerned with more than refugees, displaced persons, escapees, migrants, and all the other victims of political and military conflict. The term *inter-church* has a twofold reference: it includes the churches' help to one another and the churches' united service to the world at points of special need. This calls for speedy action in times of disaster—earthquake, famine, or flood. Some funds (contributed from member churches or through the national committees) are held in Geneva to make possible quick action in these emergencies. Within a few hours of the occurrence of earthquakes in Greece, Algeria, and Morocco, volcanic eruptions in Chile, floods in India and Pakistan, hurricanes in Japan, Haiti or Madagascar, money was cabled from Geneva to the places of need in the name of the churches, while information and appeals were also cabled to the national committees. Similarly, while most of the field-work in all these situations, whether amongst refugees or in relation to sudden disasters, is locally and nationally organized, the

World Council of Churches maintains its own staff of field workers, located in various parts of the world and with the necessary mobility. This staff—much of it constantly changing with changing needs—now numbers about five hundred; a great variety of nationalities and denominational allegiances, languages and professional skills are represented in it.

It is scarcely possible to assess fully and accurately the amount of money—the result of voluntary giving on the part of churches—raised and spent annually in this beneficent ministry. There is no completely co-ordinated picture of the money-value of the service rendered by national committees or by the kind of national organizations already named, by the member churches of the World Council, and by closely-related international Christian agencies such as Lutheran World Service. On the basis of available data it was estimated that these organizations and their constituent bodies contributed in 1950 about $10,000,000 (a little over £3,500,000); in 1955 the figure was more than four times this. As the range of this service increases—and it does so every year—it becomes less practicable to make a reliable over-all estimate: what can safely be asserted is that the annual money total of the churches' giving to these great works of mercy now far exceeds the figures just quoted. Within this total, the direct responsibilities carried within the World Council of Churches Division of Inter-Church Aid involve an annual budget of about $900,000 (£320,000). Rather more than half of this goes to work amongst refugees; the remainder —apart from administration costs—is allocated to other forms of emergency service and to that inter-church aid which is the giving of help from church to church.

Figures, however, in these areas of Christian service, need constantly to be translated into persons if their meaning is to be properly understood. Even then it is all too easy to blur the personal and spiritual significance of what is being done if we simply apply the numbers to people instead of pounds. It is, for example, true to say that in 1960 the World Council was carrying a 'caseload' of 60,000 refugees and that, of these, about 33,000 were awaiting emigration while the remaining 27,000 were listed as non-settled. This is, in fact, the wording of a memorandum which was circulating in the office of the Division of Inter-Church Aid and Service to Refugees at that time. It was a statistical record concerning 'unpersons in uncountries', as *The Times* once described them. But— ' "Master, the multitudes throng thee and press thee; how sayest thou '*Who* touched me?' " And Jesus said, "Some *one* hath touched me" . . .'.

Try another figure. To date, 200,000 refugees have been found a home and livelihood by the World Council. About 12,000 are resettled every year. About a thousand every month, about thirty every day. I remember turning over the pages of a large day-book or journal in an office where some part of this operation was being administered. This was not just a series of numerical items adding up to a grand total. Each page was headed by a name and there followed notes about the history of the person. There were blanks in most of these histories, blanks between the different countries or camps in which the 'case' had stayed for a time. There were intermittent references to escapes and deportation. There was information about nearest relative (so often 'none'), about illness, employment, and (especially) unemployment. There were references to children, to hospitals, to physical defects. And each page was a moving story of some *one*. Twelve thousand a year, about one thousand a month, thirty a day: thirty tomorrow, thirty today; one of the thirty, this minute, in my office or home. Today, no passport, no citizenship, no means of livelihood, no home. Tomorrow, or later today— *now*, before the 'case' says goodbye and the 'caseload' is reduced by one, this *one* has touched me.

This is what the vast operation called Inter-Church Aid and Service to Refugees comes down to, or rises up to. It is to this end that the churches have come together, across national frontiers and denominational differences in a unity of concern and obedience springing from the one Spirit.

★   ★   ★

'Rapid Social Change'

'What stands most in jeopardy is not bread but freedom; not the body but the spirit; not material well-being and the progress of technics but social justice, love and peace. . . . Christendom should be disquieted.' These words were written by one of the French pioneers in the ecumenical movement (Pastor Elie Gounelle) a quarter of a century ago. They have since been endorsed by happenings in almost every part of the world and they still express the deepest concern of Christians who are busy in distributing bread to the hungry.

Alongside the work of the World Council's Division of Inter-Church Aid and Service to Refugees there was initiated in 1955 a series of studies under the title: 'The common Christian Responsibility towards Areas of Rapid Social Change'. Not many countries are free from changes of this character. The title is applicable to new towns and re-housing areas in Britain, or to the constant movement of families and communities in the United States, no less than to the break-up of village and tribal patterns in Asia and Africa. But the points of concentration in these studies were, in the first instance, areas in Asia, Africa, and Latin America where the pace and radical nature of the social change are most revolutionary in their effects. It is in such areas as these that questions of 'material wellbeing and the progress of technics' raise in their most searching form problems of 'social justice, love and peace'. In launching the studies the committee responsible for the project said:

The problems of areas of rapid social change in Asia, Africa and Latin America must be seen as world problems. The social awakening of these countries has come about through the impact of western technology, education and religion; and the way in which the West responds will help to determine whether this awakening will find its creative fulfilment in the development both of a better community life in Asia, and Africa and of human solidarity. Whether for good or ill we are one family under heaven.

In the initial discussion of the studies it became clear that while the character of the West's response to the social revolution in Asia and Africa was supremely important—its response both in attitude and sympathy and in terms of political and economic action—in some respects the most urgent questions were those confronting Christians at the point of the revolution itself, in Asia, Africa, or elsewhere. 'Young' churches standing within the revolutionary ferment, and young Christians involved in day-to-day decisions, made clear their need of insight and knowledge on which to act with Christian responsibility. The programme was therefore launched with a double objective:

First, to enable Christians and indigenous churches in Asia, Africa and Latin America to make a concerted study, under indigenous leadership, of the new social issues that challenge Christian social thought and action in their areas, in order to clarify the Christian responsibility for political, economic and social life. This involves the development of a social thought which is informed by the Christian faith and suited to a rapidly changing situation, and which will serve as a guide to Christians and non-Christians. It also involves rethinking and altering the pattern of the Church's life and structure in the light of its social mission.

Second, to enable Christians and churches in the West to understand their responsibilities in the evolution of economic welfare, and the building of a new community life in the lands of Asia, Africa and Latin America. This involves specifically understanding the economic implications of world community and the role of economic and technical aid from the West in the realization of social goals and spiritual values.

Even those who had been most zealous in inaugurating this programme were surprised by the speed and enthusiasm of the response to it. It immediately won the interest and active co-operation of laymen in many different countries whose daily job lies on one or other of the frontiers of this social revolution. Africans, Indians, Japanese, and Indonesian eagerly participated in it. Sociologists, economists, lawyers, trade union leaders, politicians, civil servants and education- ists all become involved, with their European or American brethren, in one aspect or another of the studies. Some of them met occasionally as an international group in Europe, America or Asia; but most of the work was done on the spot by men and women living with the daily problem. And the common starting point and common bond of them all was their membership in a world-wide Christian community and their desire to perceive and discharge a 'common Christian res- ponsibility'.

The results of this kind of enterprise are not measurable. Study, however lively the process or keen the minds engaged in it, has to be geared into action and in this complex world the gears are sometimes slow to engage. Moreover—in keeping with the nature of the ecumenical movement and of the responsibility of the churches—such an undertaking as this can go little farther than elucidating problems and pointing a way forward in terms which have then to be reckoned with outside the Church and by other agencies than a World Council of Churches. Here we run again into a principle and a necessary limitation which apply to other aspects of the ecumenical movement. What can be said with confidence about this particular undertaking, however, is that in place after place there are men and women meeting their daily responsibilities with clearer insight and greater confidence than before because of their participation in this venture. And there are local churches working on some of these frontiers with new understanding of what it means to proclaim the Lordship of Christ over the whole of life. It is at this point that studies, discussions, and experiments in the field of social responsibility prove to be inseparable from an under- standing of the Gospel in its full range and depth. A group of Asian Christians, closely involved in these Rapid Social Change studies, expressed this conviction persuasively in a report adopted by a conference of Asian church leaders in Kuala Lumpur in 1959. They said:

The Gospel is a Gospel of redemption of the whole human race and of the whole created world. By His death and resurrection Jesus Christ has reconciled all things to Himself. His purpose is not to withdraw individual spirits one by one from their involvement with material things and human communities in order to set them in a purely "spiritual" relation to Himself. Rather, His goal is 'to unite all things in Him.' . . .

The Gospel is a Gospel of the Kingship of Christ over the world. Therefore the meaning of world history, including that of modern Asian history, is to be discovered in that Kingship which today is hidden and will be revealed at the end of time. The Church must endeavour to discern how Christ is at work in the revolutions of contemporary Asia, releasing new creative forces, judging idolatry and false gods, leading people to a decision for or against Him. . . .

Our discussions as Christians about economics, politics are therefore conversations about Jesus Christ, that is to say, an attempt of faith to discern Him in the social change of our nations and to discover what it means to respond to His call in relation to these changes.

These frontier-crossing studies into the areas of rapid social change were not a new feature of the ecumenical movement. As the preceding chapter has recalled, it was upon such problems as these that the Life and Work movement and kindred endeavours focused attention. The particular significance of the rapid social change studies lies in their new and contemporary insights into the nature of Christian social responsibility, especially in certain key situations outside the Western world.

* * *

The Commission of the Churches on International Affairs

Another of the great concerns which animated the Life and Work Movement has found fresh expression in recent years through the Commission of the Churches on International Affairs. This was organized in 1946 under the sponsorship of the International Missionary Council and the Provisional Committee of the World Council of Churches for purposes which included (1) 'serving the churches as a source of stimulus and knowledge in their approach to international problems. . . .'; (2) 'studying selected problems of international justice and world order. . . '; (3) 'calling the attention of the churches to problems especially claimant upon the Christian conscience and suggesting ways in which Christians may act effectively upon these problems in their respective countries and internationally.' As the basis of these responsibilities, the Commission was charged 'to discover and declare Christian principles with their direct relevance to the relations of nations . . .', and it was instructed to maintain contact with such international bodies as United Nations on matters which included 'the encouragement of respect for and observance of human rights and fundamental freedoms, special attention being given to the problem of religious liberty'.

All this sounds like 'going into politics' in a big way. Is this the business of the churches? We are back here at questions which have recurred again and again in the course of this whole movement—indeed, throughout Christian history. What is the nature of the kingdom of God and its relation to world events, to nations and history? What is the bearing of Christ's redeeming work on the social relationships of man? 'The Gospel is a Gospel of redemption of the whole human race and of the whole created world', affirmed those Asian Christians in the report already quoted. This reflects the approach to these questions which has been characteristic of the ecumenical movement. These organizations do not 'go into politics' as political organizations: they venture across these frontiers in the conviction that Christ is Lord of history, Lord of the nations and King of kings. His realm transcends this world and his kingdom must never be equated with any temporal order; yet his Word has meaning for history and for time and it is part of the mission of the Church to seek to articulate the Word in terms which can be translated into political action. This form of frontier-crossing obedience is beset by many pitfalls; the peril of confusing the eternal and the temporal instead of allowing the one to illumine and redeem the other is always present. Moreover, in the nature of things, the task of achieving common agreement amongst Christians drawn from a diversity of historical situations and national and cultural backgrounds, is manifestly difficult. These are some of the reasons why the churches' 'pronouncements' on current affairs, whether made denominationally or ecumenically, seldom carry with them a self-authenticating prophetic accent. But the undertaking is part of our Christian obedience, even where it seems to be no more impressive than the linguistic struggles of a missionary slowly mastering a new language in the hope that eventually a vehicle will be fashioned which can be used with power by the Word.

Partly because of the nature of its task the Commission of the Churches on International Affairs is not solely an organ of the two bodies which sponsored its formation—the World Council of Churches and the International Missionary Council. It enjoys considerable autonomy, but it derives its main support from the two sponsoring organizations and is under an obligation to report to them. They, in turn, refer to the Commission matters on which its expert help is required. These have included questions concerning mission property in Israel, marriage laws in Israel, the study, with special reference to religious liberty, of draft constitutions of new States, migration and population problems, technical assistance to under-developed countries, and so on. In times of crisis—as in Korea, Kenya, Cyprus or Colombia—the Commission has initiated special studies and consultations, or it has sent delegations to confer with Christian leaders in the countries concerned. The great issues of war and peace, with the complex problems of disarmament, receive continuous attention within the Commission, and on all these matters there is close contact with United Nations whose delegates receive memoranda or personal representations from officers of the Commission. For example, on an occasion when aspects of the *apartheid* policy in South Africa were being debated in United Nations there was distributed to five hundred United

Nations delegates a memorandum which included the text of a resolution passed by the Second Assembly of the World Council of Churches on this grievous question of the frontiers that discriminate between races by means of a colour-bar. The resolution (passed in 1954) reads:

The Second Assembly of the World Council of Churches declares its conviction that any form of segregation based on race, colour or ethnic origin is contrary to the gospel, and is incompatible with the Christian doctrine of man and with the nature of the Church of Christ. The Assembly urges the churches within its membership to renounce all forms of segregation or discrimination and to work for their abolition within their own life and within society.

In doing so the Assembly is painfully aware that, in the realities of the contemporary world, many churches find themselves confronted by historical, political, social and economic circumstances which may make the immediate achievement of this objective extremely difficult. But under God the fellowship of the ecumenical movement is such as to offer to these churches the strength and encouragement to help them and individuals within them to overcome these difficulties with the courage given by faith, and with the desire to testify ever more faithfully to our Master.

From its very beginning the ecumenical movement by its very nature has been committed to a form of fellowship in which there is no segregation or discrimination. The Assembly of the World Council of Churches rejoices in this fact and confirms this practice as the established policy of the Council.

In its relationships with United Nations the Commission of the Churches on International Affairs has consultative status with the Economic and Social Council and it has maintained close contact with such organs as the Trusteeship Council and the Committee on Technical Assistance to Under-developed Countries. It played an influential part in the discussions which resulted in the Universal Declaration of Human Rights with its assertion that:

Everyone has the right to freedom of thought, conscience and religion; this right includes freedom to change his religion or belief, and freedom, either alone or in community with others and in public or private, to manifest his religion or belief in teaching, practice, worship and observance.

The Commission is also in constant touch with the work of the International Labour Organization, the World Health Organization, the Food and Agriculture Organization, and United Nations Educational, Social, and Cultural Organization (UNESCO). Concurrently with its relationship to the World Council of Churches and the International Missionary Council it works through national Commissions composed of men and women chosen for their knowledge and experience in international problems and their representative character as church members. In Great Britain the International Department of the British Council of Churches serves as this national Commission. All this work would be impossible without the generous service of busy people—especially laymen—many of whom bring outstanding gifts to the task. Amongst those who were most active in the formation of the Commission in 1946 were J. H. Oldham, Baron F. M. Van Asbeck (at that time Professor of International Law in the University of Leiden), John Foster Dulles (then a practising lawyer in the United States), Sir Alfred Zimmern, Professor Reinhold Niebuhr, Professor H. S. Alivisatos, Professor Emil Brunner, and Dr Walter Van Kirk who had for many years played a leading part in America in the churches' witness in international affairs. From the beginning the Commission has been greatly served by its chairman—Sir Kenneth Grubb, and its Director—Dr. O. Frederick Nolde.

* * *

The Laity at Home and Abroad

The crucial frontier between the Church and the world is not an institutional one; it is not the organizational line between institutions called churches and the life outside them. It is deeper and more subtle than this. It is the frontier between life in Christ and life apart from him; between the moments of insight and obedience and the moments of blindness and disobedience. It lies between our corporate experience within the fellowship of the spirit and our life in a society based on standards, assumptions, and hopes other than those which reflect the mind of Christ. This frontier may cut into 'Christian' institutions, including the organized life of the churches; in a profound and searching sense there needs to be a constant crossing of the frontiers *within* the churches so that their life may be renewed and become more perfectly the realm of Christ's Lordship. This character of the main frontier also means that the members of the Church stand at the most critical point of witness when they are living out their daily life in society. Here the most vital witnessing responsibility is not fulfilled by inviting the non-churchgoer to 'come to church', needful and important as this may be. It is fulfilled by bringing to bear upon the daily life of society convictions, judgements, standards, and graces of behaviour derived from faith in Christ and belief in his Gospel.

Sharper recognition of this truth in recent years has influenced two developments in the work of the International Missionary Council and the World Council of Churches. The first of these involves an extension in the use of the term 'missionary'. Not for the first time, but with fresh interpretation and emphasis, the International Missionary Council through its Willingen meeting in 1952 issued an appeal for what it called 'non-professional missionaries'. The term is not the most happy one for it may suggest chiefly a protest against 'professionalism' within the missionary movement. This, of course, is always to be deprecated, but the Willingen proposal was concerned with something different from this. It was a call for a recognizable 'brotherhood' of Christian men and women working in commerce, industry or government in lands other than their own and bringing to their daily work and relationships a Christian dedication and obedience.

The relevance to the foreign missionary movement of the beliefs and behaviour of Westerners resident in 'foreign' lands has long been apparent. One of the pioneer missionaries of the 'Great Century' of missions was a remarkable and somewhat eccentric German named Tobias Ringeltaube. Ringeltaube was one of the early emissaries of the London Missionary Society and his name is still honoured for the work he did in South Travancore. On foundations which he helped to lay at great cost there was built up one of the strongest churches in Asia.

Before his appointment by the London Missionary Society Ringeltaube had been in touch with the Danish Missionary Society. The Danes could not make use of him immediately but they told him that the Society for the Promotion of Christian Knowledge was looking for a man to work in Calcutta. He was required, not for service with Indians, but with English settlers in Bengal. Ringeltaube considered this and replied :

To preach the simple but saving and sanctifying word of the Cross to simple-minded men who hitherto have not experienced its power, that is my desire; not to dispute with unbelieving Englishmen in Calcutta.

To Ringeltaube there appeared to be two fundamentally different tasks—taking the Gospel to simple-minded Indians or confronting the unbelief of English settlers. This was seen as an either-or, and for the missionary the choice was clear—to preach the simple word to simple-minded men who had not experienced its power. As things turned out, this devoted missionary did try his hand at the job in Calcutta, but the effort was short-lived. Henceforth he looked upon Calcutta and other great cosmopolitan centres as being almost beyond redemption. Years later he wrote :

Long experience has taught me that in large towns, especially where many Europeans are, the Gospel makes but little progress. Superstition is too powerfully established and the example of the Europeans too baneful.

Ringeltaube is more to be commended for his achievements

than criticized for his limitations. There are diversities of gifts, aptitudes, and callings. Ringeltaube saw where his own contribution ought to lie and he made it, often at great cost and with marvellous consequences. But the Church universal was under an obligation to see its mission in its totality and not to let one part of it be outflanked by omissions elsewhere. Those two frontiers of witness—to simple-minded (and not so simple-minded) Indians and to unbelieving Englishmen in Calcutta, needed manning simultaneously in a unity of purpose which used diversities of gifts.

In renewed awareness of this need the Willingen meeting of the International Missionary Council in 1952 pleaded for a fresh advance in 'training for Christian witness and the service of the Church in secular occupations overseas'. Supporting this proposal, Canon M. A. C. Warren said:

I believe there is a call for an entirely new type of missionary activity to be developed alongside the traditional modes. We need, for instance, to envisage men and women of scientific training who will be ready to give their service in development schemes, going to their work as ordinary salaried officials and bringing their expert knowledge to bear on some local situation. But they will go, not merely as those whose Christian convictions are marginal to their work, as is commonly the case of many today. Rather, they will go with a vocation consciously and deliberately to seek to work out 'a disciplined and purified technology' in the light of Christian insights. Promotion and financial reward will, by such men, be completely subordinated to their Christian vocation. Others with the same dedication will go as experienced trade unionists, to help ensure that the young trade union movements of Africa and Asia are built up on Christian insights as to the meaning of society to individuals. Yet others will bring a Christian integrity to the development of co-operative movements . . . I envisage the possibility of such a missionary brotherhood being pioneered by a number of men who would be banded together in a dedicated fellowship, with something of the same sense of cohesion and of spiritual support that has characterized the historic missionary societies.

In Switzerland some of the churches and missions were at this time experimenting in training laymen and women for this kind of service. Subsequently in Great Britain there came into existence, on the initiative of the Conference of British Missionary Societies and the British Council of Churches, an organization called Oversea Service which provides intensive courses of study for men and women under appointment to 'secular' posts in Government or commercial undertakings overseas. Several of the missionary agencies, including the London Missionary Society, the Methodist Missionary Society, and the Church of Scotland have also instituted a procedure by which Christian men and women going abroad to appointments of this kind may become 'associates' of the missionary society or members of an 'Overseas Fellowship' in token of their Christian commitment. The full scope of the Willingen proposal has not yet been realized but these are steps towards the goal.

This same concern has found expression in the work of the World Council of Churches, both in the kind of studies and experiments initiated by the department on the Work of the Laity, and through the Ecumenical Institute at the Château de Bossey, a few miles from Geneva. This owed its inception to the generosity of Mr. John D. Rockefeller, Junior, and to the genius of the first Director of the Institute—Professor Hendrik Kraemer of Holland and Indonesia. Dr. Kraemer combines immense erudition and theological acumen with a powerful grasp of those factors in the political and economic order which constitute the most significant points of challenge and opportunity for those who believe in the lordship of Christ over the Church and the world. A missionary by calling and experience, he has an acute perception of those frontier situations which call for technical skill as well as spiritual gifts on the part of those who would testify convincingly to the meaning of the Gospel. In conferences and courses at Bossey Dr. Kraemer and his colleagues gathered together representatives of the professions—law, medicine, education, politics, the sciences and the arts, engaging them in a study of the significance of the Christian revelation for these differing areas of social and vocational responsibility. Philosophers, theologians, and pastors similarly found their way to Bossey for studies in the nature of the churches' task in the modern world. Under the leadership of Dr. Kraemer's successor (Dr. H. H. Wolf) the Ecumenical Institute continues this ministry, alongside longer residential courses of study which are linked with the Theological Faculty of the University of Geneva. These longer courses are provided under an arrangement with the university by which the Ecumenical Institute constitutes a Graduate School of Ecumenical Studies.

The frontiers on which the Church is called to witness to the world and serve men in Christ's name are as diverse as life itself. For this reason there is an element of missionary challenge wherever Christian men and women live, whether they think of themselves as being 'at home' or 'abroad'. The mission of the Church is not confined to the crossing of geographical boundaries. As is now often said, 'the home base is everywhere'. Every church, wherever situated, is—or is called to be—a base of operations for a universal mission. The field is the world, and every area of human interest and activity. Yet within this all-embracing conception of the Church's mission there continues to be the distinctive call and witness of 'foreign missions'. The call is one which impels men and women to go beyond their immediate environment, taking the world as their parish and being willing to go to the ends of the earth, remembering that 'this Gospel of the Kingdom shall be preached in all the world for a witness unto the nations; and then shall the end come'. Characteristic of the crossing of these 'foreign' frontiers, there is the breaking of familiar ties, the learning of new languages, the identification with another land and culture; there is the daily bearing of witness to a supra-national loyalty and to the power and grace of a Lord whose way it is to send men forth as heralds of a kingdom which, though it embraces the world, will appear in final splendour when the fashion of this world has passed away. This missionary imperative lies at the heart of the

Church's existence. It constrains us to cross all other frontiers in preparation for the day—and as heralds of it—when 'He might gather together in one all things in Christ, both which are in heaven and which are on earth'.[1]

[1] Ephesians i.10.

Chapter V

TOWARDS UNITY

The Change of Atmosphere

> For aught that ever I could read,
> Could ever hear by tale or history,
> The course of true love never did run smooth.

Yet it is true love and the true lover is undaunted, for

> Love is a durable fire
> In the mind ever burning.

The same has to be said about the course of Christian unity. The course is checkered. The disappointments on the way are many. But those who seek it and work for it can know it as a reality, given 'in the mind'.

As the opening chapter of this book recalls, long before there took shape those new expressions of the ecumenical movement which Edinburgh 1910 and its successor conferences illustrated, there was a widespread awareness amongst Christian people of a real and practical unity across denominational differences and national frontiers. The re-birth of the missionary movement in the eighteenth and nineteenth centuries, the creation of the Bible Societies, the rapid growth of a sense of evangelical unity resulting in such agencies as the Evangelical Alliance—all these meant that for a great many Christian people the separations of their denominational life were being overcome. They were finding fellowship, in action and to some extent in worship, with fellow-Christians of different church traditions.

So far, however, this growing sense of unity was amongst individual Christians. It was not a movement of the churches.

It was not affecting denominational structures and the relation of the churches one to another. Ministers and clergy remained ministers of particular denominations, with the range of their ministry conditioned by their Orders. Most serious of all, because of these limitations it was not possible for Christians of different denominations to express their unity at the Table of the Lord in Holy Communion. Moreover, despite the new spirit which animated many churchmen at the end of the eighteenth century and well into the nineteenth, there followed a period of recession in this movement towards a more manifest unity. This was partly due to the fear of some church leaders that the kind of evangelical unity which was being enjoyed and furthered was really an individualistic short-cut through the serious theological and ecclesiological questions which divided the churches. It was substituting 'undenomi-nationalism'—an indifference to the nature and form of the Church—for real Church unity. Apart, however, from this serious criticism of a certain type of Christian unity—a criticism which has still to be reckoned with—there occurred in the latter half of the nineteenth century, particularly in England, a fresh hardening of the denominational lines. A weighty factor in this was the emergence of the Oxford Movement, and the rebirth of a High Church party within the Church of England. In the light of history and of its own remarkable contribution to the renewal of the religious life of England, Free Churchmen can today look upon this development with an appreciation not easily felt by a previous generation. But in its origin and earlier course the movement led by Keble and Froude, Newman and Pusey could only deepen the rift between Dissenters and the Church of England. It is true that John Henry Newman's spiritual power, intellectual brilliance, and subtle mastery of language in speech and writing laid generations of Christians, whatever their denomination, in his debt. Most Free Church preachers, thirty or forty years ago, still turned to his *Parochial and Plain Sermons* as to models of pulpit utterance. But they could not easily swallow Newman's blunt assertion in one of these same sermons that 'There is not a dissenter living but inasmuch and so far as he dissents, he is in sin'. Minds less theologically subtle than Newman's not only took this assertion for granted; they expressed it with greater vigour and a forthright indication of its consequences. Mr. Somerset Maugham recalls that as a boy he went to live with a clergyman uncle (a few years before Newman's death). This uncle, says Maugham, 'hated the Dissenters in his parish and indeed thought it a monstrous thing that the State tolerated them. His consolation was that they would suffer eternal damnation.'[1]

There were non-theological factors in England at this time which no less powerfully militated against closer relationships between Anglicans and Free Churchmen. The fight for civil liberties and for the removal of disabilities imposed by law upon non-Anglicans was not yet over. Not until 1854 did the University of Oxford permit a Nonconformist to read for a Bachelor's degree; Cambridge went a little further in 1856, permitting a Dissenter to enter for the M.A. degree also; but it was only in 1871 that Oxford, Cambridge, and Durham conceded full student privileges to Nonconformists. Even then, there was the exception that Divinity degrees were not open to Dissenters. This last barrier was only removed in 1918. Oxford gave its first honorary D.D. to a Dissenter in 1920. Questions of church rates, burial rights, access to certain professional appointments, all constituted civil barriers to religious fellowship. And these legal disabilities had their social counterpart. Even more hurtful than civil injustice was that social incivility which for long treated Dissent with contempt. There are still parts of England—especially in rural areas—where some of this social discrimination lingers on. Happily it is disappearing and the general situation has changed beyond measure. But only those who have lived within such an atmosphere can fully understand the relation between Christian unity and civil behaviour—in every sense of the term. In all this it should be acknowledged that the grace of Christian civility was often wanting in the attitude of

[1] W. Somerset Maugham: *The Summing Up*, p. 154

Dissenters to the Established Church as well as *vice versa*. I rejoice to have learned more of the meaning of Christian fidelity, integrity, and charity from my father than from almost any other man I have known. Yet—at least until his later years—for him the bells of the parish church had a pagan ring which severely fretted his equanimity. For long he found it difficult to think of the Church of England as anything more than 'the Conservative Party at prayer' and, as an ardent Radical, he was inclined to doubt whether a through-going Tory and a good Liberal could really be praying to the same God.

Yet those who can recall this less happy state of things can also appreciate best the change of atmosphere which has since taken place in the sphere of church relationships. Preaching in St. Paul's Cathedral in 1952, on the tenth anniversary of the formation of the British Council of Churches, the Archbishop of Canterbury (Dr. Fisher) said:

Have not the Churches found in thought and practice that the unity they already have is not disembodied at all but is a unity *within* the Body of Christ? Are they not ready now to say that the Holy Catholic Church embraces all baptised persons and all groups of baptised persons: and that however erroneous or imperfect or even scandalous we may consider one another to be, *our divisions are within the Holy Catholic Church and not across its boundaries?*. . . . The inter-Church relations which do exist, even when they rest on nothing more than a basis of economy or courtesy, are only possible because they are relations within the family and Body of Christ.

Referring to the World Conference on Faith and Order held at Lund in this same year, the Archbishop said that the temper and subject-matter of the discussions 'were only possible between people who are all within the family and Body of Christ and speak the language of the Holy Spirit'. This is a far cry from the attitude of churches and their leaders to one another fifty years earlier.

★   ★   ★

National Councils of Churches

When Archbishop Fisher made this significant statement in 1952 he was speaking as President of the British Council of Churches as well as a representative of his own communion. Unity within a Council of Churches is not the same as the unity of the Churches. The two things can, however, be related as well as contrasted, and the growth of local and national councils in recent decades has been a vital factor in the approach to unity.

As recalled in a previous chapter, Christian co-operation on the national plane had in some countries preceded the world missionary conference at Edinburgh 1910 and this development was greatly accelerated from 1910 onwards. In many of these Christian councils the membership was, at first, not exclusively that of churches. In the Orient and Africa they were initially federations of missionary society representatives; only gradually did the membership of churches become significant and only recently has it shown signs of becoming predominant. In America and Britain, however, a somewhat different course from this was followed. The great missionary societies or mission boards developed their specialized agencies of co-operation, as in the Conference of British Missionary Societies and the Foreign Missions Conference of North America. But alongside these the churches fashioned their own national councils. America led the way in this as early as 1908 when there was created the Federal Council of the Churches of Christ in America, with the primary aim of expressing 'the fellowship and catholic unity of the Christian Church'. It is significant that at this early date the membership of the Federal Council was that of churches—the main denominations in the U.S.A., not simply individuals with a personal interest in Christian co-operation. A further declared aim was 'to bring the Christian bodies of America into united service for Christ and the world'. The Council, however, claimed no authority over its members nor was it at liberty 'to draw up a common creed or form of government or of worship, or in any way to limit the full autonomy of the

Christian bodies adhering to it'. From its inception this Federal Council enjoyed distinguished leadership, not least in its permanent secretariat, and it was strongly supported by the leading denominations. It became a powerful instrument for common Christian action and a sounding-board for Christian opinion on national and international affairs. Parallel to it there also grew up in the U.S.A. a series of national councils dealing with specialized activities—Religious Education, Home Missions, Christian Stewardship, etc., and in 1950 a number of these parallel councils, including the Foreign Missions Conference, entered into an organic relationship with the Federal Council and formed the National Council of the Churches of Christ in the United States of America. The imposing headquarters of this Council, opened on Riverside Drive, New York, at the end of 1959, and the astonishing range of activity emanating from it, constitute an impressive focal point in the religious life of America. But the significance of this Council of Churches does not lie in its dimensions. No one can become acquainted with the work of any one of the major denominations in the U.S.A. without becoming conscious of the extent to which the National Council, and its predecessor the Federal Council, have deepened in all the churches awareness of the true 'fellowship and catholic unity of the Christian Church'.

The British Council of Churches is a much more recent growth. While it had tributary movements in earlier years it was not until 1942 that it took formal shape under the Presidency of William Temple and with a whole-time secretariat. In a relatively short time it has found a very distinctive place within the religious life of Great Britain and Ireland and its twice-yearly meetings receive the close attention of denominational leaders. A small headquarters staff, working with a series of standing committees, sustains an impressive programme of work in the fields of international affairs, education, and social responsibility. Its Department of Inter-Church Aid and Service to Refugees, which works closely with the World Council of Churches, has grown rapidly in recent years, and its initiative in promoting 'Christian Aid Weeks' has produced a response beyond all expectation. Well before the end of World Refugee Year the Department had raised over a million and a quarter pounds, more than a quarter of the total national target. In most of this regular departmental work there is intimate association between the British Council of Churches and the Conference of British Missionary Societies, with interchanging committee membership and staff liaison. The headquarters of the two bodies are within two doors of one another; headquarters' facilities are shared and there is a common chapel for staff and committee worship. The membership of the British Council of Churches is that of churches, not local councils of churches, but the Council has done much to foster these local councils which now number over two hundred and fifty. These smaller embodiments in towns and cities of the aims and spirit of the ecumenical movement are a most significant part of the whole movement. While they belong to the sphere of co-operation rather than that of organic unity, it is within these relationships that growth in knowledge and under-standing between the denominations has been greatly furthered since the inception of the British Council of Churches. Much of what Archbishop Geoffrey Fisher said in the sermon already quoted had become experienced and acknowledged only because of the existence of the Council.

*   *   *

Church Relations in Britain

The growing-together which finds embodiment in councils of churches is only one expression of that search for Christian unity which lies at the heart of the ecumenical movement. During the period in which councils of churches have grown up throughout the world there have been many instances of full organic unity between churches. Even where this full unity has not been reached there have been other instances of new relationships established which have sometimes included inter-communion. Between 1910 and 1960 there were between thirty and forty major acts of union in different parts of the world. In addition to this, in a dozen or more instances new relationships involving inter-communion were reached. Some of the complete unions were between members of the same Church-family as with the union between the Church of Scotland and the United Free Church of Scotland in 1929, and as in the Methodist Union in England (1931) where the uniting churches were the Wesleyan Methodist, United Methodist and Primitive Methodist Churches. Other schemes of union brought different denominations together as in the Church of Christ in China (1927) which included Baptist, Congregational, Methodist, and Presbyterian elements; the Kyodan in Japan (1941); or the United Church of Canada (1925)—a union of Presbyterian, Methodist, and Congregational Churches. The most significant of these fully achieved unions is the Church of South India (1947) in which Episcopal, Presbyterian, Methodist, and Congregational Churches have come together on a basis which preserves and yet modifies these four historic elements in the ordering of the Church. Other negotiations or conversations regarding union are in process at the present time in several countries. An advanced stage in the process has been reached in North India and Ceylon where episcopal and non-episcopal churches are approaching union on a pattern to some extent resembling the South India achievement. In Great Britain conversations are taking place between the Church of England and the Methodist Church; there have also been long discussions between the Church of Scotland (Presbyterian) and the Church of England, with the participation of the Episcopal Church of Scotland and the Presbyterian Church of England.

These two series of conversations between episcopal and non-episcopal churches in Great Britain have behind them a lengthy history, but in both instances a new initiative was taken following a notable sermon preached by the Archbishop of Canterbury (Dr. Fisher) before the University of Cambridge in 1946. In the course of this sermon Dr. Fisher said:

There is a suggestion which I should like in all humility to make to my brethren of other denominations. . . . The road is not yet open, we are not yet ready for organic or constitutional union. But there can be a process of assimilation, of growing alike. What we need is that while the folds remain distinct, there should be a movement towards a free and unfettered exchange of life in worship and sacrament between them as there is already of prayer and thought and Christian fellowship—in short that they should grow towards that full communion with one another which already in their separation they have in Christ. . . .

Every Church's ministry is effective as a means by which the life of Christ reaches His people. Every Church's ministry is defective because it is prevented from operating in all the folds of His flock. For full communion between Churches there is needed a ministry mutually acknowledged by all as possessing not only the inward call of the Spirit but also the authority which each Church in conscience requires.

It was as a step towards this end that the Archbishop invited the non-episcopal churches 'to take episcopacy into their system' and 'try it out on their own ground', allowing the distinctive elements in each of these other systems to provide whatever safeguard might be needed against those 'abuses of episcopacy' which the non-episcopal churches fear. Dr. Fisher was here only voicing a suggestion, sketchily and tentatively; he was not formulating a procedure; but he invited serious consideration of the idea and accompanied his proposal with a moving admission:

It is because I fear a stalemate that I venture to put this suggestion forward for examination. I love the Church of England, as the Presbyterian and the Methodist love their Churches. It is, I think, not possible yet nor desirable that any Church should merge its identity in a newly constituted union. What I desire is that I should be able freely to enter their Churches and they mine in the Sacraments of the Lord and in the full fellowship of worship, that His life may freely circulate between us. Cannot we grow to full communion with each other before we start to write a constitution? Have we the wisdom, the humility, the love and the Spirit of Christ sufficient for such a venture as I have suggested? If there were agreement on it, I would thankfully receive at the hands of others their commission in their accustomed form and in the same way confer our own. . . .

As an outcome of this sermon a series of discussions took place from 1947 onwards between representatives of the Anglican and Free Churches, resulting in the report, published in 1950, called *Church Relations in England*. This reaffirmed a declaration made a year previously in an Interim Report that:

On the doctrines of God the Father, the Person and Work of Christ, the Person and mission of the Holy Spirit, the Trinity and the Life Everlasting we have found nothing which separates any one of these Communions from another.

The difficulties—as recognized by all participants in the discussions—lay in the realm of order rather than faith. These difficulties were frankly shared and clearly stated and the report set out the major problems which would need solution if the Archbishop's proposal were to become practicable. The group responsible for the report made no attempt to formulate possible solutions of the problems. Its task was to elucidate the implications of the main proposal and to define the area in which agreement would be essential if episcopacy, in a form acceptable both to the Anglican and Free Churches, were to be 'taken into the system' of the latter. While the purpose of this proposal and the spirit of these conversations were generally appreciated, it cannot be said that the result was a marked change in denominational attitudes. Nevertheless, it was as a direct result of these endeavours that official conversations were eventually started between the Anglican Church and Presbyterian and Methodist Churches. The conversations with the Methodists have so far reached only the stage of an Interim Report. Those with the Presbyterians reached a critical phase with the publication in 1957 of recommendations which had behind them the unanimous support of all who had participated in the discussions. The crux of these proposals lay in the term 'Bishops-in-Presbytery'. This referred to a suggestion that the Presbyterians should 'take into their system' a form of Episcopacy which would be responsibly related to the authority of the Presbytery, and that the Anglicans should 'take into their system' a distinctive feature of Presbyterian authority and relate this to the office of Bishop. The report suggested that:

Bishops chosen by each Presbytery, from its own membership or otherwise, would initially be consecrated by prayer with the laying on of hands by Bishops from one or more of the Episcopal Churches and by the Presbytery acting through appointed representatives. Thus consecrated, each Bishop would be within the Apostolic succession as acknowledged by Anglicans on the one hand and as required by Presbyterians on the other. He would be the President of the Presbytery and would act as its principal minister in every ordination and in the consecration of other Bishops. He would exercise pastoral oversight over his fellow-ministers in the Presbytery, and act as its spokesman to the community. . . .

The Presbytery would still retain its full and essential place in the life and government of the Church, except that a permanent Bishop-in-Presbytery would take the place of the changing Moderator. The General Assembly would retain its full existing authority in doctrine, administration, legislation, and judicature. . . .

In respect of the existing Episcopalian Churches the proposal was that:

Lay persons would be solemnly 'set apart' for some measure of pastoral responsibility towards their fellow-Christians, in an office akin to the Presbyterian eldership. Lay people would be given appropriate participation in the Government of the Church at all levels: parochial, diocesan, provincial and national. The integration of such lay persons with the Bishop and presbyters in diocesan synods would greatly strengthen their authority and importance, by fulfilling the doctrinal requirement that decisions of the Church must be made by the whole Church, by the Body of Christ in its entirety. . . .

It is unlikely that any of the members of the Joint Conference which produced this unanimous report expected the proposals to receive easy and speedy acceptance. It is certain that all of them were surprised by the nature of the reaction which the Report provoked in Scotland. The cry 'No Bishops!' seems to have run through the land with the vehemence of a 'No Popery!' battle-cry. Public discussion through the daily Press was astonishing in its volume and vigour, and the subject properly assumed major importance in successive General Assemblies of the Church of Scotland and in the deliberations of local Presbyteries. Eventually, in May 1959, the Assembly declared that the proposals of the Joint Conference were 'unacceptable in that they imply a denial of the catholicity of the Church of Scotland and of the validity and regularity of its ministry within the Church Catholic'. The Assembly, nevertheless, did not want this to be the end of the matter. It expressed the hope that conversations would be resumed, with special reference to four areas in which there had been a lack of clarity in regard to the assumptions and approaches of the conferring Churches. These were (i) the meaning of unity as distinct from uniformity in Church order; (ii) the meaning of 'validity' as applied to ministerial orders; (iii) the doctrine of Holy Communion; and (iv) the meaning of 'the Apostolic Succession' as related to all these matters. The Assembly also set up a new committee, composed of elders as well as ministers, to act on behalf of the Church of Scotland in any further conversations, and it welcomed a number of proposals made by the Joint Conference for promoting better knowledge and understanding between the Anglican and Presbyterian Churches; these included (i) full participation by the churches in the annual Week of Prayer for Christian Unity; (ii) the extension of visits of official representatives of the Anglican and Presbyterian Churches to the meetings of their respective governing bodies; (iii) the interchange of teachers and students among the theological colleges; and (iv) the fostering of unofficial groups, both clerical and lay, for the discussion of doctrinal questions and for informing one another of the distinctive forms of worship, ethos, and practice of the Anglican and Presbyterian Churches. The Archbishop of Canterbury has voiced the concurrence of the Church of England in such steps as these and has acknowledged the need for 'some further clarifying of our minds' about the questions raised by the Church of Scotland and in regard to the lines which future conversations might profitably follow. There is, therefore, a pause, though not a termination, in the process of negotiation between the Episcopal and Presbyterian Churches.

It is not the purpose of this book to study in detail any one of the schemes of union either achieved or under discussion; but these Presbyterian-Episcopal conversations call for some attention in view of their significance. Reference has already been made to the unanimity which prevailed amongst the members of the Joint Conference when they put forward their recommendations, gathering around the conception of the Bishop-in-Presbytery. Conversations of this character between the representatives of Churches are not in any sense officially related to the World Council of Churches. Yet the majority of the members of the Joint Conference which produced these proposals are themselves intimately involved in the ecumenical movement as representatives of their Churches and some of them are closely identified with the work of the World Council of Churches. Their published report, in fact, contains this testimony:

It has been of primary importance for the present series of Conversations that all four Churches represented in them have been associated with one another within the Ecumenical Movement and have also shared in the revival of interest in Biblical theology which has been a notable feature of the last few decades. This meant that the Conversations could be held from the beginning in an atmosphere of assured friendship, and that on many matters germane to them a common outlook and commonly held convictions could be taken for granted.

This is further expressed in the printed prefatory letter to the

report in which the signatories—Episcopal and Presbyterian
—say:

We have become a brotherhood of friends and we have
experienced, as our discussions have proceeded, a growing
intimacy of fellowship and an increasingly uninhibited freedom
of utterance, based on the secure confidence that whatever was
said by the spokesmen on one side or on the other would be
met by the patience, sympathy, and understanding of their
brethren of different traditions.

The recommendations thus came from a group which was
itself experiencing something of the spiritual enrichment of a
shared unity: its proposals were framed from within this
experience. They had to be weighed and discussed, however,
by Presbyteries and a General Assembly which, as corporate
entities, could not bring to them the same experience. This
difference does not alone account for the conclusion reached by
the Assembly and Presbyteries: but it is a serious reminder
that growth towards unity between churches depends on something more than growth in understanding and confidence
between a limited number of leaders or representatives.
Members of a negotiating group, after a long experience of
one another's minds and characteristics, after frank debate
and earnest corporate study, all set within the context of
common worship and deepening friendship, reach some of
those pre-requisites of fuller unity which constitute firm
ground for the next steps. But if an act of union is to be the
action of churches, a comparable process must take place
within the churches as a whole. The last chapter of this book
will return to this point.

There is, however, another fact which needs to be recognized if the seriousness of the present situation between
Episcopal and Presbyterian Churches in Britain is to be understood. The members of the Joint Conference were not trying
to frame a constitution for a united Church; they were seeking
means by which full communion could be reached between
their Churches. Now it had long been acknowledged that the

greatest problem here lay in the absence of a ministry mutually recognized by the Churches. How could this mutual recognition be attained? Thirty years earlier the Lausanne Conference on Faith and Order had unanimously adopted a report on the ministry which centred on the fact that 'the Episcopate, the Councils of Presbyters, and the Congregation of the faithful' were rooted in the history of Christendom and manifestly constituted essential elements in the existing churches. 'We therefore recognize,' said the report, 'that these several elements must all, under conditions which require further study, have an appropriate place in the order of life of a re-united Church and that each separate communion, recalling the abundant blessing of God vouchsafed to its ministry in the past, should gladly bring to the common life of the united Church its own spiritual treasures.'

Lausanne was only an expression—but a particularly significant one—of this approach to relationships which would bring together, for their mutual enrichment, these three classic elements—episcopal, presbyterian, and congregational—in the ordering of the Church and its ministry. Following Lausanne there had been widespread discussion of possible ways of achieving this relationship, especially the relationship of the 'historic episcopate' to Presbyterian and Congregational conceptions of the ministry.

The phrase 'historic episcopate' should not be confused with the term 'apostolic succession'. Apostolic Succession is a theory or doctrine concerning the manner in which continuity in Church Order and in the means of grace has been preserved. It is a theory on which there are great divergences within the episcopal churches, including the Anglican Communion. The most disputed theory of Succession is that which J. Vernon Bartlet described as 'Grace communicated as through material channels, from one bishop to another, in virtue of certain bodily acts and sacrosanct formulae'.[1] This theory implies, as a distinguished Anglican has said, that 'the Holy Spirit is no

[1] J. Vernon Bartlet: *Church Life and Church Order* (Oxford, Blackwell, 1943) p. 93.

longer, as clearly in the New Testament, a corporate possession of the whole Body of Christ, but a gift monopolized by and in a ministerial succession'.

This criticism of the theory comes from Canon Theodore O. Wedel, until recently Warden of the College of Preachers in Washington, whose book *The Coming Great Church*, presses home, from within an Episcopal Church, the challenge to the theory. 'Accept this view,' continues Canon Wedel,

and Sacraments become dependent for their efficacy on the ministry alone. They, too, convey a substantive grace—a grace endangered if the slightest flaw occurs in the genealogy of the sacerdotal succession. Hence the problem of validity leaps to a position of paramount importance. A lapse in technical validity means loss of the life-giving Spirit on which the Church's very existence depends. No valid bishop, no valid priest; no valid priest, no valid eucharist; no valid eucharist, no Body of Christ.

'This theory of the ministry,' declares Canon Wedel, 'a Biblical Protestantism will never accept. Whether it may remain as a permissive view in an ecumenical Christianity may be a question referred to future ecumenical charity. But a threat of its dominance will wreck any reunion movement in which a Reformation Church is to share.'[1]

In some of the Schemes of Union already referred to, acceptance of the historic episcopate has been dissociated from any theory concerning it. In the Constitution of the Church of South India there appear the following statements:

The Church of South India accepts and will maintain the historic episcopate in a constitutional form. But this acceptance does not commit it to any particular interpretation of episcopacy or to any particular view or belief concerning orders of the ministry, and it will not require the acceptance of any such particular interpretation or view as a necessary qualification for its ministry.

[1] Theodore O. Wedel: *The Coming Great Church* (London, S.C.M. Press, 1947) pp. 141f.

Whatever differing interpretations there may be, however, the Church of South India agrees that, as Episcopacy has been accepted in the Church from early times, it may in this sense fitly be called historic, and that it is needed for the shepherding and extension of the Church in South India. Any additional interpretations, though held by individuals, are not binding on the Church of South India.

The discussions still proceeding in Ceylon (Lanka) between Episcopal and non-Episcopal churches are based on provisions which include these words:

The uniting Churches accept the historic episcopate in a constitutional form as part of their basis of union. By 'historic episcopate' is meant the episcopate which has historic continuity with that of the undivided Church. No particular theological interpretation of episcopacy shall be demanded from any minister or member of the Church of Lanka.

This acceptance of episcopacy as an historic element in the Church and one which would serve what the South India scheme called 'the shepherding and extension of the Church' is clearly different from the endorsement of that theory of apostolic succession which Canon Wedel challenges as vigorously as any non-episcopalian would do—and in terms which should go down well in Scotland. The signatories to the Anglican-Presbyterian report certainly had no intention of confusing these two issues—the 'historic episcopate' and 'apostolic succession': their concern was with a form of episcopacy which could justifiably be called 'historic' and which would serve the shepherding and extension of the Church. The emphasis was upon the diversity of form which such an episcopate had already taken in history. As the Episcopalian participants in the discussion wrote, concerning the suggestion 'Bishops-in-Presbytery':

Such Bishops-in-Presbytery would undoubtedly, in many respects, be different from the English pattern of Episcopacy. The diversity of form taken by the historic episcopate down the centuries was, however, recalled, and few Anglicans would insist that every aspect of the Anglican Episcopate under the Establishment was essential to the order.

Notwithstanding all this, the Assembly of the Church of Scotland found the proposals as a whole unacceptable. Many considerations no doubt entered into this judgement, but amongst them was the impression that even that modification of the historic episcopate which is expressed in the phrase 'Bishops-in-Presbytery' carried with it a conception of the ministry and the means of grace incompatible with the convictions and traditions of a Reformed Church. The Presbyterian signatories to the plan did not take this view and the discussion and voting in the Assembly clearly revealed differing judgements on this crucial point. It should be added that the proceedings of the Lambeth Conference of 1958 did not remove anxieties as to the assumptions on which the Episcopal churches would interpret the office of Bishop-in-Presbytery. Lambeth had not been asked for a definitive pronouncement on the Presbyterian-Episcopal proposals; it recognized that they needed careful study by all the churches concerned before any such pronouncement could be made. But it commended the report for this purpose, with a resolution declaring that 'the Conference welcomes the taking up in a new spirit of the problem of the relations between Episcopal and Presbyterian systems of Church Order'. Nevertheless, the general effect of Lambeth 1958 was less reassuring to the non-episcopal churches than had been hoped. In particular, the tentative observations offered by the Lambeth Committee on Church Unity and the Church Universal on points raised by the Church of Scotland Assembly were felt to be both disappointing and ambiguous. Uneasiness was created by an apparent inconsistency between two of these observations. In the one it was clearly stated that 'the Anglican Churches ought to be ready to recognize the Presbyterian Churches as true parts of the One, Holy, Catholic and Apostolic Church, and that the spiritual effectiveness of their ministerial orders ought not to be implicitly or explicitly questioned'. Yet in a paragraph dealing with 'the Presbyterian desire for immediate intercommunion as the sequel to the expression of a solemn resolve on the part of the Churches concerned to seek unity and reconciliation with one another, it was declared to be 'impossible to envisage the establishment of fully reciprocal intercommunion at any stage short of the adoption of episcopacy by the Churches of the Presbyterian Order'. The position was not made any easier by the suggestion that 'such a solemn resolve as has been suggested would have the effect of making it possible to regularize, as a general practice, the admission of Presbyterians to communion at Anglican altars'.[1] So long as this could not be reciprocal, the concession hurt more than it helped. As the Senior Minister of St. Giles Cathedral, Edinburgh, wrote:

Whatever words may be used to gloss over the unpleasant fact, this statement clearly implies that in the view of the Anglican Church, Presbyterian Orders are defective.[2]

All this affected the mood of the Church of Scotland Assembly in 1959 and its action in pressing for a clarification of the questions which its resolution formulated.

It remains uncertain whether the action of the Church of Scotland in 1959 amounts to a lasting refusal to consider proposals based on acceptance of the historic episcopate in any form or whether, as a result of the clarification now sought, agreement will prove possible on a plan which still bases a 'mutually recognized' ministry on Episcopal, Presbyterian, and Congregational elements in the Church's order. If the former proves to be the case the action of the Church of Scotland will indeed mark a major departure from assumptions which have been widely held at least since Lausanne; it will constitute what Dr. Archie Craig called, in the Church of Scotland Assembly, a 'switch' in the attitude and approach of a great Church to the union question. There are, indeed, some who feel that the situation calls for as big a new departure

[1] These quotations are from the *Report of the Lambeth Conference 1958* pp. (2) 42–44 (SPCK, 1958).
[2] C. L. Warr: *The Glimmering Landscape*, p. 308.

as this. They would contend that to go on using the term 'historic episcopate' while leaving unresolved some stubborn theological questions which are raised by any attempt to define the term, will never lead to a satisfactory basis of union. This opinion is not confined to certain members of the Church of Scotland; it is widely prevalent in the English Free Churches, and there are those in the Anglican communion who—from differing standpoints—have the same misgiving about avoiding 'any particular interpretation of episcopacy or . . . any particular view or belief concerning orders of the ministry' (to use phrases taken from the South India Scheme of Union). Bishop Hensley Henson recalls that following the 'Cambridge Sermon' of 1946 he wrote to the Archbishop of Canterbury saying that the non-episcopalians 'may well ask for an answer to the inevitable question—"What kind of episcopacy do you mean that we should add to our systems—Lightfoot's or Gore's? Sir Henry Slessor's or the pre-Tractarian Church of England's?"' [1] Anglicans can, of course, meet this question by saying that the alternative conceptions of episcopacy illustrated by Hensley Henson do, in fact, exist—alongside other variants—within the unity of the Anglican Communion; the bond of unity lies elsewhere than in acceptance of a theological either-or. Members of the Church of South India could also urge that a decisive and fruitful act of union has proved possible without waiting for a final reconciliation of divergent views on this issue. Some would go further and contend that the act of accepting a basis of union which includes the 'historic episcopate' alongside other equally 'historic' elements in the ordering of the Church, can lead to an understanding of the meaning of unity in which unresolved questions find their proper place, if not their intellectual answer. This contention is one of the great considerations which have to be reckoned with responsibly by all concerned in the quest for unity. It stands alongside two other seriously held convictions. On the one hand there are those who are deeply concerned

[1] Letter to the Bishop of Chichester, 29 December 1946, in *The Letters of Hensley Henson*, p. 192.

that a church without bishops standing in an acknowledged 'Catholic' succession must remain defective at a vital point; these believe that the main course of ecclesiastical history, as well as doctrinal considerations, endorse this view. On the other hand, there are those who feel that, however great the switch involved in relation to most union discussions of recent decades, the question of what is called *episcope*—a pastoral and ministerial function exercised with a spiritual authority acknowledged by the whole Church—must be separated from the question of *bishops*, an historic office which has resulted from certain conceptions of *episcope*. Those who take this view believe that *episcope* in its New Testament connotation can and does exist in churches which do not possess the office of 'bishop' and that further progress towards either the union or inter-communion of churches must begin with the recognition and acceptance of this fact. All these things belong to the persistent and as yet unresolved issues which still lie in the path of those who seek to give visible, organic expression to the unity of Christ's people.

The course of true love. . . . With every new experience of the tenacity of some elements in the problem of Christian unity, there is the temptation to drop the whole business in disappointment or impatience. 'This reunion tomfoolery' was a phrase used—according to *The Times*—by an Anglican vicar in the Year of Grace 1960; and the mood is not peculiarly Anglican. The most serious danger is that those who care deeply about Christian unity may become weary in well-doing; they may begin to wonder whether the spending of time and energy in a quest that is fraught with so many difficulties represents the right kind of well-doing in a time when the main encounter between the Church and the world is so urgent and critical. 'The thinking that I have been compelled to do in the last two or three years,' writes someone who is deeply committed to the ecumenical movement, 'makes me sure that in some matters the Church is like a group of ancient British villagers throwing up a small earth-work round their dwellings when the whole tide of Imperial Rome is moving with its legions across Europe'; and the writer[1] adds a rueful comment on the diversion of energies into 'inter-tribal feuds'. This kind of criticism must not be softened: it needs sharpening and driving home more forcefully. Yet as this chapter has already illustrated, the churches that are most responsibly involved in the ecumenical movement, especially those that are giving the most time and thought to unity questions, are working in a very different atmosphere from that of inter-tribal feuds. The increasingly close conjunction between the missionary movement and the quest for unity means that the concern expressed in the letter just quoted is, in fact, one of the driving forces in the main discussions on Church union. There is an urgent desire that unity shall further the mission of the Church and that through a deeper sharing of the spiritual riches of the churches the Gospel shall be presented to the world with greater power.

Yet this sense of urgency and deep concern needs to become far more widespread than it is at present. The zeal of the few needs to become the temper of the many. When the parish priest and local minister, with the regular membership of the churches, care deeply enough about the need something will happen even to the tempo of theological discussion. The trouble is that we are all, to some extent, imprisoned by history. We have been born into churches already organized in separation; or, with our conversion to Christianity, our open commitment to Christ has taken the form of membership in *a* church, not *the* Church. The limitation may have been mitigated by denominational teaching which encouraged a charitable attitude to other churches, or by the claim and desire of the denomination to stand in line with the Church of the New Testament. But, in fact, history has led us to accept as normal a plurality of churches—not only in the necessary and proper sense that a universal Church finds local and parochial embodiment, but as a state of dividedness in which the People of Christ take tribalism for granted. Even if the

[1] The Rev. Alan Birtwhistle in a letter to the author.

feuds are past, the clan loyalties are assumed to be part of the essential structure. There may be some inclination to cultivate friendly relationships with the other tribes, but there is too little vivid awareness of the primary fact that—as the author of *Piers Plowman* put it centuries ago—we are all blood-brothers at the Cross of Christ. Our natural existence is within the one Household of Faith. Our first privilege, not our last luxury, is the full freedom of the household.

Experience within the organized life of the ecumenical movement reinforces this truth and lights up its significance. The greatest thing that has been happening through the movements recorded in this book is not that certain international organizations have in themselves accomplished great things— co-operation in mission, frontier crossing activities and the rest; nor is it simply that by working together for these ends churches have done more than was possible in separation. It is that through the staying-together and the doing-together representatives of the separated churches have *begun* to participate in the fuller and richer life of the one Household of Faith. They do not treat lightly those historic loyalties and privileges which are bound up with the story of the separated denominations; but they become increasingly aware of something more than any one denomination can enshrine or bestow. They become debtors, in their own spiritual life and their apprehension of the Faith, to the work of grace within other traditions than their own; and in their growing-together with others they taste more fully of that given unity which is Christ's undivided gift to his one people. Yet this experience within the organized life of the ecumenical movement is only a beginning. Even at its best it keeps running into limitations which no amount of co-operation and goodwill between separated churches can overcome. Again and again, in the closest degree of co-operation between separated groups, the sting of separation shows itself—most grievously at the point of dividedness in Holy Communion. At this point and at innumerable others of which this becomes the most searching symptom, those who have gone farthest in the long quest for unity know that they cannot and must not give up the endeavour. They are under a spiritual compulsion which is more than dogged human endeavour. It is the pressure of the spirit of unity itself, a gift already bestowed while carrying with it its own compulsion to go further. 'We could not seek God,' said Pascal, 'if we had not already found him.' We seek unity because we have already found it in Christ. Like love itself, it becomes

a durable fire
In the mind ever burning.

Chapter VI

TRENDS AND PROSPECTS

World Council and Missionary Council

It is important to think of the ecumenical movement as a movement more than as an organization. As a movement of the Spirit, quickening Christian men and women to perceive more clearly the range and depth of their fellowship and the scope of their task, it is older than any organization and more far-reaching and penetrating in its influence. Some of its most significant expressions are to be seen not in the international organizations described in this book but in the life of churches and individuals, especially in new attitudes, relationships, and insights. Nevertheless, in the course of the last half century organizations such as the International Missionary Council and World Council of Churches have played a distinctive part in the movement and their course seems far from finished. What are the main trends and prospects so far apparent within these two bodies?

In December 1961 each of these Councils will hold another Assembly. They will gather in the same place—New Delhi, and it is expected that after each has held a brief session separate from the other, the rest of the proceedings will constitute a single Assembly of an integrated or united World Council of Churches and International Missionary Council. The structural changes involved in this step can be summarized briefly. It will be recalled that the World Council of Churches operates at present through three Divisions, each with a large degree of autonomy but all closely inter-related through the Assembly, the Central and Executive Committees, and the daily staff operations. In addition to this there exist two other bodies called Commissions—the Commission on Faith and Order and the Commission of the Churches on International Affairs. There are differences in the structure and working of these two Commissions, derived from their different history and purposes. The Commission of the Churches on International Affairs is a product of the joint action of the World Council and the International Missionary Council. It reports to both and owes its main support to both and the two Councils are represented on its Executive Committee, but, largely in the interests of its specialized tasks, it is structurally separate from them. The Commission on Faith and Order is an integral part of the World Council of Churches and is finally answerable to the Assembly of the Council; nevertheless it also enjoys considerable autonomy and is able to draw into its deliberations representatives of churches not in membership with the Council. The Commission itself only meets at intervals of several years but it is linked with a Department of Faith and Order which is part of the World Council's Division of Studies. Its interests and tasks are therefore part of the regular work of the Council; its departmental committee meets annually and its secretary is a wholetime member of the central secretariat of the World Council.

With the organic merging of the International Missionary Council and the World Council of Churches there will be created both a new Commission and a new Division of the World Council. The Commission will stand in a similar relation to the Assembly as the Commission on Faith and Order but the majority of its members (80 out of 115) will be appointed by the national Christian councils which at present constitute the membership of the International Missionary Council. This will provide for as wide a representation of missionary interests as is now reflected in an Assembly of the International Missionary Council. In addition to the creation of this Commission—to be called the Commission on World Mission and Evangelism—a fourth Division will be added to the present divisional structure of the World Council; this new Division will be responsible for carrying out the aims and functions of the Commission. It will be called the Division of World Mission and Evangelism: its directing committee will meet annually; its staff will be part of the World Council staff and its principal secretary will be an Associate General Secretary of the Council.

In the proposed constitution of the new Commission on World Mission and Evangelism its aim has been defined as being:

to further the proclamation to the whole world of the Gospel of Jesus Christ, to the end that all men may believe in Him and be saved.

Its declared functions include the following:

(i) To keep before the churches their calling and privilege to engage in constant prayer for the missionary and evangelistic work of the Church;

(ii) To remind the churches of the range and character of the unfinished evangelistic task and to deepen their sense of missionary obligation;

(iii) To stimulate thought and study on the Biblical and theological bases and meaning of the Church's missionary task and on questions directly related to the spread of the Gospel in the world;

(iv) To foster among churches and among councils and other Christian bodies more effective co-operation and united action for world evangelization;

(v) To deepen evangelistic and missionary concern in the whole life and work of the World Council of Churches;

(vi) To assist in securing and safeguarding freedom of conscience and religion as formulated in declarations of the World Council of Churches on religious liberty.

In line with the character of the present International Missionary Council and of the World Council itself, the constitution of the new body explicitly states that the Commission 'shall have no mandatory authority over any of the councils related to it'.

This latest step in the organization of the World Council of Churches and the International Missionary Council is an

outcome of what may be called the inherent logic of the
ecumenical movement from Edinburgh 1910 onwards. The
World Missionary Conference of 1910 created a Continuation Committee which became the International Missionary
Council. But the continuation of all that began in 1910 is no
less clearly to be seen in those other movements and organizations which led to the creation of the World Council of
Churches in 1948. Persons and events have interlocked all
through the story. John R. Mott, while still the honorary
Chairman of the International Missionary Council, inevitably
became one of the first co-Presidents of the World Council of
Churches. J. H. Oldham, while secretary of the International
Missionary Council, became more responsible than any other
single person for shaping the 1937 Conference on Church,
Community, and State under the auspices of the Universal
Christian Council on Life and Work. When the decision to
constitute a World Council of Churches was taken, it was a
secretary of the International Missionary Council (Dr.
William Paton) who became an associate secretary of the
Provisional Committee while continuing to hold office in the
older body. The published *Message* of the Jerusalem meeting
of the International Missionary Council in 1928 was based on
the *Statement* formulated a year earlier at the Lausanne
Conference on Faith and Order. The Tambaram meeting of
the International Missionary Council in 1938 drew heavily on
material provided by the preceding year's Life and Work
Conference. Significant participants in all these gatherings
were equally active in meetings of the Faith and Order and
the Life and Work movements as well as in the International
Missionary Council.

At Tambaram in 1938 the International Missionary
Council took note of the decision to create a World Council of
Churches and approved the appointment of one of its secretaries to the staff of the new body. It also encouraged other
measures in co-operation with the World Council but made it
clear that—for the time being, at any rate—it desired to
maintain its own 'separate organization, autonomy and

independence.' To ensure adequate *rapport*, however, Tambaram recommended the appointment of a Joint Committee between the two bodies, especially with a view to ensuring the adequate representation of the 'younger' churches of Asia and Africa in the World Council. John R. Mott became its chairman and though war postponed its activity the committee met periodically from 1946 onwards. From its first meeting, it worked on the agreed conviction that the two Councils ought 'to demonstrate as fully as possible their common origin, calling and purpose' and especially to 'make clear their identity of purpose and concern for the evangelization of the world'. Immediately prior to the first Assembly of the World Council of Churches some consideration was given to a proposal that with the inauguration of the World Council the International Missionary Council should become 'the Missionary Council of the World Council of Churches'. Many people in both organizations favoured this suggestion but it was finally decided to wait until the new Council had become well established before considering the merging of the older body with it. Meantime it was agreed that the two Councils should signify in their titles their necessary inter-dependence. This was done in 1948, since when the note-heading and all official documents of the two Councils have indicated that each of them is 'in association with' the other.

On the basis of this association, expressed in the work of the Joint Committee and in regular staff liaison, a number of joint activities (already pre-visaged in the creation of the Commission of the Churches on International Affairs) followed. In 1950 a single secretariat for the two Councils was opened in the Far East. With the growth of refugee and other emergency needs in Asia and the Middle East the Division of Inter-Church Aid and Service to Refugees of the World Council acted on behalf of the International Missionary Council which nominated its own representatives to the Administrative Committee of the Division. At the Evanston Assembly of the World Council in 1954 the Research Department of the International Missionary Council was integrated with the work of the World Council and became the Department of Missionary Studies within the Division of Studies. In addition to these developments in the structure and regular programme of the two bodies there have been many *ad hoc* undertakings on a joint basis. Meantime, more of the younger churches have entered into direct membership of the World Council of Churches and some of the national Christian councils which constitute the International Missionary Council have also become 'associated councils' of the World Council. While the basic membership of the World Council is that of churches, its constitution provides that national Christian councils may 'enter into working relationships' with the World Council 'as associated councils'. 'The purpose of such working relationships', says the constitution, 'shall be to help national councils in their work and to encourage them to help the World Council of Churches in the promotion of ecumenical activities in the area concerned'. These associated councils may be represented at meetings of the World Council's Assembly and Central Committee by fraternal delegates.

It is this increasing interlocking of the two Councils in their main work and in their claim on persons which has made their proposed integration a natural step. 'It would be a failure in Christian statesmanship,' wrote Dr. Samuel McCrea Cavert in 1945, 'to divide the ecumenical forces permanently into two groups'. This feeling has become widespread, not least amongst the younger churches and especially in Asia. Behind this logic of events and organizational alignments there is the deeper unity of calling and purpose. The missionary movement cannot remain true to its essential purpose without taking into account the relation between Church and Gospel or between unity and witness. It is no accident that in the main meetings of the International Missionary Council following Edinburgh 1910 the question of the Church, its unity and its total witness to the world assumed increasing prominence. This was not only because 'younger churchmen' were assuming the leadership in the Council; it arose from concern with the meaning of the Gospel, the nature of a Christian society, and the right expression of fellowship in Christ. William Paton put his finger on this point in a letter to John R. Mott (in 1934) when some people in the International Missionary Council were questioning the wisdom of letting J. H. Oldham, the Council's secretary, give so much time to the Life and Work movement. Apart from recognizing that Oldham would go his own way anyhow ('and it is not to be expected that he will now change his methods') Paton said:

I believe there is an ultimate unity in the problem which confronts the whole Church throughout the world and that no satisfactory line can be drawn between the problems of the Christian message and of the church in its relation to society, nor can any line by drawn between these problems as they affect the mission field and as they affect the churches of the West.

Paton therefore welcomed this sharing of resources between the two movements as a step towards 'bringing fresh theological assistance to the help of the International Missionary Council quite as much as bringing fresh missionary assistance to the help of the Life and Work movement'. Oldham had expressed views comparable to this some years earlier, coupling them with an anxiety 'lest missions should drift into a backwater outside the main currents that are shaping the life of the world'. 'The tremendous task to which we are called,' he added, 'is to restore the missionary effort to a central place in the life of the world' and 'to lift the whole missionary enterprise to a new level of vision and achievement'.

It is fair to claim that this kind of thinking has been amongst the incentives leading to the new step in World Council–International Missionary Council relationships. Within the contemporary phase of the ecumenical movement the word *mission* is one of the key words in thought and action. Biblical and theological study keep focusing upon it; thought and aspiration concerning the 'renewal' of the Church are constantly attuned to the note of Emil Brunner's dictum:

'The Church lives by mission as a fire exists by burning'.[1]
The nature of the Church's mission to a war-time world
dominated the period in which the World Council of Churches
was 'in process of formation'. When the first member-
churches of the Council declared at Amsterdam 'We intend
to stay together' they were not thinking in terms of staying
put. They were committing themselves to a new relationship
in obedience to a Lord who was sending them forth. The same
Message, speaking of 'God's unchanging Word to the world',
said:

Millions of our fellow-men have never heard it. As we are
met here from many lands, we pray God to stir up His whole
Church to make this Gospel known to the whole world, and
to call on all men to believe in Christ, to live in His love and
to hope for His coming. . . . Our coming together to form a
World Council will be vain unless Christians and Christian
congregations everywhere, commit themselves to the Lord of
the Church in a new effort . . . to be His witnesses.

This note recurs in the Message of the Evanston Assembly
six years later. Speaking 'through our member churches
directly to each congregation' the Assembly said:

The Church of Christ is today a world-wide fellowship, yet
there are countless people to whom He is unknown. How much
do you care about this? Does your congregation live for itself,
or for the world around it and beyond it? Does its common
life, and does the daily work of its members in the world,
affirm the Lordship of Christ or deny it?

Throughout this period since Amsterdam, as in the earlier
'process of formation', the activities of the Council and the
kind of questions dominant in its discussions could appro-
priately be described as variations on the theme 'We intend
to *go* together'. The General Secretary of the World Council
was expressing more than a personal conviction and hope
when, in relation to the proposed integration of the Council
with the International Missionary Council, he wrote:

[1] Emil Brunner: *The Word and the World*, p. 108.

It should mean that, even more definitely than has been the case, the evangelistic and missionary dimension of the task of the Church becomes a central concern of the whole ecumenical movement. The common obligation of all churches to finish the unfinished task of the evangelization of the world must cease to be a concern of specialists and colour the prayer, the life and thought of the whole fellowship and of all its parts. And the question must be raised whether it is not the normal duty of each church to participate in the fulfilment of that obligation.[1]

For reasons to which fuller reference will be made in the next chapter, the proposed integration of the World Council of Churches and the International Missionary Council has not gone uncriticized or unchallenged. But if—as now seems certain since the step has been approved by the Central Committee of the World Council and the Administrative Committee of the International Missionary Council—integration takes place at the end of 1961, there will be no doubt about its intention. That intention is not merely organizational tidiness: it is Gospel obedience.

* * *

The Role of the World Council

Every fresh recognition of the obligations which faithful witnessing lays upon a Council of Churches compels any such body to look anew at its own capacities and mandate. Christian obedience is as large as life and in the profoundest sense there is no limit either to the obligations or resources of any Christian organization. Nevertheless, for reasons rooted in the Incarnation, there is an economy of tasks and functions within the sphere of grace. The World Council has repeatedly affirmed that it is not a 'super-church' and the affirmation is sincere. The Council could not have come into being if this were not true, nor could it continue many months longer. In the sphere of action—action that may have to be translated

[1] W. A. Visser 't Hooft: *The Pressure of our Common Calling*, p. 43.

into administration—it is only authorized by its constitution to 'take action on behalf of constituent churches in such matters as one or more of them may commit to it'. Its primary responsibility is 'to offer counsel and provide opportunity of united action in matters of common interest'. In 'providing opportunity of united action' it is not assumed that the Council shall itself provide the administrative instrument; this may be constituted by the churches themselves through opportunities and relationships initiated by the Council. Within both these agencies of the ecumenical movement—the International Missionary Council and the World Council of Churches—there has been a constant endeavour to ensure that action shall be through the authority and resources of their constituent members, churches or national councils as the case may be.

The churches have nevertheless taken full advantage of their right to commit responsibility for action in some matters to the World Council itself. They have also made it clear that they expect initiatives and challenges to proceed from the Council. Nowhere is this more obvious than in the work of the Division of Inter-Church Aid and Service to Refugees in which the responsibilities carried by the Council as well as those discharged directly by the churches have grown year by year. To begin with it was assumed that the Council's part in these undertakings would be of a temporary character. This was reflected in the words 'relief' and 'reconstruction', used in earlier titles of the operation. Yet, in this world of plenty and this age of astonishing technological achievement, emergency needs prove either to be tragically recurrent or, by a grim paradox, to become 'chronic emergencies'. Inter-church aid in the double sense of the churches' aid to one another and their joint aiding of human need, is seen more and more as a permanent element in Christian witness. 'It has proved possible,' writes Dr. Visser 't Hooft:

to arrive at widespread spontaneous collaboration between the churches with regard to great emergencies such as floods, earthquakes and famine. But why should such general co-operation be confined to times of sudden emergency and not

also take place with regard to *continuing* human needs? . . .
It is time to complement the various forms of international
technical assistance to nations which need such service by
projects of international Christian assistance.[1]

Aims and undertakings of this character involve an inescapable
element of central initiative and direction. The field of need
has to be seen, as far as possible, as a whole, and policies
worked out accordingly. For this reason the work of the
World Council's Division of Inter-Church Aid and Service
to Refugees seems likely to grow rather than diminish in the
years immediately ahead. This will be so even if, mercifully,
the needs of the refugees become less—a prospect which,
however, still grievously recedes. Yet as this task grows it
will become more than ever important to devise policies and
procedures which will keep to the minumum the scale of the
work having to be done directly by the Council's committees
and staff. While doing everything possible to ensure that the
task is seen as a whole, the principle of placing responsibility
for action elsewhere than at the centre will need most faithful
application. In this connexion (and this applies to the work of
other Divisions of the World Council as well as that of the
Division of Inter-Church Aid) a recent development generally
referred to as 'regionalism' is of significance. Its best illustration is to be seen in the formation, in 1959, of the East
Asia Christian Conference.

When Dr. Rajah Manikam (subsequently Lutheran Bishop
of Tranquebar) began his work as secretary in East Asia for the
World Council of Churches and the International Missionary
Council, he was surprised to discover how little the Asian
churches knew of one another. Many of them were well-
informed about the churches in Europe and America and some
of them had strong personal links with the churches in the
West. Yet these same churches were often unaware of vital
happenings within their neighbouring churches in Asia; sometimes even, they were ignorant of one another's existence. It
soon became evident that while it was desirable to strengthen

[1] W. A. Visser 't Hooft: *The Pressure of our Common Calling*, p. 60.

relationships through the ecumenical movement between churches in Asia and the West, it was also of vital importance for the Asian churches to find one another in mutual knowledge and enrichment. A great deal has happened in the last decade towards this end. There have been interchanges of students, pastors and teachers; conferences on matters of common concern—Christian literature, Christianity and Asian culture, Home and Family Life, the training of the Ministry; joint undertakings in evangelistic and missionary work and the sharing of experience and judgement on the significance for the churches of the 'Asian revolution'. Largely as an outcome of all this, the churches and Christian councils in Asia have together constituted a standing conference, with a whole-time secretariat, called the East Asia Christian Conference. It provides a clearing-house for information and a forum for the working out of common policies. It draws the attention of churches to special evangelistic opportunities and needs within the region and stimulates the missionary outreach of the churches within Asia and beyond. At its inaugural Assembly it was possible to report that the Asian churches represented within the Conference already had more than two hundred of their own members serving as missionaries outside their homeland; some of these are in Africa and one is at work in the dockland of London with the Missions to Seamen.

This East Asia Conference was formally inaugurated soon after the historic Bandung conference of Asian politicians, though it was, in fact, taking shape many years before the Bandung meeting. There were some who feared that this development amongst the churches in Asia might signify a kind of ecclesiastical Bandung—an expression of Asian solidarity and self-consciousness over against the West. If this had been the case there would have been a set-back in the ecumenical movement; a group of regional *blocs* is not the equivalent of ecumenical relationships. There has not been the slightest sign, however, of this tendency. Asian Christian solidarity is finding rich expression, yet it is coupled with increased recognition of the necessity to keep the fellowship and con-

tribution of a particular region in living relationship with the
Christian fellowship and mission throughout the world. There
was a great sense in which the inaugural assembly of the East
Asia Christian Conference was a world missionary meeting:
it conjoined local commitment and 'togetherness' with world-
wide vision and concern.

This Asian Conference is an autonomous body: it is not an
integral part of the World Council of Churches or the International Missionary Council although there are close ties
between these two bodies and the Conference. The Conference
secretariat serves the two international organizations and
replaces their former East Asia secretariat. Certain responsibilities in, for example, the World Council's Division of
Inter-Church Aid and Service to Refugees are being devolved
upon it and it shows promise of making a very significant
contribution to the question of balancing central and regional
authority within the whole movement. It does not follow that
this particular development in East Asia sets the pattern for
other parts of the world, but there is a general recognition of
the importance of what Dr. John Mackay calls 'dynamic
regionalism' as a contribution to and expression of that
ecumenical movement which is larger than one or two organizations. Early in 1958 there was held at Ibadan in Nigeria an
exciting All-Africa Church Conference under the chairman-
ship of a distinguished African Christian, Sir Francis Ibiam.
One consequence of this has been the setting up of a provisional
committee representing the main territories in Africa to
explore ways and means of furthering African Christian
solidarity within the world-wide fellowship of Christians. In
1960 a Zulu educationist from the Union of South Africa—
Dr. Donald M'Timkulu, sometime Senior Lecturer in
Education at Fort Hare University College—was appointed
whole-time secretary to this provisional committee and he
has entered upon the kind of roving ministry which Dr.
Manikam so helpfully fulfilled in Asia. Again, in Latin
America, where regionalism is most obviously dynamic, there
was held in 1961 an all-Latin America conference in which

a great deal of consideration was given to possible ways and means of pursuing these same ends in another wonderfully significant region of the world.

Essentially, these regional developments are within the ecumenical movement; they are responses to and expressions of the same Spirit. But they are not merely organizational extensions of a structure called the World Council of Churches or of its older partner the International Missionary Council. As with the national Christian councils, which vary greatly in their composition and functions, there are effective relationships between the different organizations; there is a fruitful interplay in knowledge, experience, and purpose: but local and regional autonomy are kept in balance within a movement which is essentially a *movement*.

All this emphasizes the fact that such a structure as the World Council of Churches, enlarged and affected as it is likely to be by its integration with the International Missionary Council, remains a flexible instrument and one which may well be subject to further changes in the light of experience and of the Spirit's leading. Its emphasis is not upon its own life as an institution but upon what it stands for in terms of relationships; on what it may help to facilitate in further relationships within the fellowship and mission of the whole Church. This raises other questions which are likely to claim increased attention during the next few years. What is the nature of the unity being sought within the ecumenical movement and what is the proper role of a World Council of Churches in the pursuit of this? It is sometimes assumed, by those not sufficiently informed, that the World Council is either pressing the churches towards a type of unity already clearly seen and determined upon, or that it constitutes in itself a union of the churches. Both these assumptions are wide of the mark. The clearest expression of the Council's mandate in this matter is to be found in its constitution where authority is given for the work of the Faith and Order Commission. The functions of the Commission are here declared to be:

(i) To proclaim the essential oneness of the Church of Christ and to keep prominently before the World Council and the Churches the obligation to manifest that unity and its urgency for the work of evangelism;

(ii) to study questions of faith, order and worship with the relevant social, cultural, political, racial and other factors in their bearing on the unity of the churches;

(iii) to study the theological implications of the existence of the ecumenical movement;

(iv) to study matters in the present relationships of the Churches to one another which cause difficulties and need theological clarification;

(v) to provide information concerning actual steps taken by the Churches towards reunion.

In the more detailed constitution of the Commission itself it is laid down that:

Its main work is to draw Churches out of isolation into conference, in which none is to be asked to be disloyal to or to compromise its convictions, but to seek to explain them to others while seeking to understand their points of view. Irreconcilable differences are to be recorded as honestly as agreements.

Only Churches themselves are competent to take actual steps towards reunion by entering into negotiations with one another. The work of the Movement is not to formulate schemes and tell the Churches what they ought to do, but to act as the handmaid of the Churches in the preparatory work of clearing away misunderstandings, discussing obstacles to reunion, and issuing reports which are submitted to the Churches for their consideration.

This question of the nature of the obligation—and its limitations—resting upon the World Council in respect of unity matters has always been regarded as a vital one. It is significant that at the inaugural Assembly in Amsterdam the Council found it desirable to draw special attention to it, even though the constitution then adopted dealt so explicitly with the matter. A resolution on 'the authority of the Council' was passed in terms which included the following:

The council desires to serve the Churches, which are its constituent members, as an instrument whereby they may bear witness together to their common allegiance to Jesus Christ, and co-operate in matters requiring united action. But the Council is far from desiring to usurp any of the functions which already belong to its constituent Churches, or to control them, or to legislate for them, and indeed is prevented by its constitution from doing so. Moreover, while earnestly seeking fellowship in thought and action for all its members, the Council disavows any thought of becoming a single unified church structure independent of the Churches which have joined in constituting the Council, or a structure dominated by a centralized administrative authority.

The purpose of the Council is to express its unity in another way. Unity arises out of the love of God in Jesus Christ, which, binding the constituent Churches to Him, binds them to one another. It is the earnest desire of the Council that the Churches may be bound closer to Christ and therefore closer to one another. In the bond of His love, they will desire continually to pray for one another and to strengthen one another, in worship and in witness, bearing one another's burdens and so fulfilling the law of Christ.

Two years later the Central Committee returned to the subject at its meeting in Toronto. The Committee then remitted to the churches for study an important document bearing the title 'The Church, the Churches and the World Council of Churches'. This again makes the position clear, first, in a series of disclaimers concerning 'What the World Council is not'. Two of these read:

(a) The purpose of the World Council of Churches is not to negotiate unions between Churches, which can only be done by the Churches themselves acting on their own initiative, but to bring the Churches into living contact with each other and to promote the study and discussion of the issues of church unity.

(b) The World Council cannot and should not be based on any one particular conception of the Church. It does not prejudge the ecclesiological problem.'

Secondly, the statement makes certain affirmations, including :

(*a*)   The member Churches of the World Council believe on the basis of the New Testament that the Church of Christ is one.'

(*b*)   The member Churches recognize that the membership of the Church of Christ is more inclusive than the membership of their own church body. They seek, therefore, to enter into living contact with those outside their own ranks who confess the Lordship of Christ.

(*c*)   The member Churches of the World Council recognize in other Churches elements of the true Church. They consider that this mutual recognition obliges them to enter into a serious conversation with each other in the hope that these elements of truth will lead to the recognition of the full truth and to unity based on the full truth.

This important document—commonly referred to as 'the Toronto statement'—was, in procedural terms, 'received' by the Central Committee and remitted to the member churches. This process illustrates one of the ways in which a fairly complex international organization seeks to engage its members in responsible deliberation. On many important issues it would be irresponsible to be content with a 'pronouncement' formulated at a single gathering, however representative the meeting might happen to be. What is needed is the judgement of the churches, based on their own full consideration of the matter and then subjected to wider discussion and correspondence. The procedure is necessarily slow; church assemblies meet annually or even less frequently and these in turn are dependent upon their own committee procedures. But anything less thorough and careful than this would fall short of responsible, world-wide 'conversation'. This process is continuing in regard to the Toronto statement. Meantime, both its disclaimers and affirmations have proved to be in line with the general assumptions and aims of the member churches and with the meaning they attach to membership in the World Council.

The resulting situation is not without its paradoxical features. For example, the Eastern Orthodox churches may feel compelled to assert, as their delegates did at the Evanston Assembly of the World Council, that:

We are bound to declare our profound conviction that the Holy Orthodox Church alone has preserved in full and intact the faith once delivered unto the saints.

and further:

When we are considering the problem of Church unity we cannot envisage it in any other way than as the complete restoration of the total faith and the total episcopal structure of the Church which is basic to the sacramental life of the Church.

Nevertheless these same Orthodox churches are committed unreservedly to the World Council of Churches and are engaging in its discussions and responsibilities at a depth which can best be described in the words of the Toronto statement:

The member churches recognize that the membership of the Church of Christ is more inclusive than the membership of their own church body. They seek, therefore, to enter into living contact with those outside their own ranks who confess the Lordship of Christ.[1]

The words 'living contact' provide the best term in which to describe what is happening. It is a situation in which deep divergences are held within a fellowship constituted by something more than goodwill or amiability. The divergences are not merely 'held' in a static sense or poised in a fashion which results in a paralysing fear lest the balance shall be upset. The much-used word 'encounter' comes nearer the mark; not conflict but real meeting—the meeting of mind with mind and heart with heart; the endeavour to expound the truth as one sees it, with unreserved frankness and fidelity, and at the same time to understand the truth as another sees it, with

[1] The Russian Orthodox Church applied for membership of the World Council of Churches in 1961.

unreserved sympathy and humility. The process is not easy. There are occasions when patience is near exhaustion and sympathy wanes and hope is daunted, but repeatedly the spirit of the movement itself (surely the Spirit in the movement) takes charge of the situation and renews in the participants clarity of vision and strength of purpose. In the illustration just given, the commitment of the Orthodox churches to the fellowship of the Council has proved to be one of the most significant elements in its life. Not all the Orthodox churches are members. The great exception is the Russian Church. After prolonged absence of contact between the World Council and any of the churches in Russia—whether Orthodox or Evangelical—communications have happily been restored; there has been some interchange of visits and at the Central Committee of the Council in Rhodes in 1959 official observers from the Moscow Patriarchate were present; a message was also read from the Metropolitan Nikolai of Moscow declaring that the Church in Russia views the ecumenical movement with a sympathy 'inspired by the fact that in spite of separation all Christians continue to pray "Our Father", that all of us keep the Word of God, which is given to us in the Bible and in the Holy Gospel, and that we are all bound together by love for our Lord Jesus Christ'. Other Orthodox churches, including the Patriarchates of Alexandria, Antioch, and Constantinople, are members of the Council and their contribution to its fellowship—both in giving to others and receiving from others out of the heritage of each— has marked a new chapter in Church history. The renewed contact of these churches with churches from which they had been insulated for centuries has resulted in manifest benefits and the process of enrichment is a two-way one. There are many churches in the West and younger churches in Asia which have learned through this process to think in a new way about the significance of the historic Eastern churches in the total Christian heritage and to be thankful for the grace bestowed in such an experience.

All this means that in its own life the World Council of

Churches does not regard itself as having 'arrived'; although the organization ceased constitutionally at Amsterdam to be 'in process of formation', in fact the process continues. The 'living contact' goes on within the fellowship. It is not therefore claimed, or assumed by any of the member churches, that the Council itself provides the final answer to the question of church relationships or Church order. Nor is it assumed or intended that, within the fellowship, all the churches will some day accept the Orthodox view of the Church, any more than it is expected that some day all will accept the Quaker views held by the Friends General Conference of the U.S.A. (also a member of the World Council). It is not even assumed that the ultimate pattern of the visible church will be identical with one of those exciting 'United' churches which comprise within their order episcopal, presbyterian, and congregational elements. To the question 'What, then, is the form of the church towards which all this is leading?', the answer, in the most serious and reverent sense, is 'God only knows'. The *form* of a Church on earth which will more faithfully and clearly manifest the unity given by Christ to his People is still being sought in prayer, thought, and obedience. In the seeking, the World Council serves the churches by bringing them together, confronting them and helping them to confront each other with tasks and questions bearing on the search. At the last Central Committee of the Council at St. Andrews in 1960 it was decided, for example, to ask the member churches whether the unity they are seeking (whatever its form may prove to be) could be expressed by saying that:

. . . the unity which is both God's will and His gift to His Church is one which brings all in each place who confess Christ Jesus as Lord into a fully committed fellowship with one another through one baptism into Him, holding the one apostolic faith, preaching the one Gospel and breaking the one bread, and having a corporate life reaching out in witness and service to all; and which at the same time unites them with the whole Christian fellowship in all places and all ages in such wise that ministry and members are acknowledged by all, and that all can act and speak together as occasion requires for the tasks to which God calls the Church.

The churches will return to this question—as to many other aspects of their life together and their witness to the world—at the Third Assembly in New Delhi at the end of 1961. Meantime and all the time, within the life of the Council and the relationships which it fosters there is experienced with increasing power and promise the unity that is already given in Christ. For the rest, the future will disclose its own answers to those who stay together, grow together, and go together in their common acceptance of Jesus Christ as God and Saviour.

Chapter VII

RESISTANCES, APPREHENSIONS, AND QUESTIONS

Members and Non-Members

When the Third Assembly of the World Council of Churches meets in December 1961, thirteen years will have passed since the inaugural assembly at Amsterdam. Twenty-three years will have gone by since the decisive meeting at Utrecht which laid the constitutional foundations of the Council. Edinburgh 1910 will be more than half a century distant. These periods are not long when seen within the total sweep of Christian history. In the story of organizations, however, especially organizations of this character, they constitute a critical as well as formative spell of time.

The one hundred and seventy eight member churches of the World Council provide an impressive representation of the major denominational and confessional families within the Christian scene today. Lutheran and Reformed, Episcopalian, Presbyterian, Methodist, Congregational, and Baptist churches appear in the Council in considerable strength. Mennonites, Brethren, Disciples, Friends, and the Salvation Army are all well in evidence. The Orthodox Patriarchates already named, the Coptic churches of Egypt and Ethiopia, the Armenian, Syrian, Assyrian, and Mar Thoma churches, play their part in the life of the Council, and there is a steady increase in the number of 'younger' churches of Asia and Africa, including some significant united churches, in the active membership of the Council.

Yet the Council is far from being inclusive of all the non-Roman churches in the world today, even the larger ones.

There were churches from China in the initial membership of the Council, but these are now absent. One of the largest of all the denominations in the U.S.A.—the Southern Baptists—stands outside. There exist many other Baptist and Presbyterian churches which are unwilling to consider membership and there is still too small a representation of the newer indigenous churches of Asia and Africa. Then there are great groupings of churches, such as the very diversified sections of the Pentecostal movement, with many others which lay special claim to the word 'Evangelical', which have so far refrained from seeking membership. With some of these there exist helpful fraternal relationships even where the question of membership in the Council seems unlikely to arise. At Assemblies and some other meetings of the World Council there have been 'observers', or 'fraternal delegates', from, for example, the World Pentecostal Fellowship and the Southern Baptist Convention, and there are good and frequent personal contacts between some of the leaders of these churches and officers of the World Council. Nevertheless the gaps in the membership of a Council bearing the word 'World' in its title are significant.

If the International Missionary Council and the World Council of Churches become one in 1961 there will be brought into closer relationship with the World Council, through the new Commission on World Mission and Evangelism, more of the churches of Asia and Africa and of the great missionary agencies which are serving with them. These missionary societies or boards are, it will be recalled, grouped within the membership of such organizations as the Conference of British Missionary Societies, the Division of Foreign Missions of the National Council of the Churches of Christ in the U.S.A., and comparable missionary councils on the continent of Europe and in Australia and New Zealand which are all part of the International Missionary Council. Yet the councils which comprise the membership of the International Missionary Council are far from being comprehensive of the contemporary missionary movement. Few missionary societies have a more distinguished record than that of the China Inland Mission some of whose leaders participated in Edinburgh 1910. The mission was for some years a member of the Conference of British Missionary Societies and was thus linked with the International Missionary Council. It withdrew from the Conference, however, primarily on the ground that the Message of the Jerusalem meeting of the International Missionary Council did not adequately 'express its own convictions concerning the Commission it believed God had given to it as a mission'. Behind this action there had been a growing fear that 'modernist' influences were affecting the International Missionary Council. For many years, also, the Board of Foreign Missions of the Southern Baptist Convention was a member of the Foreign Missions Conference of North America, but when this Conference became an integral part of the National Council of the Churches of Christ in the United States the mission terminated its membership. In both cases good relationships have continued but the break in membership was a loss to the life of the movement. Beyond this there are very large missionary organizations, chiefly in the U.S.A., which have never co-operated with the International Missionary Council. Since the end of the Second World War there has been a very large and rapid increase in these missionary forces. Some of them are well-organized missionary agencies associated with well-established denominations in the U.S.A. Others take the form of undenominational missions which draw their support from individuals in various churches. Many of them are independent groups of no definable denominational category and some of them are short-lived in their activities. In the United States there exist two large and influential organizations which provide a kind of federal framework within which many of these missions operate. One of these is the Evangelical Foreign Missions Association; the other is the Interdenominational Foreign Mission Association. Both stand for an 'Evangelicalism' which tends— regrettably—to withhold the term Evangelical from those who do not come within their membership or who do not concur in their doctrinal position. The missionaries associated with these two organizations now comprise more than half the total number of American missionaries serving overseas. Further, recruitment for missionary service is proceeding much faster within these groups than it is through the mission boards in membership with the Division of Foreign Missions of the National Council. The number of missionaries alone is not an adequate measure of the strength of these different organizations, for important differences in missionary policy have also to be taken into account. Far more of the resources, for example, of the historic mission boards associated with the National Council's Division of Foreign Missions are devoted to the support of national or indigenous leaders, pastors and teachers, and to the maintenance of schools, colleges and hospitals, than is generally the case with the other groups of missions. Yet this numerical contrast in missionary strength is not without its significance.

This situation is part of that revival of what is generally called 'Evangelicalism', often based on 'Fundamentalism', which has been characteristic of the post-war years. Both the terms just used have a confusing ambiguity. It is deeply distressing that such a word of grace as the word 'Evangelical' should have come to be used with a party connotation and an exclusiveness which denies to others the right to employ it. It is equally regrettable that a word suggestive of the Christian fundamentals should have become the designation of those whose test of orthodoxy lies in acceptance of a particular theory of inspiration. Happily, grace has its own ways of ignoring our classifications; hence, many of those who enclose themselves, or try to lock others, within these terms often find themselves hard put to it to discern the boundaries. Yet there exist certain broadly observable separations. As regards the two large American missionary organizations just referred to, the Interdenominational Foreign Mission Association in the main stands far apart from and sometimes in opposition to the agencies of the World Council of Churches and International Missionary Council. It doubts the theological integrity of the whole movement, suspects 'ecclesiasticism', fears 'Romanizing tendencies', and tenderness towards 'Communism'. Some of these suspicions and hesitancies also appear within the Evangelical Foreign Missions Association but this Association also includes many who are sympathetic towards the International Missionary Council though they may have less liking for the World Council of Churches. At the present moment there are signs of an increase in understanding and mutual respect between this group and the leadership of both the International Missionary Council and the World Council of Churches. Nevertheless, the proposed integration of these two bodies has produced a good deal of apprehensiveness within the Evangelical Foreign Missions Association. This has also made itself felt in other parts of the world whether in groups which have links with the American organization or within movements based on a similar doctrinal position. Some of the grounds of this apprehension are discussed later in this chapter.

There is one element in this general situation to which it is distasteful to have to refer in a book of this kind. These chapters are written in the conviction that the ecumenical movement is a movement of the Spirit which is not confined to one or two organizations; the Spirit bloweth where it listeth and may be expected to extend its gracious, reconciling, and empowering activity beyond all our limiting judgements and loyalties. There is, however, one agency at work in this sphere of relationships between the churches which continues to be the source of much misunderstanding and mischief. It bears the impressive title of the International Council of Christian Churches and is closely related to another body called the American Council of Churches. These two American organizations are the creation of the same man and owe their continuing activity to him. The American Council of Churches was avowedly set up to combat the then Federal Council of Churches and to deliver innocent Americans from what was described as the 'darkness and paganism' of the churches within the Council. The International Council of Christian

Churches was launched in the same spirit to oppose the World Council of Churches which was perceived to be the Woman of Babylon inadequately disguised once more. The originator of these two organizations is Carl McIntyre who was at one time a minister of the Presbyterian Church in the U.S.A. As an extreme 'fundamentalist' he joined a rebel movement within the Presbyterian Church whose Assembly eventually deposed him, with others, from its ministry. This action was taken, not for doctrinal reasons, but on the ground that these men had 'defamed the character of their fellow Christians . . . and were instrumental in causing dissension and strife' within the Church. Being thus disciplined the group established itself as 'the Presbyterian Church in America'. McIntyre, however, seceded from this new church and established his own denomination—the 'Bible Presbyterian Church'.

'Dissent' is an honourable word with an honourable history. Without it something would be lacking in our present understanding of the wholeness of the Church and the manifold gifts of grace. But it is impossible to follow the activities and read the publications for which McIntyre is responsible through his two organizations—the American Council of Churches and the International Council of Christian Churches—without concluding that they constitute nothing more honourable than the 'smear campaign' which Dr. John A. Mackay has called them. Anyone associated with the ecumenical movement is target for attack. To Carl McIntyre Billy Graham is 'modernist' and 'apostate'; the Revised Standard Version of the Bible is 'the work of Satan and his agents'; the great concerted broadcast appeal of the American churches for service to refugees, launched under the title 'One Great Hour of Sharing', was derided as 'socialist propaganda'; and the leaders of the World Council of Churches are alleged to be (by some strange process) at one and the same time 'modernists', 'Communists' and 'Romanizers'.

I write this as—I believe—a tolerant creature with no love of controversy; I even cherish a sneaking affection for the tender-hearted schoolgirl who wrote that 'even the Devil in any other walk of life would have been a good man'. Bickerings within the Household of Faith 'hurt my understanding' and I would be charitable to others even as I need the charity of men and the mercy of God. The preceding lines have been written in deep regret but out of concern for many good men and women whom I have met all over the world whose thought of the ecumenical movement has been sullied because of this strange campaign which has all too successfully exploited the techniques of propaganda in the interests not of Dissent but of dissension.

★ ★ ★

Evangelicalism and Mission

Very different from this travesty of Evangelicalism, there continues to be active an historic organization which played an important part in an earlier phase of the ecumenical movement. This is the Evangelical Alliance to which reference is made in the opening chapter of this book. Several countries can claim to have originated the Alliance but its constitutive meeting in 1846 took place in London. Branches of the Alliance (or independent Alliances) were formed in several European countries and these continue today. For some years there was a strong American branch, created in 1867, but its influence waned at the turn of the present century; it was dissolved in 1944 and some of its functions were taken over by the Federal Council of Churches. The main leadership in the Alliance—at any rate up to the end of the Second World War —was provided by the British section. Throughout its history the Alliance has successfully provided a meeting point for Christians of various denominations; in Great Britain individual Anglicans have been as active in its service as have Free Churchmen. In membership it is 'a voluntary union of individual Christians of different churches', not a federation or council of churches. In contrast to the single article which constitutes the Basis of the World Council of Churches, the Basis of Faith of the Alliance reads as follows:

That the parties composing the Alliance shall be such persons only as hold and maintain what are usually understood to be Evangelical views, in regard to the matters of doctrine understated, namely:

1. The Divine Inspiration, Authority and Sufficiency of the Holy Scriptures.
2. The Right and Duty of Private Judgment in the Interpretation of the Holy Scriptures.
3. The Unity of the Godhead, and the Trinity of Persons therein.
4. The utter Depravity of Human Nature, in consequence of the Fall.
5. The Incarnation of the Son of God, His work of Atonement for sinners of mankind, and His Mediatorial Intercession and Reign.
6. The Justification of the sinner by Faith alone.
7. The work of the Holy Spirit in the Conversion and Sanctification of the sinner.
8. The Immortality of the Soul, the Resurrection of the Body, the Judgement of the World by our Lord Jesus Christ, with the Eternal Blessedness of the Righteous, and the Eternal Punishment of the Wicked.
9. The Divine Institution of the Christian Ministry, and the obligation and perpetuity of the Ordinances of Baptism and the Lord's Supper.

With the disappearance of the American Evangelical Alliance other organizations arose with a similar basis and emphasis, though many of these tended towards an even more 'conservative' position. One of the most influential is the National Association of Evangelicals, 'a voluntary association of Bible-believing Christians from various denominations, who wish to bear positive and united witness to the Christian faith once delivered as it is revealed in the New Testament'. The Evangelical Foreign Missions Association is closely related to this National Association of Evangelicals.

In 1951 the American National Association of Evangelicals and the British Evangelical Alliance convened a conference in Holland which led to the formation of a World Evangelical

Fellowship with a membership composed of 'national fellowships of believers in any country which represent an adequate cross section of evangelical life and interests, always providing that they are truly interdenominational in character'. The members of this international organization are the British and American groups which took the initiative in 1951, some of the Evangelical Alliances in the European continent, and a number of more recently formed national Alliances or Fellowships in Africa and Asia. The World Evangelical Fellowship has adopted the following Statement of Faith, which may be compared with the original Basis of the Evangelical Alliance:

The Fellowship believes in,

1. The Holy Scriptures as originally given by God, divinely inspired, infallible, entirely trustworthy; and the supreme authority in all matters of faith and conduct.
2. One God, eternally existent in three persons, Father, Son and Holy Spirit.
3. Our Lord Jesus Christ, God manifest in the flesh, His virgin birth, His sinless human life, His divine miracles, His vicarious and atoning death, His bodily resurrection, His ascension, His mediatorial work, and His personal return in power and glory.
4. The salvation of lost and sinful man through the shed blood of the Lord Jesus Christ by faith apart from works, and regeneration by the Holy Spirit.
5. The Holy Spirit by whose indwelling the believer is enabled to live a holy life, to witness and work for the Lord Jesus Christ.
6. The unity in the Spirit of all true believers, the Church, Body of Christ.
7. The resurrection of both the saved and the lost; they that are saved unto the resurrection of life, and they that are lost unto the resurrection of damnation.

In a Statement of Purpose it is declared that:

The Fellowship is not a council of churches nor is it in opposition to any other international or inter-denominational organization. It seeks to work and to witness in a constructive manner ever 'maintaining the truth in love'.

Uniformity of opinion and temper is no more characteristic of 'Evangelicals' than it is of any other group of Christians. There are some individuals within the national units of the World Evangelical Fellowship who are less successful than others in 'maintaining the truth in love' and witnessing 'in a constructive manner'. Some of these—especially in the U.S.A.—would prefer to see this international body move into sharp hostility to the World Council of Churches. If increasing emphasis were thus put upon its *anti* characteristics there could be a serious loss to the ecumenical movement as a whole, in the sense in which this book understands the movement. There are, however, very many individuals in the Alliances which constitute the World Evangelical Fellowship who belong to member-churches of the World Council of Churches. Most of these welcome their dual relationship and regard the two loyalties as complementary rather than conflicting. The main leadership of the World Evangelical Fellowship is also deeply committed to the spirit of its declared Purpose. It may therefore be hoped that the Evangelical Alliances in their new international relationships will continue to maintain, and find new ways of fulfilling, that ecumenical vision and conviction which brought the original Alliance into being more than a century ago.

The fulfilment of such a hope may well include the salutary service of criticism, especially if this is offered in relationships which make possible mutual growth in knowledge and the correction of misunderstandings. The process also needs to be of a kind which facilitates the real meeting of mind with mind and spirit with spirit in the endeavour to discern what the ecumenical movement, as a movement of the Spirit, signifies. What is the nature of our unity as Christians? What is its essential basis? To what end are we brought together in Christ and what constitutes the full obedience of Christians to the demands of Christ's mission to the world? Questions of this kind really lie behind much of the discussion provoked by the proposed integration of the World Council of Churches and the International Missionary Council. For example, it has been contended by some of the 'Evangelical' critics of the step that integration will identify the missionary movement with a single conception of unity and a 'rigid ecclesiasticism'. Enough has been said in preceding chapters to show how mistaken this assumption is. It must also be said that in the quest (the end of which is not predetermined) for a right understanding of Christian unity there is a contribution, theological and experimental, of critical importance to any understanding of the nature and unity of the Church, which can and ought to be made in full by those whose standpoint is illustrated in the history of the Evangelical Alliance and kindred movements. On the other hand, the tendency of those within these movements to be content with a 'spiritual' interpretation of unity, requiring no radical re-thinking of denominationalism or of existing church orders, needs also to be challenged on the basis of what has happened—especially on 'mission fields'—between Edinburgh 1910 and 1960, as well as on Biblical and theological grounds. The integration of the World Council of Churches and the International Missionary Council will not close the great debate on these questions. It can bring to bear upon them, more forcefully and responsibly than hitherto, convictions and experience bound up with that apprehension of evangelical Christianity which has been one of the mainsprings of the modern missionary movement.

Another of the criticisms voiced from this same quarter is that the International Missionary Council is about to become part of an organization theologically weak in its Basis. Incidentally it is a little curious that when this argument is used, no criticism is levelled against the International Missionary Council for having no theological basis at all in its constitution. The Council has contented itself with a Purpose which lays upon it the responsibility 'to further the effective proclamation to all men of the Gospel of Jesus Christ, as Lord and Saviour'. This Purpose becomes the Aim of the proposed Commission on World Mission and Evangelism and in the new constitution it reads: 'to further the proclamation to the whole world of the Gospel of Jesus Christ, to the end that all men may believe in Him and be saved'. This becomes part of the constitution of a council which requires from its member churches a declaration that they 'accept our Lord Jesus Christ as God and Saviour'. The Basis is thus Christologically centred; there is no ambiguity about its acknowledgement of the Deity and saving work of Christ. Is this inadequate as a basis of Christian fellowship, as the starting point of that 'togetherness' in obedience, study, and prayer, which seeks to learn more of the mind of Christ for the Church and for the world? Can there be no truly Christian meeting in mind and heart unless such comprehensive statements of belief as those which appear in the constitutions of the Evangelical Alliance and the World Evangelical Fellowship are made the starting point? This question concerns something more than a comparison of creeds; it is a question of the nature and basis of Christian fellowship.

There is another misgiving in relation to the new pattern of the World Council of Churches and International Missionary Council which has been voiced from within these bodies as well as by those who stand in the tradition of the Evangelical Alliance. It is that the word 'mission' and the reality it denotes will lose their cutting-edge amidst the many interests and concerns of the World Council. Assurance on this point can, of course, only be given in experience. Preceding chapters have made clear the declared intention and hope. It is that 'mission', which has been the central thread of recent ecumenical history, especially the period 1910 to 1960, shall be kept central to the future course of the movement. One of the guarantees of this lies in the awareness within both the existing Councils that failure to accomplish this aim would be a fatal loss to the whole movement. The answer to the anxiety is not a complacent assertion that the danger does not exist. It does. It can exist even within 'missionary societies' and 'evangelical movements', especially as the jubilees and centenaries pass. It is the constant peril of every Christian institution, whether the institution be called Society, Church,

Alliance, or Council. It is the peril of letting the institution quench the spirit which the institution exists to serve and express. There is no escape from exposure to the danger; eternal vigilance is the price of freedom to overcome it.

Yet this does not simply mean that responsibility for alertness in this matter will depend solely on the strength which the missionary movement, as represented in the International Missionary Council, will bring into the integrated council. In what has been said already there is much evidence not only of a concern within the existing World Council of Churches for the missionary purpose which found vivid expression at Edinburgh 1910. There are indications that some of the new dimensions of the missionary task in the world today have been perceived within the World Council of Churches all through its short history. There are insights and experiments, as well as relationships, deeply relevant to the world mission of the Church in this new day. Such terms as 'world wide evangelization', 'foreign missions', 'the home-base of missions', 'missionary policy' and 'missionary vocation' all need to be deepened and sometimes challenged by thought and experience within a more completely ecumenical conception of the Church and its calling. Very specially, this new stage in evangelical and missionary obedience requires the insight and vision which the emerging churches of Asia and Africa (many of them more than just emerging) can bring to a world-wide undertaking. An organizational step, such as the integration of the International Missionary Council and the World Council of Churches, will not in itself ensure all these things; but both in symbol and in action this more integral relationship of two historic expressions of a great movement, will—by grace—be enabled to serve this movement of the Spirit more faithfully. In this endeavour the integrated council will need the widest and richest possible range of relationships with all who accept our Lord Jesus Christ as God and Saviour.

*   *   *

The Orthodox Churches

Some of the hesitancies and apprehensions which have found expression through those who are most at home in the tradition of the Evangelical Alliance and similar movements have naturally had their counterpart in another area of the ecumenical scene. The growing interest of the Eastern Orthodox churches in the World Council of Churches and the deep commitment to the movement of many of their representatives has been one of the most signal events in the sphere of Church relationships during the present century. Those who have participated in the regular deliberations of the World Council, especially in the smaller committees and groups which facilitate more intimate contact of mind and heart, testify eagerly to the enrichment that this has brought; and the testimony is every bit as generous and heartfelt on the part of the Orthodox participants. A meeting without an Orthodox voice would now be an impoverished one. This is far from saying that fundamental differences no longer exist between these churches and other members of the World Council. They do, and the occasions are frequent in which the deeply significant character of the differences is sharply in evidence. Correspondingly, Orthodox and non-Orthodox are aware that staying together and growing together in this relationship is an experience which makes searching demands spiritually even while it bestows immeasurable blessing.

The closer relationship of the International Missionary Council and the World Council of Churches has given many Orthodox churchmen a kind of obverse pang to that experienced by certain 'Evangelicals'. In a large part of the Orthodox world the term 'missions' has been mainly suggestive of free-lance fanatics whose chief aim is to proselytize amongst the Orthodox flock, especially in the Middle East. Conversely, the representatives of some missionary societies have hitherto scarcely thought of the Orthodox churches except as ancient monuments incapable of possessing missionary zeal or Gospel fervour. Humanly speaking, there are those in both groups who would be content permanently to keep their distance from one another. 'Ecumenical conversation', however, is an experience which constantly moves its participants to a level of discourse deeper than 'humanly speaking'. Contact, of the kind nurtured within the fellowship of the World Council of Churches—contact in service towards the needy, in mutual assistance, in worship as well as in theological discussion—has resulted, during the last few decades, in much new understanding and mutual appreciation, not least at points where differences remain unresolved. This progress has also attended discussions about the integration of the World Council of Churches and the International Missionary Council. On the one hand, there is already apparent, amongst leading Orthodox representatives, a fuller knowledge and better judgement of the modern missionary movement, and many representatives of this movement have learned more about the historic witness of the Orthodox churches and the bearing of this witness on the Christian mission. In two current studies which involve both the World Council of Churches and the International Missionary Council —one on 'Christian Witness, Proselytism and Religious Liberty' and another on the 'Theology of Mission'—there is fruitful Orthodox participation with other member churches of the World Council and representatives of the International Missionary Council. Again, this debate is not ended. It is a continuing ecumenical conversation involving more than argument and sometimes more than speech; but it is another illustration of that 'living contact' between different members within the Household of Faith which can be so fruitful, spiritually and practically.

*   *   *

The Roman Catholic Church

Are there no limits to this outreaching of fellowship in the name of the ecumenical movement? There are some who would say—and who are uneasy because the World Council of Churches does not say it—'We draw the line at Roman Catholics; they are the limit.' In the middle and late nineteenth century when some of the forces which led to Edinburgh 1910 were beginning to be felt, there was a good deal of co-operation amongst Protestants on a basis which included a strong anti-Roman Catholic note. One of the pioneers of the Evangelical Alliance summoned these interdenominational movements to 'lift up a standard against papal and prelatical arrogance'. Another, carried away in the rush of his alliteration, saw a common foe in 'Popery, Puseyism and Plymouth Brethrenism'—a less common, if suggestive, conjunction. Yet amongst those who spoke with a different accent from this at Edinburgh 1910, and even there talked of fellowship between Protestants, Orthodox, and Roman Catholics, were leading British Free Churchmen.[1]

It takes two to make relationships and to provide the obedience which God will turn into Christian fellowship. As already noted, Rome gave a decisive 'no', nearly fifty years ago, to an invitation addressed to 'all Christian Communions throughout the world which confess our Lord Jesus Christ as God and Saviour'. This was the invitation which, following the initiative of Bishop Brent, led to the first World Conference on Faith and Order. It was consistent with the Roman Catholic conception of the Church that this invitation should be declined. There cannot, in Rome's view, be a permanent organization called, with any validity, a Council of *Churches*. The Church is one, not many. Its visible unity is to be seen in 'the Holy, Catholic, Apostolic, *Roman* Church'. Rome cannot enter into any formal relationships which would qualify—or even seem to qualify—its claim to be the sole true Church of Christ. This view may be—and frequently is—accompanied by charity towards 'separated brethren' and by willingness to meet with 'dissidents' in theological discussion. The inflexible position regarding the one true visible Church may also be accompanied by the recognition that baptism in the threefold Name, even when administered heretically, possesses a certain validity;

[1] See Chapter III, p. 45.

but significant as are these qualifications of the main Roman Catholic position they do not fundamentally affect that position. It is not lack of goodwill or charity, in the every-day use of these terms, which prevents the Roman Catholic Church from officially participating as a member in the non-Roman organs of the ecumenical movement. It is fidelity to certain presuppositions without which Rome would cease to be what she is.

Nevertheless, contacts on a basis other than that of church dealing with church are frequent and are by no means of recent origin. In chaplaincy work in hospitals, prisons, and the armed forces; in movements for social betterment; in the dealings of Christian minorities with non-Christian governments; and in service to refugees, there is a long story of co-operation, often characterized by personal relationships of the most enriching kind. In Egypt there existed for many years a council in which Roman Catholics joined forces with others in negotiations with the Egyptian Government on such matters as Christian education. In the Middle East there is an important and active committee on work amongst the refugees in which Roman Catholics participate with members of other churches. When the International Missionary Council initiated its survey of African marriage problems in 1947 there was Roman Catholic collaboration in the field work. When the World Council of Churches launched its theological study of 'the Lordship of Christ over the Church and the World', a parallel study on the same theme was undertaken by a group of Roman Catholic scholars, with some interchange of papers and correspondence between this group and the World Council's Study Division. The *International Review of Missions*, the journal of the International Missionary Council, annually devotes a section of its 'Survey of the Year' to the progress of Roman Catholic missions and there is reciprocal action on the part of certain Roman Catholic journals. There are several quarterly journals published under Roman Catholic auspices whose main purpose is, on the one hand, the presentation to Roman Catholic readers of information concerning the ecumenical movement, and, on the other hand, the interpretation of the Roman Catholic position to non-Romans. The journals *Unitas* (published in Rome), *Istina* (published in France), *Irenikon* (published in Belgium), and the *Heythrop Journal* (recently launched in England) are all of a high order, both in their presentation of factual material and their eirenical spirit. Most of these publications have behind them influential groups within the Roman communion which exist for the sympathetic study of developments within the non-Roman churches and there are many personal contacts of a treasured kind between these groups and members of other churches. Prominent amongst these movements is the Society of Catholic Ecumenists with its headquarters in France and with an international membership.

In 1960 a step was taken in Rome which, while not affecting the fundamental position, may contribute towards the right kind of climate in which questions of Church relationships can be discussed. Pope John XXIII announced the creation of a new Secretariat for Promoting Christian Unity. It was subsequently stated that the functions of the Secretariat would be, first, to help the churches not in communion with Rome to follow the work of the forthcoming Vatican Council, and, secondly, to help the churches not in communion with Rome to arrive at unity with the Roman Catholic Church. The first secretary appointed to this new Secretariat is Monsignor Willebrands who has long been deeply and sympathetically interested in the ecumenical movement and has attended various meetings of the World Council of Churches in a personal capacity as an observer. It is far too soon to estimate the real significance of this step. The most that can be said at the moment is that the informal contacts between individual Roman Catholics and other Christians already referred to may in future be supplemented at certain points by more official contacts. To use a word which now tends to become part of a technical jargon, there may be some possibility of a 'dialogue' between the Roman Catholic and other churches. This is much to be welcomed, but a reminder voiced in the report of the Executive

Committee of the World Council of Churches to the Central Committee at St. Andrews in 1960 has also to be noted:

It should be remembered that the creation of the Secretariat does not mean that any of the fundamental differences which exist between the Roman Catholic Church and the churches in the World Council of Churches have been solved. The change is a change in procedure and in climate. The opportunity for dialogue is to be grasped, but it means that the real problems will come to the fore.

'Opportunity for dialogue'. 'A change in climate'. It was in recognition of this and as a contribution to it that the Archbishop of Canterbury made his historic courtesy visit to Pope John XXIII in December, 1960. The term 'courtesy visit' was strictly true. It in no sense constituted an opening of official negotiations between the Anglican Communion and the Roman Catholic Church. As Pope John said, he and the Archbishop 'remained at the threshold of great problems'. Yet the word courtesy is a profoundly important one and a deeply Christian one. The Archbishop went to the Vatican because—as he said—'the Pope had expressed his great desire to increase brotherly feelings among all men, especially among all Christians'. 'Cordiality and sympathy'—in another phrase of the Archbishop's—were the main characteristics of the meeting. No one can say when and by what ways personal relationships between representative churchmen may progress from this starting-point in the grace of courtesy to fruitful dialogue concerning other matters within the realm of grace; but this historic meeting was clearly within that climate which has become characteristic of the ecumenical movement.

There is a point in this grave and complex problem of the deep division between Roman Catholics and others at which the individual Christian, of whatever communion, can most surely make a constructive contribution. It is in the prayer-life of the believer. Amongst other aids to prayer for Christian unity there is a movement associated with the name of a French Roman Catholic, the late Abbé Couturier. Through

Couturier's initiative an 'octave' (or eight-day period) of prayer for unity has become widely observed every January by Christians of many denominations as a time of special prayer 'for the unity of the Church of Jesus Christ, as He wills and when He wills'.

Is none of this worth while? Does it constitute, on the part of the World Council of Churches or the International Missionary Council, a 'betrayal of history', 'papistical leanings' and what not? Would the cause of Christ be better served by fulminating against 'papal and prelatical arrogance'? A glance through the membership of the World Council of Churches, with its strong representation of Lutherans, Presbyterians and Reformed, Baptist and Congregational Independents, Methodists, Disciples, Salvationists and Quakers, scarcely gives ground for fear that the Protestant witness is in danger or that the case of the non-Roman churches against Rome, theologically and historically, is undefended. In fact, at almost all the points just enumerated, where there is the opportunity of contact between Christian and Christian, the serious nature of the differences between Rome and the rest of the churches constantly becomes apparent and it is met, not dodged. Another of the present studies of the World Council of Churches is concerned with religious liberty. The study is being directed by a representative international commission (including missionaries in its membership) and with the whole-time staff service of an expert in Roman Catholic philosophy and practice in the matter. This undertaking is designed to penetrate more effectively than hitherto the root of the differences between Protestants and Roman Catholics and to strengthen the witness of the World Council of Churches and its members on an issue which contemporary history makes burningly relevant. On this and many other contemporary problems, discussions with Roman Catholics often heighten rather than diminish awareness of the profound differences between the standpoint of Rome and that of member churches of the World Council. But the differences are approached not merely in terms of an encounter between protagonists who must for ever stand on opposite sides of a great divide. They are approached in the name of Christ and in concern for that unity and catholicity which have their source and meaning in him.

Within foreseeable history there may never be any fundamental change in the relationship between the Roman Catholic Church and other churches. For all who love our Lord Jesus Christ in sincerity this should give cause for grief more than for recrimination. Meantime, small as the contribution may seem to be, it is possible, in response to that ecumenical movement which is a movement of the Spirit, to establish and deepen contacts which grace may use to further the unity and mission of Christ's Church 'as He wills and when He wills'. This can be done in full fidelity to truth as well as love and this is the ground on which the hand of fellowship is offered to 'all Christian Communions throughout the world which accept our Lord Jesus Christ as God and Saviour'.

* * *

Organization

The World Council of Churches and the International Missionary Council are organizations seeking to be responsive to that ecumenical movement which is larger than any organization. The closer conjunction of these two councils, which seems likely to be effected at the end of 1961, is being contemplated as a further response to the pressure of this deeper movement of the Spirit. But every organizational development, especially if it be towards the enlargement of an administrative structure, ought to be accompanied by a fresh look at the scale of the organization and the demands it is making upon the resources of its members. As a matter of fact, the word 'administration' should not be given too much weight in connexion with these two international councils, whether in their present or prospective manner of working. The International Missionary Council does not 'administer' the missionary work of the agencies within its membership, nor does the World Council 'administer' the work of its member churches. There are occasions and areas of responsibility in which, as this book has illustrated, special tasks are undertaken on behalf of the churches, as in the service to refugees. Even here, a good deal of the administration, in the strict sense of the word, is not handled by the World Council staff: responsibility lies with national organizations or with member churches. Nevertheless, even where the emphasis lies on consultation, co-ordination, common planning, the exchange of information and so on, there is no escape from desk work or from demands on the minds and hands of competent people. More especially, the whole process of study and consultation necessitates meeting and writing; the organization of committees, commissions, working-parties and groups. And in the shaping of the Council's policy and the maintenance of its corporate life, assemblies and committees make their inescapable demand on time and energy as well as money. Further, the claims of the World Council and International Missionary Council on their members by no means constitute the total, or even the chief, demand on the physical, intellectual, and spiritual resources of the men and women involved. If the Council is to act responsibly it must have within its counsels those in positions of responsibility in their own churches. These are necessarily the people who are already subject to exacting claims in their denominational assemblies, councils, dioceses, synods, and committees. In the last decade or so, apart from other multiplying causes, there has been a significant development commonly referred to as 'world confessionalism'. This refers to such international organizations as the Lutheran World Federation, the Methodist World Council, the Presbyterian World Alliance, the Baptist World Alliance, the International Congregational Council, and various 'pan-Anglican' gatherings on a world-wide basis of which the periodical Lambeth Conferences are the chief, but not the only, example. The fear is sometimes expressed that these organizations and gatherings represent a counter-move to the ecumenical movement. Is denominationalism digging itself in against the more radical consequences of the ecumenical movement? It is true that the instinct of self-preservation is as strong in institutions as in individuals. Unconscious motives may also be as powerfully at work in a corporate entity as in a single mind. Yet it is doubtful if 'world confessionalism' is to be accounted for in these terms. Most of these organizations have a fairly long history; there is nothing new-fangled about the idea of world-wide gatherings of the denominationally like-minded. They have proved to be spiritually enriching and to make for enlargement of vision. Moreover, the denominations in which this trend is most noticeable are also those most deeply committed to the ecumenical movement, both through the service of their leaders and in the responsible participation of the denomination in the work of the World Council. One new emphasis may nevertheless be discerned in the current phase of this movement. There seems little doubt that the contact with other churches and traditions engendered by the ecumenical movement has encouraged the denominations to look afresh at their own inheritance and at the character of their 'distinctive witness'. This could constitute a period of institutional introversion: it could also be a step towards a deeper theological and spiritual sharing with other communions of gifts and graces which all need to apprehend in their fullness. This latter is certainly the hope and intention which animates the present leadership of the world confessional organizations. Nevertheless, in this present phase of the movement there has of necessity been an increase in, so to speak, the machinery of world confessionalism. International gatherings which were formerly convened at irregular intervals on an *ad hoc* basis are now the regular meetings of standing organizations. These have their permanent officers and committees and are invariably equipped with those duplicating machines which give the impression of churning out material on their own volition and through force of habit. No doubt he who runs may read but with the pace of things today it is increasingly difficult to keep up with all the available memoranda.

It is, of course, easy to deride all this—and to escape from responsibility in so doing. Theologically speaking, the Holy Spirit and the Incarnate Son are 'consubstantial'. A movement of the Spirit carries flesh-and-blood consequences for the obedient. If it is right to dare to claim that the ecumenical movement is a movement of the Spirit—however imperfectly apprehended—organizational obedience becomes one of the Christian imperatives. Moreover, in a period of history when events as well as principles are calling for thought and action in international terms, organizations of a more than parochial character are essential. Most important of all, if Christians of all nationalities and divers cultures and languages, are to grow together—in knowledge of one another, in their experience of Christian fellowship and in fidelity to a world-wide mission—it is only to be expected that certain people must accept the responsibility for meeting, working, and even 'organizing' within a larger and more complex pattern than hitherto. At this point such words as 'administration' and 'organizing' ought not to be dismissed as of the Devil or be set over against the word 'spiritual'. They must be read within the realm of grace and seen as part of the discipline by which Christ's people seek to 'discern the body'.

This does not excuse the careless multiplication of offices, officers, and meetings. It calls for a proper sense of responsibility in relation to their growth and implications. The question of what constitutes responsible growth in the operations of the World Council of Churches is much under discussion and it will inevitably become more important in relation to an integrated World Council of Churches and International Missionary Council.[1] Hitherto the great Assemblies, with their maximum demands, have been convened at six- or seven-yearly intervals (though the Constitution provides for Assemblies every five years). The Central Committee, with consultants, fraternal delegates and staff in addition to its ninety members, meets annually for ten or twelve days and is usually accompanied by divisional

[1] See also the note on structure on pp. 184 ff.

and departmental committees and meetings of special commissions. This annual cluster of meetings covers three or four weeks and may involve the attendance of two or three hundred people for varying lengths of time. The small Executive Committee meets twice yearly for a few days. Some people would favour changing this time-table, providing for an Assembly every ten years and Central Committee every other year with longer intervals than at present between meetings of other committees. Meetings of the Executive Committee could scarcely be reduced beyond their present number. The problem is how to avoid two dangers in the life of such a Council. On the one hand, it is clearly imperative to guard against excessive demands on key people; either they or their work, including their work for the Council, will suffer, or they will refuse to serve and their place may have to be taken by men and women less equipped to reflect the mind of their churches. On the other hand, if the main directing committees meet too infrequently too much responsibility will have to be left with the staff, and the Council may become a less effective meeting point of the churches. A not unimportant consideration touching the frequency and size of meetings lies in the opportunity they provide for gradually drawing a greater number of people into the experience of international and ecumenical discussion with its peculiar disciplines as well as delights; there is an art to be learned in these matters. It is hoped—and this very frequently proves to be so—that such people will take back into their local and national situations better knowledge of what the ecumenical movement is and greater zeal in furthering it.

In trying to find the right course between varied considerations of this kind the distinctive role of the World Council has constantly to be remembered. It is not itself a Church or Missionary Society, still less is it a super-Church or super-Mission. It is not its purpose to gather to itself responsibilities which belong to the churches any more than it can (or wishes to) claim the authority belonging to them. Yet it is more than a clearing house and post office between the churches. It is not merely an agency for arranging meetings of church representatives or convening conferences on important topics. It is, at certain points, an instrument through which separated churches can act together with a deep degree of commitment one to another in tasks which cannot be done—or done so effectively—by the churches separately. The work of the Council's Division of Inter-Church Aid is the most notable instance of this. It can thus, in itself, constitute an expression of Christian solidarity. Further, through its total activities it can be instrumental in bringing the churches into new and profounder relationships with one another and in its own life it can provide the means by which—at any rate for the time being—aspects of the given unity of Christ's people can be more clearly apprehended and its demands and promises realized. It can in some measure constitute a manifestation of the unity already experienced by the churches. Yet it is not an end in itself and does not provide the goal of Christian unity: it is an aid to people on pilgrimage and—by grace—it may help to nourish them on the way and keep their vision clear. For these great purposes its structure must not be too slight or makeshift; but in providing and maintaining a worthy instrument for its own obedience, it must not mistake the process for the end.

Chapter VIII

ECUMENICAL AND LOCAL

Local Awareness

'Here at Halton we are discovering Amsterdam, Lund, Travancore and Evanston writ small.'[1] This was written concerning an Anglican parish church, a single congregation in Halton on the outskirts of Leeds. It was exciting testimony to the fact that the ecumenical movement as a movement of the Spirit was disturbing, renewing and enriching a local group of Christians. The forces that made so significant and memorable the great ecumenical gatherings with their delegates from many nations were doing the same 'in our street'. The size and scale were different; the experience and its significance were the same. The greatest test of the adequacy of such agencies as the World Council of Churches is whether they help towards this local and parochial experience of all that the word *ecumenical* signifies.

This involves something more than learning *about* the kind of events recorded in this book. Local discovery of the meaning of the word *ecumenical* is an experience deeper than that of receiving information about world movements. But awareness of what has been happening to the churches and missions in their wider relationships is relevant to this deeper experience. This turbulent twentieth century seems likely to pass into recorded history—unless the record is finally broken within the century—as one packed with mighty events. It is darkened by grievous tragedies—it has already been called, with justification, the Century of the Homeless Man. Behind the

[1] E. W. Southcott: *The House Church* (British Council of Churches, 1956); see also his *The Parish Comes Alive* (Mowbray, 1956).

plight of the vast refugee population there are regressions to barbarism all the more terrible because they have co-existed with sophistication, and all the more baffling because the same century is witnessing unparalleled advances in social welfare. It is the century of astounding scientific and technological progress; a century of discovery, searching out worlds beyond worlds. It is the Century of the East and its renaissance; it may well be the Century of Africa and Latin America, radically changing the power centres of the world. It is a century of an intellectual ferment the end of which cannot yet be seen, of acute criticism and startling experiment in the arts, all of which may yet make it a period of permanent cultural achievement. So far, it seems scarcely likely that it will be ranked as one of the great Ages of Faith—though it still has forty years to go and the Word of God is not bound. It is clear that it includes happenings in the life of the churches that are momentous in themselves. It is a time of no mean achievement in theology and biblical studies, and though these advances are not the product of the ecumenical movement (for at some points they are its source) they are closely related to it. Further, the movement itself is one of the great happenings of the century. It includes an approach to Christian unity which constitutes a new trend as compared with the main course of church history for centuries past. Within it there have been great missionary advances and it has given rise to the search for a fuller and more dynamic conception of the Church's redemptive mission to the world. With all this there is a growing sense of community amongst Christians in every land, a solidarity in purpose and resources within the Domain of Christ. Whatever the rest of the century holds for better or worse, these events matter. They are of immeasurable significance for all who profess and call themselves Christian. It is of importance, therefore, to every local congregation and parish that there should be awareness of the ecumenical significance of the age. Once more it must be said that the ecumenical movement is more than one or two organizations; nevertheless the movement is using the organizations, and people in all the churches should know of it. Following this chapter there is a chart and, in summary form, a sketch of the main organization which has resulted from the long and variegated process described in the rest of this book. Indications are there given of some of the links by which a local congregation is related to the wider movement.

If these things are to become better known in a local parish somebody in that parish must be faithful in the prosaic business of disseminating information. Yet spreading information is, in this connexion, telling good news—no merely prosaic task. There needs to be in every local congregation at least some one person committed to this privilege and service. It need not and should not be left to the parson, but whoever does it should bring thought and alertness to the task. It means keeping in touch with a good deal of published material, using and adapting it imaginatively to local conditions. The Information Department of the World Council of Churches publishes the main informative material and this is generously supplemented by publications of the British Council of Churches and of comparable councils in other countries. In the Appendix to this book there are detailed references to these information sources. Parish magazines and their equivalent ought to draw regularly on this material. The programmes of various types of church meeting—guilds, fellowships, discussion groups and so on— should make full use of it. Local newspapers are generally open to receiving contributions from budding amateur journalists who can serve the cause and practise their skill by using or recasting good 'copy' of a kind that is readily available.

The principle, frequently enunciated in preceding chapters, that the main centres of responsibility and action lie with the member churches of the World Council or the member councils of the International Missionary Council, applies to this educational process. Some of the churches are fulfilling this responsibility well. It is becoming a regular practice for annual reports of denominational assemblies, synods or councils, to include some account of the work of the World Council and of the denomination's participation in it; but there is need for more of this and especially for its transmission through dioceses and synods, rural deaneries, circuits and presbyteries to every local congregation.

A vital part of this information concerns developments within the national Christian councils and such regional councils as are taking shape. At this point the process of receiving news about the ecumenical movement should become one with experience in the movement locally. This involves at once the question of relationships between churches of different denominations in any given locality. How close and deep are these? In most towns and villages do the churches 'stay together' in relationships which result in the kind of growing together that is characteristic of the ecumenical movement? Local situations are infinitely varied. As was discovered in some of the Asian countries a few years ago, a church may become greatly interested in an international movement and remain a stranger to its immediate neighbours. The weakness is not peculiarly Asian. It can be more exciting and less demanding to attend a meeting a thousand miles away than to go round the corner to the local Baptist or Anglican church. It is possible to enjoy an enriching contact with members of other communions during a few days' conference amidst new scenes and yet to remain daunted by the prospect of getting any closer to that 'sticky Anglican' or 'rabid Evangelical' or 'stubborn Presbyterian' down the road. Yet, in the long run, the place where we now are is the place of testing and is meant to become the place of revelation— revelation of what the ecumenical movement means.

* * *

Local Action

An important contribution to all this can be made by a local council of churches—a council coterminous with a single town. More than two hundred and fifty of these councils now exist in

Britain and more are being formed. Again, they vary enormously. Some plod along, or totter along, without becoming points of living contact and spiritual enrichment across the denominational lines. Some are kept going, for a few necessary and worthy purposes, out of a reluctant sense of duty. Yet others are real meeting points in which there is a lively sharing of Christian judgement and experience. Just as doing things together internationally has contributed so greatly to relationships within the World Council of Churches, so local co-operation between the churches—in social welfare or civic responsibility—can serve more than a pragmatic end. All depends upon the depth of the conviction and concern which the churches and their representatives bring to one another and to their common tasks.

Yet doing things together, even in the most efficient local council or through such admirable undertakings as Christian Aid Weeks, does not meet the whole need. If the doing has been effective and worth while, the question soon arises: 'What next?' Sooner or later this leads to a full stop, especially when certain forms of Christian witness are contemplated. What of the central task of evangelism? How far can the churches—as they are—act together here? In some situations they can go a long way, as instanced in some notable campaigns and especially in the long-term 'Tell Scotland' venture. Yet the nearer such evangelistic campaigns get towards touching the genuinely unevangelized—as distinct from fostering revival amongst nominal Christians—the more embarrassing becomes the question: 'Which church?' when the new convert looks for anchorage and the means of growth within the Christian fellowship. It is not enough to say 'Any one' and to offer no guidance or invitation. And if the guidance or invitation are to be offered, on what worth-while grounds is the advice tendered and the decision made? There are clergy and ministers who cannot go far, if at all, along the road of unity in evangelism if such questions as these are not to be faced in their deepest significance. To pass them over lightly or to attribute concern about them merely to unwillingness to co-operate or to lack of an accommodating spirit is to deal too casually with history, loyalty, conviction and the gravity of our present disunity. Local togetherness, for the sake of the Gospel and its propagation, needs to be at a depth where the real differences between the churches as well as their common possessions are frankly faced. At no point is this more crucial than when members of different churches who are learning to grow together realize what it means to have to stop short of meeting at the Table of the Lord. Some members of churches which, by tradition and conviction, are free to practise 'open Communion' sometimes assume that those who take a different line and have to refuse fellowship in Holy Communion are lacking in brotherliness and goodwill. It is essential to realize that there is more at stake than this and that both viewpoints —grievous as is the resulting situation—can be based on serious convictions that are inseparable from a Christian's obedience. Not indifference to these obstacles but acceptance of the cost of learning together and growing together at greater depth is the only way forward here.

This deeper encounter may be facilitated by the existence of a local council of churches and by the relationships engendered within it. But opportunities for contact of a more intimate kind are also needed. These may take the form of very small and informal groups, to begin with, meeting in the homes of church members, for conversation about the standpoint and traditions of the several churches. If these can also become groups for united Bible study there is promise of still deeper growing together.

In any ventures of this kind the problem of time for 'one more meeting' is a genuine one nowadays; though it usually begins to look less intractable when at least a few people really care about the matter. If this whole business is as important as the nature of the ecumenical movement indicates, there is need in many instances to look afresh at the normal calendar of 'church activities' and see at what point it can be adjusted to serve this purpose of local ecumenical growth. 'All life is meeting', said Martin Buber, and the dictum springs from a profound realization. It is not quite the same, however, when it becomes 'All life is meetings', and if growing together locally mainly seems to involve one more rush in a crowded day, the spiritual gain is by no means assured. There are types of united gatherings which ought to be substituted for— not added to—certain items in the normal weekly or monthly programme. This includes meetings for the consideration of the nature of the Church's witness to the immediate neighbour-hood, in civic affairs and in its special concern for the needy. It should also include meetings for the presentation of the overseas' mission of the Church in its fullness. It is one of the paradoxes of the missionary movement that starting with a world view, it can become reduced to a new parochialism in the minds of many of its supporters in a local parish or congregation. Missionary societies each have their own proper sphere of service and there is a right and necessary concentration upon this 'field'. For excellent reasons there may be a further delimitation in the mind of the local congregation, occasioned by support and prayer for 'our own missionary'. But all this needs to be kept in living fashion within the con-text of a world-wide calling and fellowship. 'Look at big maps,' once counselled Lord Salisbury, and the advice is pertinent to more than the task of a Government's Foreign Office. In any town or village where there are three, four, or more churches there are links of loyalty, devotion, and knowledge with half-a-dozen historic missionary societies. Between them these repre-sent Christian relationships with a dozen or more countries, including all the major crisis-points of this present time in history. When a storm blows up in the Middle East, Korea, Kenya, Central Africa, or Latin America, it is not difficult to find within the missionary resources of these three or four churches a personal link with the area concerned. Local 'missionary meetings' of every denomination could profitably be set on a wider canvas than is commonly the case.

In these local relationships nothing is more important than growth in praying together. One of the most far-reaching contributions of the Evangelical Alliance to the ecumenical movement was its initiation over a century ago of the annual week of prayer normally held in the first week of every new year. Its support and vitality vary greatly in different countries and areas but it represents a point of meeting in worship and intercession that ought not to be neglected or treated casually. The annual octave of prayer for unity, already referred to, is of more recent origin. It is specifically concerned with the unity of the Church and provides a point of contact in prayer with Roman Catholics. Important as are these annual occasions, their significance is diminished if their support does not grow out of the regular prayer-life of the churches and their members. One of the greatest needs in every locality is for men and women who will regularly pray for neighbouring churches as well as their 'own' and will grow together in informed and understanding prayer for the unity and mission of the whole Church.

All such undertakings as these depend on the right initiative as well as on continuous support. It may be a commonplace to say that things happen when and where there appears a man or woman with vision, conviction, caring, and initiative: but this is one of the commonplaces that are crucial. Support can be won when the lead is given, but too many people wait for the lead. It has been said that when a great need arises the reaction of most people is: 'Somebody must do it, but why should I?' But a few people will say: 'Somebody must do it, so why not I?' It is due to people of this second kind that significant movements, locally and internationally, have begun to move.

In this necessity for initiative and for the leadership which assists towards convinced and sustained following, a special responsibility is bound to fall upon ministers and clergy. Parochial demands are many and exacting; denominational and public responsibilities add to them and the more truly a minister perceives the nature of his pastoral responsibilities in the 'cure of souls', the more jealously will he guard his time and try to avoid diffusing his energies and gifts. Participation in the ecumenical movement, locally or internationally, becomes a claim which has to be weighed responsibly. Yet the claim also has to be seen as something more than 'one more thing'. Even before it may resolve itself into a summons to action and therefore to the use of time and resources, it confronts the Christian minister with a question concerning the significance of his calling and the nature of the Church of which he is a minister. Fundamentally and primarily, is a Christian minister a *Methodist* minister, an *Anglican* priest, a *Congregational* minister and so on? The ministry, of course, for reasons rooted in history, now falls into these denominational or confessional categories; ministerial 'orders' and their exercise are conditioned accordingly. Yet—without raising here the technical and ecclesiastical issue of Orders—every minister of the Word and Sacraments knows that his primary and fundamental calling is that of a minister of Jesus Christ. The Church in which he is allowed of God to minister is the Church of Jesus Christ. There are, at least, moments of insight and realization when he knows that to think in terms of the Methodist Church, the Anglican Church, or the Congregational Church is almost as wrong as thinking in terms of a Methodist Jesus, or an Anglican Jesus, or a Congregational Jesus. The Christian minister is a minister of Christ. Is Christ divided? Does my ministry point to the undivided Christ and to the unity of his people in him?

In meeting this question we may not by-pass the theological and ecclesiastical question of 'orders'; the solution of it is part of the total task of giving visible expression to Christian unity. But by the very nature of his calling the Christian minister should keep before himself and before his people the fact that essentially there is only one People of Christ, even as there is only one Gospel and one Lord.

Such a minister will not deal lightly with the responsibilities and loyalties which the legacy of history has laid upon him, still less with the convictions on which these have rested and still rest. Yet the problem of the relation between the Church and the churches will never be far from his thought and concern; he will not lightly esteem those whom history has involved in the same problem from the standpoint of other churches; nor will he too readily assume that past mistakes and present error are confined solely to denominations other than his own or that God has been gracious only to a few of his people. Most of all, in prayer and praise, in the study and proclamation of the Word, in the leadership, the teaching and the service of his flock, he will remember that his and their calling and obedience are within the *oikoumene*, a world-wide people of Christ on pilgrimage in a world-wide mission.

This awareness that a local minister and his people are at a place where a world-wide fellowship and a world-wide mission are focused is one of the great reminders of the ecumenical movement. When it could be said of that parish in Leeds that 'Here at Halton we are discovering Amsterdam, Lund, Travancore and Evanston writ small', what had happened was not merely that this congregation had read and studied the reports of the international conferences held over the years at these places. The congregation was seeing its own calling and mission in a new way and in a larger context. One of the more original features of this Halton awakening lies in its development of what has come to be known as the 'house church'. The parish church is still the main focal point of the congregation's worship and allegiance, but instead of simply saying to the people of the parish 'Come to church,' the church has sought new ways of going to the people. An increasing number of homes have become meeting places for Bible study, prayer, discussion and—in some instances—the celebration of Holy Communion. In these 'house churches' there takes place—to quote the vicar of the parish, Canon Southcott—the 'meeting of regular worshippers from house to house; of regular worshippers and irregular worshippers; of regular worshippers with outsiders and of regular worshippers of one confession with regular worshippers of another'.

Variations of this 'house church' idea are being tried out in other local situations and on the initiative of representatives of different denominations. Experiments will—and ought to—differ from one another and not all of them may prove lasting.

The significant thing is the response of a local congregation to a movement which is constraining it to see itself in a fellowship-relationship towards all the gathered companies of Christ's people and in a missionary-relationship to the world outside the Church.

'God so loved *the world* that He gave. . . .' The Church exists for the Glory of God and serves this end through its ministry of the Word and Sacraments, through its worship and fellowship and through its nurture of those whom Christ has saved and is gathering into one. But the Glory of God has also to be declared by evidence that the Church of his beloved Son bears the marks of his Sonship and obedience, the obedience of him who humbled himself and took upon him the form of a servant and who said:

> *A disciple is not above his master nor a servant above his lord. It is enough for the disciple that he should be as his master and for the servant that he should be as his Lord.*

> *As the Father hath sent me, even so send I you. . . . All power is given unto me in heaven and upon earth. Therefore go. . . .*

A NOTE ON STRUCTURE

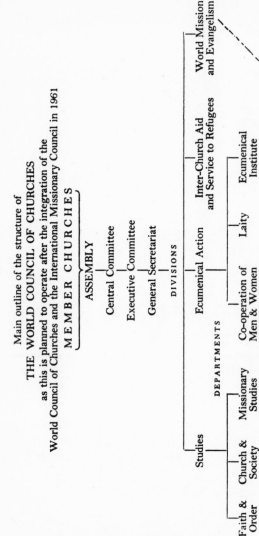

Main outline of the structure of
THE WORLD COUNCIL OF CHURCHES
as this is planned to operate after the integration of the
World Council of Churches and the International Missionary Council in 1961

MEMBER CHURCHES

ASSEMBLY

Central Committee

Executive Committee

General Secretariat

DIVISIONS

Studies   Ecumenical Action   Inter-Church Aid   World Mission
                                                    and Service to Refugees   and Evangelism

DEPARTMENTS

Church &   Missionary   Co-operation of   Laity   Ecumenical
Society   Studies   Men & Women   Institute
Faith &   in Church, Family
Order   & Society

COMMISSIONS

Faith & Order   Commission of the Churches   Commission on
Commission   on International Affairs   World Mission
                                                                and Evangelism

A NOTE ON STRUCTURE

—◦◉◦—

The sketch on the opposite page sets out the main structure of the World Council of Churches as this will operate from the end of 1961 onwards. The new features structurally are (i) a fourth Division (World Mission and Evangelism) added to the present three Divisions; (ii) a third Commission (on World Mission and Evangelism); (iii) a slight enlargement of the Central and Executive Committees. The figures quoted below are the revised ones.

Member Churches. At the time of writing these number 178. They comprise a great diversity of denominations and they vary in size from churches with membership numbered in millions to some with a membership of a few thousand only. Every member church is entitled to representation at the Assembly by a delegate or delegates with the right to vote.

Assembly. This is the principal organ of authority in the Council. The Constitution provides for a meeting of the Assembly every five years. It consists of approximately 600 delegates appointed by the member churches, plus other participants variously described as Advisers, Observers, Fraternal Delegates etc. Only the delegates appointed by the member churches have the right to vote. Seats are allocated to member churches on a basis related to the size of the church. The numbers are determined by the Central Committee which is required by the Constitution to take into account not only the size of the church but the need for adequate confessional or denominational representation and for adequate geographical distribution. The Constitution aims at securing that approximately one-third of the Assembly shall consist of lay persons and the churches are urged to bear this in mind in appointing their delegates. The expenses of the delegates are paid by the member churches but endeavours are made (by united action) to assist some churches where there is difficulty about this. A meeting of Assembly normally occupies two weeks. Some indication of the size of church delegations to an Assembly is given in the following approximate figures, based on New Delhi allocations:

(United Kingdom)		(U.S.A.)	
Church of England	19	Methodist Church	35
Methodist Conference	8	United Presbyterian	
Church of Scotland	9	Church	17
Baptist Union	5	Protestant Episcopal	
Congregational Union	4	Church	11
Presbyterian Church		United Lutheran Church	
of England	1	in America	9
		American Baptist Con-	
		vention	12

Evangelical Church in Germany	19
Church of Sweden	8
Church of Norway	5
Church of South India	6
Burma Baptist Convention	3
Coptic Church in Egypt	6
Orthodox Patriarchates of Alexandria, Antioch and Jerusalem, each	4
Russian Orthodox Church	16

Central Committee. As the Assembly only meets every five years, much of its authority is devolved upon the Central Committee which normally meets annually. It has a membership of 100 and is appointed by the Assembly. It regularly surveys the whole work of the Council on the basis of reports submitted to it by the various Divisions and Departments. The usual procedure is for these reports to be presented at a full session early in the meeting, with opportunity for questions and preliminary discussion. They are then remitted to sub-committees for detailed consideration; later in the meeting they are brought back to the full session, with the sub-committees' comments, for final discussion and action. In addition to this survey of the on-going work of the Council, the Central Committee receives substantial reports from the Executive Committee and the General Secretary; these often touch on matters of public concern—disarmament, international relations, racial tensions etc—as well as on the life and mission of the churches. It is customary, also, to provide at each Central Committee for a major address, with discussion, on some special theme. In recent years these have included such subjects as the nature of Christian unity, the moral problems posed by a nuclear age, the population problem, the Eastern and Western traditions in Christendom, etc. Ten days are usually set aside for Central Committee meetings.

General Secretariat. This is the main executive centre. It is responsible for the day-to-day work of the Council and all the preparatory work of Assemblies, Central and Executive Committees. The principal secretary of each Division (see below) is an Associate General Secretary working with the General Secretary. Directly related to the General Secretary's office are the Departments of Finance and Administration, the Department of Information and the Committee on Relationships with National Councils.

The Divisions represent, not a departmentalizing of the total interests of the Council but their organization in a compassable form. The work of each Division is guided by a Divisional Committee; these vary in size from 10 to 25 members. Intervals between committee meetings vary from one to two years. The Committee is appointed by Central Committee but for the Committee of the Division of World Mission and Evangelism nominations are made by the Commission on World Mission and Evangelism.

Departments may be created within the Divisions where the nature of the work requires it. The chart shows that two Divisions operate on this basis. Departments are served by Working Committees, appointed by Central Committee and numbering from 15 to 20 members. They normally meet annually.

Commissions. Although three bodies bear this name they are all differently constituted and have different histories and characteristics.

(i) *The Commission on Faith and Order* (closely related to the Department of Faith and Order in the Division of Studies) has its origin in the World Conferences on Faith and Order which preceded the formation of the World Council of Churches. It provides for a larger and wider representation of churches than is possible within the Divisional and Departmental structure and its triennial meetings are major events in the life of the movement. The Commission has a membership of 85 people (with facilities for co-optations) appointed by Central Committee. Amongst other distinctive responsibilities the Commission takes the initiative in convening world conferences on Faith and Order for the study of special themes bearing on Christian unity.

(ii) *The Commission on World Mission and Evangelism* carries forward (*inter alia*) the work of the former Assembly of the International Missionary Council. Its basic membership is appointed—as was the membership of the I.M.C. Assembly—by the National Christian Councils which previously constituted the I.M.C. Eighty delegates are appointed on this basis. Another thirty-five members are appointed by Central Committee and there is provision for consultants, advisers, etc. The Commission— ordinarily meeting every five years—formulates the general lines of policy and programme of the Division of World Mission and Evangelism.

(iii) *The Commission of the Churches on International Affairs* was created two years before the First Assembly of the World Council of Churches, being sponsored by the International Missionary Council and the Provisional Committee of the World Council of Churches. With the integration of the W.C.C. and I.M.C. the Commission becomes, in the terms of the revised Constitution, an

'agency' of the World Council of Churches. Its membership is composed of 'Commissioners', individuals chosen
for their special competence in the fields of the Commission's concerns. They are nominated by the Commission's own Executive Committee and appointed by
the Assembly or Central Committee, which also have the
responsibility for determining the size of the Commission.

All This and The Churches. The previous chapters in this
book have tried to give some account of the living movement
which is served by the above structure. They have also tried
to indicate the relevance of the movement and its organization
to the Churches. In Appendix I, which follows, some more
detailed information is given about publications and other
sources of information easily accessible to members of local
congregations and parishes. Two reminders may be emphasized again here:

(i) The basic life of the World Council of Churches is in its
member churches. Here is the point of chief responsibility. Many of the churches are taking this seriously
and providing their own clergy, ministers and congregations with information concerning the denomination's participation in the movement. Some churches
now have, within their own denominational structure, a
committee on church relations or ecumenical relations.
Ministers and members of local congregations keen
about this movement should ask their denominational
headquarters (or whatever the equivalent term may
be) for regular information. Requests should be made
for the services of the denomination's delegates to
W.C.C. Assembly, Central Committee etc. Requests for
direct information from the World Council of Churches,
subscriptions to publications etc. may be sent to 17
Route de Malagnou, Geneva; 475 Riverside Drive,
New York 27; or 10 Eaton Gate, London, S.W.1.

(ii) *Membership* in the World Council of Churches is that of
churches; but *National Christian Councils, National*

Missionary Conferences and other such organizations are vitally related to the movement, as this book has illustrated. The Appendix shows that some National Councils, including the National Council of the Churches of Christ in the U.S.A. and the British Council of Churches, are 'associated councils' of the World Council of Churches. This is a responsible relationship of two-way significance. Local churches should be in close touch with their national council in regard to the life of the World Council of Churches. Further, the Christian councils listed in the Appendix as being members of the International Missionary Council are those which have the right, when the integration of the two Councils takes place, immediately to become affiliated Councils of the Commission on World Mission and Evangelism, with voting responsibility in the Commission. All churches, through their own missionary committees, societies or other agencies, should be in lively contact with one or other of these affiliated Councils of the Commission on World Mission and Evangelism (e.g. the Conference of British Missionary Societies, 2 Eaton Gate, London, S.W.1, or the Division of Foreign Missions, 475 Riverside Drive, New York 27.)

> Somebody should do it,
>   but why should I ?

> Somebody must do it, ·
>   so why not I ?

APPENDIXES

APPENDIX I

A NOTE ON SOURCES AND FURTHER READING

I didn't think this morning there was half so
many Scarers in Print. But I'm in for it now.

MR. BOFFIN *after his first lesson.*

Chapter I

The standard work of reference, mentioned in the Preface, is
A History of the Ecumenical Movement by Ruth Rouse and
S. C. Neill (S.P.C.K., 1954). Parallel reference volumes
include *Ecumenical Foundations, a History of the International
Missionary Council and its Nineteenth Century Background* by
William Richey Hogg (New York, Harper & Brothers,
1952); *Addresses and Papers of John R. Mott* (6 vols: New
York, Association Press, 1946); *The World's Student
Christian Federation* by Ruth Rouse (S.C.M. Press, 1948);
*The Story of the Student Christian Movement of Great Britain
and Ireland* by Tissington Tatlow (S.C.M. Press, 1933);
*The Goodly Fellowship, a Centenary Tribute to the Life and Work
of the World's Evangelical Alliance, 1846–1946,* by J. W.
Ewing (Marshall, Morgan & Scott, 1946). In this chapter
I am also indebted to Dr. W. A. Visser 't Hooft's 'Burge
Memorial Lecture' on *The Meaning of Ecumenical* (S.C.M.
Press, 1953). The reference to William Carey's 'pleasing
dreams' occurs in a letter from Andrew Fuller to William
Ward, quoted in S. Pearce Carey's *William Carey.* It is the
subject of an article in the *International Review of Missions,*
April 1949, in which Ruth Rouse speculates on what might
have happened in the ecumenical movement if Carey had been
taken more seriously. There is no 'definitive' biography of
John R. Mott but Basil Mathews' *John R. Mott, World
Citizen* (S.C.M. Press, 1934), written while Mott was still
in full harness, tells the story up to that date. The official

report of 'Edinburgh 1910' was published in Edinburgh by Oliphant, Anderson & Ferrier under the title *World Missionary Conference 1910* (9 vols.). A one-volume popular account of the conference (from which some of the allusions in this chapter have been taken) is by W. H. T. Gairdner: *Edinburgh 1910, an Account and Interpretation of the World Missionary Conference.* J. H. Oldham's *Devotional Diary* is published by the S.C.M. (1925 and subsequently). Another key to Oldham's thinking appears in his book *Life is Commitment* (S.C.M. Press, 1953). *The International Review of Missions* is published quarterly by the Oxford University Press and ought to be in every good reference library.

Kenneth Maclennan wrote a good short account of the growth and work of the Conference of British Missionary Societies in *Twenty Years of Missionary Co-operation* (Edinburgh House Press, 1927). This was supplemented in 1944 by A. M. Chirgwin in his *Coming Together: the Churches Co-operate* (Edinburgh House Press, 1944). Two publications written in connexion with the Jubilee celebrations of 1910–60 are to be specially commended. They are Hugh Martin's *Beginning at Edinburgh* (Edinburgh House Press, 1960) and Kenneth Slack's *The Ecumenical Movement* (Edinburgh House Press, 1960).

Chapter II

The official reports of the International Missionary Council meetings are:

Reports of the Jerusalem Meeting of the International Missionary Council (8 vols., O.U.P., 1928)

Reports of the Tambaram (Madras) Meeting (7 vols., O.U.P., 1938)

Renewal and Advance, edited by C. W. Ranson (Edinburgh House Press, 1948) (report of the Whitby 1947 meeting)

Missions under the Cross, edited by Norman Goodall (Edinburgh House Press, 1953) (report of the Willingen 1952 meeting)

The Ghana Assembly of the International Missionary Council, edited by R. K. Orchard (Edinburgh House Press, 1958) (report of the Ghana 1957 meeting)

A summary of the International Missionary Council's work for 'Orphaned Missions' appears in a booklet written by Kenneth Scott Latourette and W. Richey Hogg: *World Christian Community in Action* (International Missionary Council, 1949). Some of the principal Research publications are *Modern Industry and the African* by J. Merle Davis (Macmillan 1933), *New Buildings on Old Foundations, a Handbook on Stabilizing the Younger Churches in their Environment* by J. Merle Davis (International Missionary Council, 1945); a series of *Surveys* on the *Training of the Ministry* in Africa and Madagascar, published between 1950 and 1957; and the *I.M.C. Research Pamphlets* of which 8 numbers on various aspects of missionary policy have been published since 1954 by the S.C.M. Press. Some of the national Christian councils which compose the membership of the I.M.C. publish periodical bulletins giving valuable information about the work of the churches and missions in the various countries. One of the oldest and best edited of these is the *Review* of the Christian Council of India which may be obtained through the Edinburgh House Press.

In the study of Christianity and the non-Christian religions, the book which was the basis of the great debate at Tambaram in 1938 is Hendrik Kraemer's *The Christian Message in a Non-Christian World* (Edinburgh House Press, 1938). This should now be read in conjunction with the same author's *Religion and the Christian Faith* (Lutterworth Press, 1956). Good brief introductions to this great theme are *The Gospel and the Religions* by Walter Freytag (S.C.M. Press, 1957), and *Glad Encounter* by George Appleton (Edinburgh House Press, 1959). An interesting symposium on the relation of Christianity to Judaism appears in *The Church and the Jewish People*, edited by Göte Hedenquist (Edinburgh House Press, 1954). Other relevant material, with regular reports of the work of the International Missionary Council's Committee on the Christian Approach to the Jews, appears in the Committee's quarterly *News Sheet* (obtainable from the International Missionary Council).

The quotations in this chapter on p. 32 are (regarding Hinduism) from *A History of the London Missionary Society 1895–1945* by Norman Goodall (O.U.P., 1954) and (regarding Islam) from Vol. I of the *Report of the Jerusalem*

1928 meeting of the International Missionary Council. An outstanding illustration of a contemporary Christian approach to Islam is *The Call of the Minaret* by A. Kenneth Cragg (O.U.P., 1956). Dr. Cragg is the Director of one of the Study Centres in Islam referred to on p. 34. An indication of the nature of the studies in the life of the younger churches can be seen in the I.M.C. Research Pamphlet *Processes of Growth in an African Church* by J. V. Taylor (1958). The completed study towards which this pamphlet points is J. V. Taylor's *The Growth of the Church in Buganda* (S.C.M. Press, 1958). Pamphlets which touch on some of the deeper issues in theology and policy now engaging the attention of the International Missionary Council are *Towards a Theology of Mission* by Wilhelm Andersen (S.C.M. Press, 1955), *One Body, One Gospel, One World, the Christian Mission Today* by Lesslie Newbigin (International Missionary Council, 1958), and *Out of Every Nation; a Discussion of the Internationalizing of Missions* by R. K. Orchard (S.C.M. Press, 1959).

Significant allusions to or accounts of the events recorded in this chapter, as well as in later chapters, occur in a number of excellent biographies such as *Temple Gairdner of Cairo* by Constance E. Padwick (S.P.C.K., 1929); A. E. Garvie's *Memories and Meanings of My Life* (Allen & Unwin, 1938); *William Paton* by Margaret Sinclair (S.C.M. Press, 1949); *David Cairns, An Autobiography* (S.C.M. Press, 1950); *Randall Davidson* by G. K. A. Bell (O U.P., 1935); *Cosmo Gordon Lang* by J. G. Lockhart (Hodder & Stoughton, 1949); *William Temple* by F. A. Iremonger (O.U.P., 1948); *Cyril Forster Garbett* by Charles Smyth (Hodder & Stoughton, 1959).

Chapter III

The official reports of the Faith and Order Movement are:

Faith and Order: Proceedings of the World Conference, Lausanne, edited by H. N. Bate (S.C.M. Press, 1927)

Second World Conference on Faith and Order, Edinburgh 1937, edited by L. Hodgson (S.C.M. Press, 1937)

The Third World Conference on Faith and Order, Lund, 1952, edited by O. S. Tomkins (S.C.M. Press, 1953)

More informal descriptions and interpretations of the Faith and Order conferences are contained in E. S. Woods'

Lausanne, 1927 (S.C.M. Press, 1927); Hugh Martin's *Edinburgh 1937* (S.C.M. Press, 1937); and E. H. Robertson's *Lund, 1952* (S.C.M. Press, 1952). The literature bearing on the great Faith and Order themes, including books provoked or stimulated by the world conferences, is enormous. The following small books and pamphlets useful for starting discussion and study may be noted: H. G. G. Herklots: *These Denominations* (S.C.M. Press, 1946); Hugh Martin: *Towards Reunion: What the Churches Stand For* (S.C.M. Press, 1937), O. S. Tomkins: *The Wholeness of the Church* (S.C.M. Press, 1949), Eric Fenn: *How Christians Worship* (S.C.M. Press, 1942), Hugh Martin (ed.): *The Holy Communion* (S.C.M. Press, 1947), *Rules and Customs of Churches Concerning Intercommunion and Open Communion* (Faith and Order Pamphlet No. 99), *Intercommunion, Ways of Worship* and *The Nature of the Church*—three pamphlet reports prepared for the Lund Faith and Order Conference (Faith and Order Department, 1951), *Social and Cultural Factors in Church Divisions* by C. H. Dodd, G. R. Cragg and Jacques Ellul (S.C.M. Press, 1952). One of the best books on the Church and the meaning of its unity is J. E. Lesslie Newbigin's *The Household of God* (S.C.M. Press, 1953). A standard source for official pronouncements on unity questions is *Documents on Christian Unity*, edited by G. K. A. Bell, four volumes published in 1924, 1930, 1948 and 1958 by the Oxford University Press.

The official reports of the world conferences on Life and Work are *The Stockholm Conference, 1925*, edited by G. K. A. Bell (O.U.P., 1926) and *The Churches Survey Their Task, the Report of the Conference at Oxford, July 1937, on Church, Community and State* (Geo. Allen & Unwin, 1937).

The *official reports* of the *First and Second Assemblies of the World Council of Churches* were published in 1949 and 1955, edited by W. A. Visser 't Hooft (S.C.M. Press). Amongst many brief popular accounts of the Assemblies, mention may be made of *Pilgrimage to Amsterdam* and *Looking at Evanston*, both by H. G. G. Herklots (S.C.M. Press). The late Bishop of Chichester (G. K. A. Bell) told the story of the formation of the Council and described its method of working in a 'Penguin' *The Kingship of Christ* (1954) from which the quotation from Bishop Berggrav on pp. 66 f. of this chapter is taken.

Chapter IV

The far-reaching work of the World Council of Churches' Division of Inter-Church Aid and Service to Refugees can best be followed in the periodical Bulletins issued by the Division through the Council's Department of Information, Geneva. These are obtainable, together with much additional detailed information from the main national organizations working with the Division, such as Church World Service in the United States and the British Council of Churches' Department of Inter-Church Aid and Service to Refugees. Timely pamphlets on the refugee service include Leslie E. Cooke's *The Church is There* (Seabury Press, U.S.A., 1957) and Janet Lacey's *Refugees* (Edinburgh House Press, 1959). A vivid and comprehensive account of the refugee problem and of the relation between the work of voluntary agencies (including the churches) and Governmental and inter-Governmental policies is given in *The High Tower of Refuge* by Edgar H. S. Chandler (Odhams Press, 1959).

Detailed information about such studies as those in 'The Common Christian Responsibility towards Areas of Rapid Social Change' appear in the periodical Bulletins of the Division of Studies of the World Council of Churches, issued by the Council's Information Department. An important survey of this problem and an account of the studies to date will be found in *Dilemmas and Opportunities: Christian Action in Rapid Social Change* (Geneva, W.C.C., 1959). The report quoted on p. 90 of this chapter has been published under the title *Witnesses Together, being the official report of the Inaugural Assembly of the East Asia Christian Council*, edited by U Kyaw Than (Rangoon, East Asia Christian Conference, 1959).

The Commission of the Churches on International Affairs publishes an annual report summarizing its activities in many fields of public concern. It may be obtained through the national Commissions, of which the International Department of the British Council of Churches (10 Eaton Gate, London, S.W.1.) is one. An account of the aims and formation of the Commission of the Churches on International Affairs, with reflections by various writers on the first ten years of its work, appears in a special number of *The Ecumenical Review* for July, 1956. Studies closely related to the work of the Commission are provided by the annual 'Burge Lectures', delivered in London and subsequently published: two of the most notable of these are C. H. Dodd's *Christianity and the Reconciliation of the Nations* (S.C.M. Press, 1952) and Carl von Weizäcker's *Ethical and Political Problems of the Atomic Age* (S.C.M. Press, 1958).

Chapter V

The references under Chapter III, above, concerning Faith and Order questions are equally relevant here. Reports of progress in Unity negotiations appear regularly in *The Ecumenical Review* and in periodical Bulletins of the Faith and Order Department of the World Council of Churches. The Archbishop of Canterbury's 'Cambridge Sermon' of 1946 is quoted in Bell's *Documents on Christian Unity*, Vol. 4 and appears in full in *Church Relations in England, being the Report of Conversations between Representatives of the Archbishop of Canterbury and Representatives of the Evangelical Free Churches in England* (S.P.C.K., 1950). Official comments on this report were published by the Baptist Union of Great Britain and Ireland under the title *Church Relations in England* (Carey Kingsgate Press, 1953) and by the Methodist Church in its *Report of the Faith and Order Committee on Church Relations in England* (Methodist Publishing House, 1952). The Anglican-Presbyterian discussions are reported in *Relations Between Anglican and Presbyterian Churches: a Joint Report* (S.P.C.K., 1957). The interim report of the Anglican-Methodist conversations is called *Conversations between the Church of England and the Methodist Church; an Interim Statement* (S.P.C.K. and Epworth Press, 1958). *The Constitution of the Church of South India* is published by the Christian Literature Society, Madras (latest edition 1956) which also publishes the *Plan of Church Union in North India and Pakistan* (latest edition 1957) and the *Proposed Scheme of Church Union in Ceylon* (latest edition 1949). One of many pamphlets describing the Church of South India is *South India's New Church* by C. S. Milford (Edinburgh House Press, 1947). Two of the best larger studies in the history and significance of the Church of South India are B. G. M. Sundkler's *Church of South India; the Movement towards Union 1900–1947* (Lutterworth Press, 1954) and J. E. Lesslie Newbigin's *The Reunion of the Church*

(S.C.M. Press, 1948). Very differing approaches to the Unity question (all of which need to be appreciated) are illustrated by A. C. Outler's *The Christian Tradition and the Unity We Seek* (O.U.P., 1958), E. L. Mascall's *The Recovery of Unity* (Longmans, 1958) and M. J. Congar's *Divided Christendom* (Geoffrey Bles, 1939).

Chapter VI

The constitutional documents concerning the proposed integration of the World Council of Churches and the International Missionary Council appear in the published *Central Committeee Minutes* of the World Council (Geneva, 1959 and 1960) and are obtainable from the Joint Committee, 10 Eaton Gate, London, S.W.1. Reflections and speculations on possible developments within the ecumenical movement abound in various publications. In addition to material included in the above sections of the Appendix, the following are directly relevant: W. A. Visser 't Hooft: *The Renewal of the Church* (S.C.M. Press, 1955), W. A. Visser 't Hooft: *The Pressure of our Common Calling* (S.C.M. Press, 1959), *A Decisive Hour for the Christian Mission*, being the John R. Mott Memorial Lectures given at the inaugural Assembly of the East Asia Christian Conference, Kuala Lumpur, 1959, by J. E. Lesslie Newbigin, W. A. Visser 't Hooft and D. T. Niles (S.C.M. Press, 1960), *The Unfinished Task* by S. C. Neill (Lutterworth Press, 1957).

Chapter VII

Two reprints of articles from *The Ecumenical Review* deal with some of the more widespread anxieties and misunderstandings concerning the ecumenical movement: *Some Illusions and Errors* by Ernest A. Payne (*Ecumenical Review*, April 1958, Vol. X, No. 3) and *The Super-Church and the Ecumenical Movement* by W. A. Visser 't Hooft (*Ecumenical Review*, July 1958, Vol. X, No. 4). A good deal of information about some of the more aggressively hostile groups to which this chapter alludes can be found in an unedifying chronicle called *Apostles of Discord* by Ralph Lord (Boston, The Beacon Press, 1953). A refreshing contrast to this is a booklet published by the Evangelical Alliance *The Fellowship of the*

Gospel: a New Testament Study in the Principles of Christian Co-operation by Frank Colquhoun (1955). Regular information about the Evangelical Alliance is provided by the *Evangelical Broadsheet* (Evangelical Alliance). A critical and charitable appraisal of 'Fundamentalism' is Gabriel Hebert's *Fundamentalism and the Church of God* (S.C.M. Press, 1957). A good symposium representing at its best the standpoint of 'conservative evangelicalism' in the U.S.A. is *Contemporary Evangelical Thought* edited by Carl F. H. Henry (New York, Channel Press, 1957). In slighter form the booklet series (Crusade Booklets) published by the Evangelical Alliance in Britain excellently represents a similar standpoint. Roman Catholic reflections on the ecumenical movement can be studied in the quarterly journals referred to in this chapter or in the columns of *The Tablet*. An outstanding appraisal of the movement by a sympathetic Jesuit scholar is Bernard Leeming's *The Church and the Churches: a Study of Ecumenism* (Darton, Longman & Todd, 1960).

Chapter VIII

See *The House Church* and *The Parish Comes Alive* by E. W. Southcott. Amongst other stimulating books on the renewal of the local church there are *The Face of My Parish* by Tom Allen (S.C.M. Press, 1954), and *The Parish in Action* by Joost de Blank (Mowbray, 1954). The British Council of Churches offers helpful suggestions for local ecumenical action, with special reference to local councils of churches, in *Growing Together Locally* (British Council of Churches, 1958). The Council also publishes many reports which make excellent study documents for inter-denominational groups, on such matters as *The Church and Industry*; *Technology and Purpose in Higher Education*; *Everyman's Concern* and *Review in Central Africa* (both dealing with African problems); and *Christians and Atomic War*. The Bulletin of the British Council of Churches—*The Church in the World*—should be available in all the churches.

Standard journals which should be accessible in every public library are *The Ecumenical Review*, the official quarterly of the World Council of Churches, and the *International Review of Missions*, the publication of the International

Missionary Council. The Information Department of the World Council of Churches produces information and illustrated Bulletins on all aspects of the Council's work. *Ecumenical Press Service*, giving summary news of the churches throughout the world, is an invaluable source for editors and journalists, professional and amateur. The quarterly *Frontier* now incorporates an older missionary journal *World Dominion* and the *Christian News-Letter* (another of J. H. Oldham's characteristic creations). This conjunction results in a stimulating periodical concerning the Church and its contemporary witness.

One of the choicest collections of prayers, compiled and written from within the ecumenical movement, is *In His Name: A Book of Prayers for the Church and the World* prepared by George Appleton (Edinburgh House Press, 1956). Two pamphlets about prayer for unity are *The Life and Work of Abbé Paul Couturier* by Maurice Villain and *Praying for Unity* by Olive Wyon. The latter has been followed by a second pamphlet by Olive Wyon under the same title but containing prayers for unity related to the Christian year. Suggested orders of service appropriate for united local worship are published by the British Council of Churches.

Appendix II. 8 and Preface to Second Edition

The New Delhi Assembly and its background are dealt with in three publications: *From Evanston to New Delhi* (Geneva, W.C.C., 1961); *New Delhi Speaks* (London, S.C.M. Press, 1962); and *Report of the Third Assembly of the W.C.C.* (London, S.C.M. Press, 1962).

APPENDIX II

SOME DOCUMENTARY LANDMARKS

Note. Extracts from constitutional and other documents which appear in the text of this volume are as follows:

1. *THE LAUSANNE MESSAGE*
of the Faith and Order Conference, 1927

The message of the Church to the world is and must always remain the Gospel of Jesus Christ.

The Gospel is the joyful message of redemption, both here and hereafter, the gift of God to sinful man in Jesus Christ.

The world was prepared for the coming of Christ through the activity of God's Spirit in all humanity, but especially in his revelation as given in the Old Testament; and in the fulness of time the eternal Word of God became incarnate, and was made man, Jesus Christ, the Son of God and the Son of Man, full of grace and truth.

Through his life and teaching, his call to repentance, his proclamation of the coming of the Kingdom of God and of judgement, his suffering and death, his resurrection and exaltation to the right hand of the Father, and by the mission of the Holy Spirit, he has brought to us forgiveness of sins, and has revealed the fulness of the living God, and his boundless love towards us. By the appeal of that love, shown in its completeness on the Cross, he summons us to the new life of faith, self-sacrifice, and devotion to his service and the service of men.

Jesus Christ, as the crucified and the living One, as Saviour and Lord, is also the centre of the world-wide Gospel of the Apostles and the Church. Because he himself is the Gospel, the Gospel is the message of the Church to the world. It is more than a philosophical theory; more than a theological system; more than a programme for material betterment. The Gospel is rather the gift of a new world from God to this old world of sin and death; still more, it is the victory over sin and death, the revelation of eternal life in him who has knit together the whole family in heaven and on earth in the communion of saints, united in the fellowship of service, of prayer, and of praise.

The Gospel is the prophetic call to sinful man to turn to God, the joyful tidings of justification and of sanctification to those who believe in Christ. It is the comfort of those who suffer; to those who are bound, it is the assurance of the glorious liberty of the sons of God. The Gospel brings peace and joy to the heart, and produces in men self-denial, readiness for brotherly service, and compassionate love. It offers the supreme goal for the aspirations of youth, strength to the toiler, rest to the weary, and the crown of life to the martyr.

The Gospel is the sure source of power for social regeneration. It proclaims the only way by which humanity can escape from those class and race hatreds which devastate society at present into the enjoyment of national well-being and international friendship and peace. It is also a gracious invitation to the non-Christian world, East and West, to enter into the joy of the living Lord.

Sympathising with the anguish of our generation, with its longing for intellectual sincerity, social justice and spiritual inspiration, the Church in the eternal Gospel meets the needs and fulfils the God-given aspirations of the modern world. Consequently, as in the past so also in the present, the Gospel is the only way of salvation. Thus, through his Church, the living Christ still says to men 'Come unto me! . . . He that followeth me shall not walk in darkness, but shall have the light of life.'

2. THE EDINBURGH AFFIRMATION
of the Faith and Order Conference, 1937

We are one in faith in our Lord Jesus Christ, the incarnate Word of God. We are one in allegiance to Him as Head of the Church, and as King of kings and Lord of lords. We are one in acknowledging that this allegiance takes precedence of any other allegiance that may make claims upon us.

This unity does not consist in the agreement of our minds or the consent of our wills. It is founded in Jesus Christ Himself, Who lived, died and rose again to bring us to the Father, and Who through the Holy Spirit dwells in His Church. We are one because we are all the objects of the love and grace of God, and called by Him to witness in all the world to His glorious gospel.

Our unity is of heart and spirit. We are divided in the outward forms of our life in Christ, because we understand differently His will for His Church. We believe, however, that a deeper understanding will lead us towards a united apprehension of the truth as it is in Jesus.

We humbly acknowledge that our divisions are contrary to the will of Christ, and we pray God in His mercy to shorten the days of our separation and to guide us by His Spirit into fulness of unity.

We are thankful that during recent years we have been drawn together; prejudices have been overcome, misunderstandings removed, and real, if limited, progress has been made towards our goal of a common mind.

In this Conference we may gratefully claim that the Spirit of God has made us willing to learn from one another, and has given us a fuller vision of the truth and enriched our spiritual experience.

We have lifted up our hearts together in prayer; we have sung the same hymns; together we have read the same Holy Scriptures. We recognize in one another, across the barriers of our separation, a common Christian outlook and a common standard of values. We are therefore assured of a unity deeper than our divisions.

We are convinced that our unity of spirit and aim must be embodied in a way that will make it manifest to the world, though we do not yet clearly see what outward form it should take.

We believe that every sincere attempt to co-operate in the concerns of the kingdom of God draws the several communions together in increased mutual understanding and goodwill. We call upon our fellow-Christians of all communions to practise such co-operation; to consider patiently occasions of disunion that they may be overcome; to be ready to learn from those who differ from them; to seek to remove those obstacles to the furtherance of the gospel in the non-Christian world which arise from our divisions; and constantly to pray for that unity which we believe to be our Lord's will for His Church.

We desire also to declare to all men everywhere our assurance that Christ is the one hope for the world in face of the distractions and dissensions of this present time. We know that our witness is weakened by our divisions. Yet we are one in Christ and in the fellowship of His Spirit. We pray that everywhere, in a world divided and perplexed, men may turn to Jesus Christ our Lord, Who makes us one in spite of our divisions; that He may bind in one those who by many worldly claims are set at variance; and that the world may at last find peace and unity in Him; to Whom be glory for ever.

3. *A MESSAGE TO ALL PEOPLES*
Adopted by the International Missionary Council, Madras, 1938

The reports that have been brought to us from every quarter of the globe have made us realize that the ancient pestilences which destroy mankind are abroad with a virulence unparalleled. In every country the fact of war or the fear of it casts its paralysing shadow over human hope. Race hatred, the ugly parent of persecution, has been set up as a national idol in many a market place and increasingly becomes a household god. Everywhere the greed of money continues to separate those who have from those who have not, filling the latter with angry plans of revolution and the former with the nervousness of power.

Again and again a sense of penitence has come over us as we have realized that these consuming evils are all of them man-made. They bear upon them the marks of human manu-facture as clearly as the motor car or the aeroplane. Neither flood nor earthquake nor dark mysterious force outside of our control produces wars or economic tensions. We know that we live involved within a chaos which we ourselves have made.

Again and again we have been forced to note that the evils that we face are not the work of bad men only, but of good as well. The gravest of our disasters have been brought upon us not by men desiring to make trouble for mankind but by those who thought they did their best in the circumstances surrounding them. We do not know the man wise enough to have saved the world from its present sufferings—and we do not know the man wise enough to deliver us now.

But it is just at this point that we are forced back upon our Faith and rescued from pessimism to a glorious hope. We know that there is One who, unlike ourselves, is not defeated and who cannot know defeat. In the wonder of Christ's revelation we see God not as a remote and careless deity sufficient to Himself, but as a Father with a love for mankind, His children, as indescribable as it is fathomless. We who have looked at Christ, His Messenger, His Son, torn with suffering on a cross on which only His love for man has placed Him, have a tragic but transfiguring insight into the richness and reality of God's passion for His own. It is this insight which has taken the Christians to glad martyrdoms through the centuries and sent them to the ends of the earth to spread the great Good News. And in humility we record our gratitude that even in this present time evidences multiply that men and women still go forth as faithful and untiring ambassadors of Christ.

It is clear that only God can save the peoples, and that the God and Father of our Lord Jesus Christ not only can but will.

It must become clearer to us all, however, that the instruments He demands are not men and women of ideals as such, but those who constantly in prayer and worship verify those same ideals before His august will—verify and improve and never cease to re-verify them. It is not the merely moral person whom God requires in the present crisis, or in any other, but the person who keeps his morality alive and growing through the constant refreshing of His creative touch. We can, none of us, become faultless agents of His grace, but the only hope before the world lies in those who at least attempt to know Him and to follow in His way.

National gods of any kind, gods of race or class, these are not large enough to save us. The recognition of God in Christ by no means robs a man of his nation or his family or his culture. When Christ is taken seriously by a nation or an ancient culture, He destroys no whit of good within it but lifts it rather to its own highest destiny. He does destroy exclusiveness, but in its place He causes a new quality to grow—good will—a good will which is wider than national or cultural loyalties and corresponds to the largeness of God's love.

In our midst we have seen anew that devotion to the things of Christ will work a miracle among men and women. We have prayed, and as we prayed the barriers of nationality and class have melted. Knit by the Holy Spirit the one to the other and all to God, we have known the meaning of fellowship. We feel this to be a promise of what may be in all the earth.

We call upon our fellow Christians throughout the world to join us in a new dedication. Surely God is summoning us in these times to let go our self-sufficiency, to frequent His altars, to learn of Him, and to make His ways known in all the relationships of life. To make Him known in the State involves labour for the establishment of justice among all the people. In the world of commerce it involves the ending of unregulated competition for private gain and the beginning of emulation for the public good. Everywhere it involves self-sacrificial service. God grant to His Church to take the story of His love to all mankind, till that love surround the earth, binding the nations, the races and the classes into a community of sympathy for one another, undergirded by a deathless faith in Christ.

4. WHITBY STATEMENTS

Extracts from Report of the International Missionary Council, 1947

(A) *From the Statement on 'The Supra-nationality of Missions'*

Missionaries, like other Christians, own two citizenships—their citizenship in the Kingdom which is not of this world and the citizenship of the land of their birth or adoption. Neither their immediate national loyalty nor their historic cultural and social inheritance are to be denied or belittled. The present world situation, however, in which racialism and a narrow nationalism threaten to destroy the life of mankind demands in us a vivid awareness of the fact that missionaries are ambassadors of Christ and messengers of a Gospel which bears witness to a fellowship that transcends all national and racial boundaries and in which there is neither Jew nor Greek, German nor English, European nor Asiatic. The task before us is to show how, as missionaries, by birth belonging to various nations and cultural traditions, we can give a more unequivocal expression to the fact that our primary loyalty is to Christ and that our responsibility as servants of the ecumenical Church must dominate our whole thinking and behaviour and not merely influence a part of it. The great temptation for the Church, for all Christians, and also for missionaries as ambassadors of Christ is that, while honestly confessing our primary loyalty to Christ with all the conflicts and tensions which this includes, in practice we subordinate this loyalty to others. In this respect a vigilant self-criticism is one of the greatest requirements in our whole missionary conduct. . . .

This new and acute sensitiveness to the implications of our ambassadorship of Christ can only prove effective by deeper consciousness of the fact that belonging to Christ means at the same time responsibility for and solidarity with the world and our fellowmen, along with a sense of being strangers and sojourners in the world and in our nation. Because our real desire, hope and joy are in the Kingdom that is not of this world, in the core of our being we are no more able unreservedly to identify ourselves with our nation, its self-willed destiny and aspirations. The Christian—and still more the missionary—by his special position as ambassador of Christ—will always view his nation in the light of the Word of God. This is not a ready-made test and its implications are not always easy to determine. Moreover, we have to confess that in claiming to be ruled by the Word of God we may only be trying to give a religious sanction to our own self-assertiveness. We can only guard against this danger by a continual readiness to submit ourselves to the judgement of the Word and in the light of it to amend our ways.

Another consequence of our being essentially 'strangers' though bound in the solidarity of love and service to the world, is that the Christian, in a sense peculiar to him, feels and suffers by the tension arising out of the dual character of all social, political and cultural life, which is at once good and evil. We can never forget that to take seriously in this broken world the problems of nationalism and racialism, that is to say of politics, means for a Christian always suffering and the possibility of sacrifice. This suffering and sacrifice, however, have to be seen in the light of Christ's victory over the world. They then become privilege and joy, the marks of our citizenship in that Kingdom which will endure when the fashion of this world has passed away.

(B) *From the statement on 'Christian Witness in a Revolutionary World'*

The experience of those who have taken part in the enlarged meeting of the International Missionary Council may be summarized in the words: 'one world, one Christ'. We have entered as never before into the reality and meaning of the world-wide Church. It has been brought before us by the testimony of many voices. It has been seen by us against the background of a world torn and scarred by intolerable suffering and sorrow, a world at one only in its agonies and perplexities. And more than ever before, we have been convinced of the sufficiency of Christ. Evangelism means the proclamation of His Cross to a world which is baffled by the tragedy of apparently meaningless suffering; it means the proclamation of His risen life to a world which, athirst for life, seems to be sinking down into death without hope.

We have been burdened with the sense of two great needs—the desperate need of the world for Christ, and the unsatisfied yearning of Christ over the world. We are impelled to this task both by the authority and by the compassion of Christ. As Christians, we are pledged to the service of all those who are hungry or destitute or in need; we are pledged to the support of every movement for the removal of injustice and oppression. But we do not conceive these things, good in themselves, to be the whole of evangelism, since we are convinced that the source of the world's sorrow is spiritual and that its healing must be spiritual, through the entry of the risen Christ into every part of the life of the world.

The task of world evangelism starts today from the vantage ground of a Church which, as never before, is really worldwide. This universal fellowship is, in the oft-quoted words of William Temple, the great new fact of our era. It is working itself out today in a real partnership between older and younger churches. The sense both of a common faith in Christ, and of a common responsibility for an immense and unfinished task, have brought us out of the mists of tension and readjustment to a higher level, from which we have been able to see our world task in a new perspective.

The Gospel is to be preached to all men. Can it be so preached in our generation? To preach to men is not the same as to convert them. God alone can command success, and it is always open to men to resist His will. Yet, when we consider the present extension of the Church, and the divine and human resources available, we dare to believe it possible that, before the present generation has passed away, the Gospel should be preached to almost all the inhabitants of the world in such a way as to make clear to them the issue of faith or disbelief in Jesus Christ. If this is possible, it is the task of the Church to see that it is done.

5. THE AMSTERDAM MESSAGE
of the World Council of Churches, 1948

The World Council of Churches, meeting at Amsterdam, sends this message of greeting to all who are in Christ, and to all who are willing to hear.

We bless God our Father, and our Lord Jesus Christ, who gathers together in one the children of God that are scattered abroad. He has brought us here together at Amsterdam. We are one in acknowledging Him as our God and Saviour. We are divided from one another not only in matters of faith, order and tradition, but also by pride of nation, class and race. But Christ has made us His own, and He is not divided. In seeking Him we find one another. Here at Amsterdam we have committed ourselves afresh to Him, and have covenanted with one another in constituting this World Council of Churches. We intend to stay together. We call upon Christian congregations everywhere to endorse and fulfil this covenant in their relations one with another. In thankfulness we commit the future to Him.

When we look to Christ, we see the world as it is—His world, to which He came and for which He died. It is filled both with great hopes and also with disillusionment and despair. Some nations are rejoicing in new freedom and power, some are bitter because freedom is denied them, some are paralysed by division, and everywhere there is an undertone of fear. There are millions who are hungry, millions who have no home, no country and no hope. Over all mankind hangs the peril of total war. We have to accept God's judgment upon us for our share in the world's guilt. Often we have tried to serve God and mammon, put other loyalties before loyalty to Christ, confused the Gospel with our own economic or national or racial interests, and feared war more than we have hated it. As we have talked with each other here, we have begun to understand how our separation has prevented us from receiving correction from one another in Christ. And because we lacked this correction, the world has often heard from us not the Word of God but the words of men.

But there is a word of God for our world. It is that the world is in the hands of the living God, Whose will for it is wholly good; that in Christ Jesus, His incarnate Word, Who lived and died and rose from the dead, God has broken the power of evil once for all, and opened for everyone the gate into freedom and joy in the Holy Spirit; that the final judgment on all human history and on every human deed is the judgement of the merciful Christ; and that the end of history will be the triumph of His Kingdom, where alone we shall understand how much God has loved the world. This is God's unchanging word to the world. Millions of our fellow-men have never heard it. As we are met here from many lands, we pray God to stir up His whole Church to make this Gospel known to the whole world, and to call on all men to believe in Christ, to live in His love and to hope for His coming.

Our coming together to form a World Council will be vain unless Christians and Christian congregations everywhere commit themselves to the Lord of the Church in a new effort to seek together, where they live, to be His witnesses and servants among their neighbours. We have to remind ourselves and all men that God has put down the mighty from their seats and exalted the humble and meek. We have to learn afresh together to speak boldly in Christ's name both to those in power and to the people, to oppose terror, cruelty and race discrimination, to stand by the outcast, the prisoner and the refugee. We have to make of the Church in every place a voice for those who have no voice, and a home where every man will be at home. We have to learn afresh together what is the duty of the Christian man or woman in industry, in agriculture, in politics, in the professions and in the home. We have to ask God to teach us together to say 'No' and to say 'Yes' in truth. 'No', to all that flouts the love of Christ, to every system, every programme and every person that treats any man as though he were an irresponsible thing or a means of profit, to the defenders of injustice in the name of order, to those who sow the seeds of war or urge war as inevitable; 'Yes', to all that conforms to the love of Christ, to all who seek for justice, to the peacemakers, to all who hope, fight and suffer for the cause of man, to all who—even without knowing it—look for new heavens and a new earth wherein dwelleth righteousness.

It is not in man's power to banish sin and death from the earth, to create the unity of the Holy Catholic Church, to conquer the hosts of Satan. But it is within the power of God. He has given us at Easter the certainty that His purpose will be accomplished. But, by our acts of obedience and faith, we can on earth set up signs which point to the coming victory. Till the day of that victory our lives are hid with Christ in God, and no earthly disillusion or distress or power of hell can separate us from Him. As those who wait in confidence and joy for their deliverance, let us give ourselves to those tasks which lie to our hands, and so set up signs that men may see.

Now unto Him that is able to do exceeding abundantly

above all that we ask or think, according to the power that
worketh in us, unto Him be glory in the Church by Christ
Jesus, throughout all ages, world without end.

6. *A WORD TO THE CHURCHES*
issued by the Lund Conference on Faith and Order, 1952

We have been sent to Lund by our Churches to study
together what measure of unity in matters of faith, church
order and worship exists among our Churches and how we
may move towards the fuller unity God wills for us. We give
thanks to the Lord of the Church for what He has wrought
among us in and through our fellowship of conversation and
prayer and for evidences that in several parts of the world
Churches are drawing closer together. We have made many
discoveries about one another's Churches and our perplexity
in the face of unresolved differences has been surpassed by our
gratitude for the manifold grace of God which we see at work
in the life of the Churches all over the world.

We have seen clearly that we can make no real advance
towards unity if we only compare our several conceptions of
the nature of the Church and the traditions in which they are
embodied. But once again it has been proved true that as we
seek to draw closer to Christ we come closer to one another.
We need, therefore, to penetrate behind our divisions to a
deeper and richer understanding of the mystery of the God-
given union of Christ with His Church. We need increasingly
to realize that the separate histories of our Churches find their
full meaning only if seen in the perspective of God's dealings
with His *whole* people.

We have now reached a crucial point in our ecumenical
discussions. As we have come to know one another better our
eyes have been opened to the depth and pain of our separations
and also to our fundamental unity. The measure of unity
which it has been given to the Churches to experience together
must now find clearer manifestation. A faith in the one Church
of Christ which is not implemented by *acts* of obedience is
dead. There are truths about the nature of God and His
Church which will remain for ever closed to us unless we act
together in obedience to the unity which is already ours.
We would, therefore, earnestly request our Churches to

consider whether they are doing all they ought to do to
manifest the oneness of the people of God. Should not our
Churches ask themselves whether they are showing sufficient
eagerness to enter into conversation with other Churches, and
whether they should not act together in all matters except
those in which deep differences of conviction compel them to
act separately? Should they not acknowledge the fact that they
often allow themselves to be separated from each other by
secular forces and influences instead of witnessing together
to the sole Lordship of Christ who gathers His people out of
all nations, races and tongues?

Obedience to God demands also that the Churches seek
unity in their mission to the world. We share the failure to
convey the Christian message to the mass of mankind. But it is
precisely to these masses that we have the obligation to preach
the one Gospel and to manifest the oneness of the Church.

The word penitence has been often on our lips here at
Lund. Penitence involves willingness to endure judgement—
the judgement of the Lord to whom has been given the power
to sift mankind and to gather into one the scattered children
of God. We await His final triumph at the end of history. But,
in God's mercy, tokens of judgement which are also calls
to a new and active obedience come to us in our day also, here
and now. Surely we cannot any longer remain blind to the
signs of our times and deaf to His Word.

The Lord says once again: 'He that gathereth not with me,
scattereth.'

7. THE EVANSTON MESSAGE
of the World Council of Churches, 1954

To all our fellow Christians, and to our fellowmen everywhere, we send greetings in the name of Jesus Christ. We
affirm our faith in Jesus Christ as the hope of the world, and
desire to share that faith with all men. May God forgive us
that by our sin we have often hidden this hope from the world.

In the ferment of our time there are both hopes and fears.
It is indeed good to hope for freedom, justice and peace, and it
is God's will that we should have these things. But He has
made us for a higher end. He has made us for Himself, that
we might know and love Him, worship and serve Him.

Nothing other than God can ever satisfy the heart of man. Forgetting this, man becomes his own enemy. He seeks justice but creates oppression. He wants peace, but drifts towards war. His very mastery of nature threatens him with ruin. Whether he acknowledges it or not, he stands under the judgement of God and in the shadow of death.

Here where we stand, Jesus Christ stood with us. He came to us, true God and true Man, to seek and to save. Though we were the enemies of God, Christ died for us. We crucified Him, but God raised Him from the dead. He is risen. He has overcome the powers of sin and death. A new life has begun. And in His risen and ascended power, He has sent forth into the world a new community, bound together by His Spirit, sharing His divine life, and commissioned to make Him known throughout the world. He will come again as Judge and King to bring all things to their consummation. Then we shall see Him as He is and know as we are known. Together with the whole creation we wait for this with eager hope, knowing that God is faithful and that even now He holds all things in His hand.

This is the hope of God's people in every age, and we commend it afresh today to all who will listen. To accept it is to turn from our ways to God's way. It is to live as forgiven sinners, as children growing in His love. It is to have our citizenship in that Kingdom which all man's sin is impotent to destroy, that realm of love and joy and peace which lies about all men, though unseen. It is to enter with Christ into the suffering and despair of men, sharing with them the great secret of that Kingdom which they do not expect. It is to know that whatever men may do, Jesus reigns and shall reign.

With this assurance we can face the powers of evil and the threat of death with a good courage. Delivered from fear we are made free to love. For beyond the judgement of men and the judgement of history lies the judgement of the King who died for all men, and who will judge us according to what we have done to the least of His brethren. Thus our Christian hope directs us towards our neighbour. It constrains us to pray daily, 'Thy will be done on earth as it is in heaven', and to act as we pray in every area of life. It begets a life of believing prayer and expectant action, looking to Jesus and pressing forward to the day of His return in glory.

Now we would speak through our member churches directly to each congregation. Six years ago our churches entered into a covenant to form this Council, and affirmed their intention to stay together. We thank God for His blessing on our work and fellowship during these six years. We enter now upon a second stage. To stay together is not enough. We must go forward. As we learn more of our unity in Christ, it becomes the more intolerable that we should be divided. We therefore ask you: Is your church seriously considering its relation to other churches in the light of our Lord's prayer that we may be sanctified in the truth and that we may all be one? Is your congregation, in fellowship with sister congregations around you, doing all it can do to ensure that your neighbours shall hear the voice of the one Shepherd calling all men into the one flock?

The forces that separate men from one another are strong. At our meeting here we have missed the presence of Chinese churches which were with us at Amsterdam. There are other lands and churches unrepresented in our Council, and we long ardently for their fellowship. But we are thankful that, separated as we are by the deepest political divisions of our time, here at Evanston we are united in Christ. And we rejoice also that, in the bond of prayer and a common hope, we maintain communion with our Christian brethren everywhere.

It is from within this communion that we have to speak about the fear and distrust which at present divide our world. Only at the Cross of Christ, where men know themselves as forgiven sinners, can they be made one. It is there that Christians must pray daily for their enemies. It is there that we must seek deliverance from self-righteousness, impatience and fear. And those who know that Christ is risen should have the courage to expect new power to break through every human barrier.

It is not enough that Christians should seek peace for themselves. They must seek justice for others. Great masses of people in many parts of the world are hungry for bread, and are compelled to live in conditions which mock their human worth. Does your church speak and act against such injustice? Millions of men and women are suffering segregation and discrimination on the ground of race. Is your church willing to declare, as this Assembly has declared, that

this is contrary to the will of God and to act on that declaration? Do you pray regularly for those who suffer unjust
discrimination on grounds of race, religion or political
conviction?

The Church of Christ is today a world-wide fellowship, yet
there are countless people to whom He is unknown. How
much do you care about this? Does you congregation live for
itself, or for the world around it and beyond it? Does its
common life, and does the daily work of its members in the
world, affirm the Lordship of Christ or deny it?

God does not leave any of us to stand alone. In every place
He has gathered us together to be His family, in which His
gifts and His forgiveness are received. Do you forgive one
another as Christ forgave you? Is your congregation a true
family of God, where every man can find a home and know
that God loves him without limit?

We are not sufficient for these things. But Christ is
sufficient. We do not know what is coming to us. But we know
Who is coming. It is He who meets us every day and who
will meet us at the end—Jesus Christ our Lord.

Therefore we say to you: Rejoice in hope.

8. THE NEW DELHI ASSEMBLY, 1961:
A. MESSAGE OF THE ASSEMBLY
TO THE CHURCHES

The Third Assembly of the W.C.C. meeting in New Delhi
addresses this letter to the member churches and their congregations. We rejoice and thank God that we experience here a
fellowship as deep as before and wider. New member
churches coming in considerable numbers and strength both
from the ancient Orthodox tradition of Eastern Christendom
and from Africa, Asia, Latin America and other parts of the
world visibly demonstrate that Christianity now has a home
in every part of the world. In this fellowship we are able to
speak and act freely, for we are all partakers together with
Christ. Together we have sought to understand our common
calling to witness, service and unity.

We are deeply grateful for the prayers of countless Christian
people and for the study of our theme 'Jesus Christ the Light

of the World' by which many of you have shared in our work. Now we return to our churches to do, with you, the things that have been shown to us here.

All over the world new possibilities of life, freedom and prosperity are being actively, even passionately, pursued. In some lands there is disillusionment with the benefits that a technically expert society can produce; and over all there hangs the shadow of vast destruction through war. Nevertheless mankind is not paralysed by these threats. The momentum of change is not reduced. We Christians share men's eager quest for life, for freedom from poverty, oppression and disease. God is at work in the opening possibilities for mankind in our day. He is at work even when the powers of evil rebel against him and call down his judgement. We do not know by what ways God will lead us: but our trust is in Jesus Christ who is now and always our eternal life.

When we speak to men as Christians we must speak the truth of our faith: that there is only one way to the Father, namely Jesus Christ his Son. On that one way we are bound to meet our brother. We meet our brother Christian. We meet also our brother man; and before we speak to him of Christ, Christ has already sought him.

Christ is the way and therefore we have to walk together witnessing to him and serving all men. This is his commandment. There is no greater service to men than to tell them of the living Christ and no more effective witness than a life offered in service. The indifference or hostility of men may check our open speaking but God is not silenced. He speaks through the worship and the sufferings of his Church. Her prayers and patience are, by his gracious acceptance of them, made part of the witness he bears to Christ.

We need to think out together in concrete terms the forms of Christian service for today and together act upon them. In no field has Christian cooperation been more massive and effective than in service to people in every kind of distress. There is no more urgent task for Christians than to work together for community within nations and for peace with justice and freedom among them, so that the causes of much contemporary misery may be rooted out. We have to take our stand against injustice caused to any race, or to any man on account of his race. We have to learn to make a Christian contribution to the service of men through secular agencies. Christian love requires not only the sharing of worldly goods but costly personal service. All over the world young people are giving an example in their spontaneous offering of themselves.

We must together seek the fullness of Christian unity. We need for this purpose every member of the Christian family, of Eastern and Western tradition, ancient churches and younger churches, men and women, young and old, of every race and every nation. Our brethren in Christ are given to us, not chosen by us. In some things our convictions do not yet permit us to act together, but we have made progress in giving content to the unity we seek. Let us therefore find out the things which in each place we can do together now, and faithfully do them, praying and working always for that fuller unity which Christ wills for his Church.

This letter is written from the World Council of Churches' Assembly. But the real letter written to the world today does not consist of words. We Christian people, wherever we are, are a letter from Christ to his world 'written not with ink but with the spirit of the living God, not on tablets of stone but on tablets of human hearts'. The message is that God in Christ has reconciled the world to himself. Let us speak it and live it with joy and confidence 'for it is the God who said "Let light shine out of darkness", who has shone in our hearts to give the light of the knowledge of the glory of God in the face of Jesus Christ'.

1st Sunday in Advent 1961.

The Assembly decided that the following affirmations, which were said by all in the closing service of the Assembly, should be sent to the Churches with the Message, so that they can be used in congregational worship and especially in united services.

We confess Jesus Christ, Saviour of men and the light of the world;

Together we accept his Command;

We commit ourselves anew to bear witness to him among men;

We offer ourselves to serve all men in love, that love which he alone imparts;

We accept afresh our calling to make visible our unity in
  him;
We pray for the gift of the Holy Spirit for our task.

B. AN APPEAL TO ALL GOVERNMENTS AND PEOPLES

1. The Third Assembly of the World Council of Churches,
at which are gathered Christians from all parts of the world,
addresses this appeal to the government and people of every
nation.

2. Today, war itself is a common enemy. War is an offence
to the nature of man. The future of many generations and the
heritage of ages past hang in the balance. They are now easy
to destroy, since the actions or miscalculations of a few can
bring about a holocaust. They are harder to safeguard and
advance, for that requires the dedicated action of all. Let there
be restraint and self-denial in the things which make for war,
patience and persistence in seeking to resolve the things
which divide, and boldness and courage in grasping the things
which make for peace.

3. To turn back from the road towards war into the paths
of peace, all must renounce the threat of force. This calls for
an end to the war of nerves, to pressures on small countries,
to the rattling of bombs. It is not possible to follow at the
same time policies of menace and of mutual disarmament.

4. To halt the race in arms is imperative. Complete and
general disarmament is the accepted goal, and concrete steps
must be taken to reach it. Meanwhile, the search for a
decisive first step, such as the verified cessation of nuclear
tests, should be pressed forward despite all obstacles and
setbacks.

5. To substitute reason for force and undergird the will
to disarm, institutions of peace and orderly methods to effect
change and to settle disputes are essential. This imposes a
duty to strengthen the United Nations within the framework
and spirit of the Charter. All countries share this duty,
whether aligned with the major power blocs or independent
of them. The non-aligned can contribute through their
impartiality; with others they can be champions of the
principles of the Charter.

6. To build peace with justice, barriers of mutual distrust must be attacked at every level. Mutual confidence is the most precious resource in the world today: none should be wasted, more must be found. The fundamentals of an open society are essential that contacts may freely develop, person to person and people to people. Barriers to communication must go, not least where they divide peoples, churches, even families. Freedom of human contact, information, and cultural exchange is essential for the building of peace.

7. To enhance mutual trust, nations should be willing to run reasonable risks for peace. For example, an equitable basis for disarmament involves, on the one hand, an acceptance of risks in an inspection and control which cannot be fool-proof, and, on the other, the danger that inspection may exceed its stated duties. Those who would break through the vicious circles of suspicion must dare to pioneer.

8. There is a great opportunity for constructive action in the struggle for world development. To share the benefits of civilization with the whole of humanity is a noble and attainable objective. To press the war against poverty, disease, exploitation, and ignorance calls for greater sacrifice and for a far greater commitment of scientific, educational, and material resources than hitherto. In this common task, let the peoples find a positive programme for peace, a moral equivalent for war.

9. A creative strategy for peace with justice requires universal recognition of the claims of humanity—of all people, whatever their status, race, sex or creed. Lest man's new powers be used to degrade his human freedom and dignity, governments must remember that they are the servants of their citizens and respect the worth of each individual human being. The supreme achievement for a government is to enhance the dignity of man and free him for the creative exercise of his higher powers.

10. In making this appeal to all governments and peoples, we are constrained by obedience to the Lord of history, who demands righteousness and mercy and is a light unto the nations and the hearts of men. For the achievement of peace with justice, we pledge our unremitting efforts and call upon the Churches for their support in action and in prayer.

C. A MESSAGE TO CHRISTIANS IN
SOUTH AFRICA

The members of the Third Assembly of the World Council of Churches, meeting in New Delhi, have been aware of the developments within the past eighteen months in the relationships between Christians and churches in South Africa and the World Council of Churches, and wish to send fraternal greetings to you in the name of Jesus Christ, our Lord.

Our concern at this Assembly has been to testify to Jesus Christ as the Light of the World, and to seek God's guidance for our witness to him, our service in his name and our unity in him. In our worship together, in corporate study of the Bible and in all our discussions, we have become increasingly and vividly conscious of the power of the Spirit to lead his Church amid our troubled times, and of his bringing us into deepened fellowship with one another and with him. We have rejoiced as twenty-three churches have joined our fellowship at this Assembly, eleven of them from the continent of Africa. Nor have those churches which to our regret have felt bound to leave our fellowship been forgotten in our prayers.

During the Assembly, our convictions concerning the unity of the Church have grown. A year ago, our representatives shared with South African Christians at Cottesloe in declaring: 'The Church as the Body of Christ is a unity and within this unity the natural diversity among men is not annulled but sanctified. No one who believes in Jesus Christ may be excluded from any church on the ground of his colour or race. The spiritual unity among all men who are in Christ must find visible expression in acts of common worship and witness, and in fellowship and consultation on matters of common concern.' We subscribe to this principle to the full, and we stretch out our hands to all our fellow Christians to encourage them to manifest such unity in Christ.

Gathered here at New Delhi from all parts of the world, we have heard again God's clear call to us to fulfil the mission of the Church, both in its unfinished evangelistic task and in the submission of the world in which we live to the Spirit of Christ. Specially heavy obligations for both types of mission rest upon Christians in countries where the Church is strong. Those at Cottesloe said: 'We give thanks to Almighty God for bringing us together for fellowship and prayer and consultation; we resolve to continue in this fellowship, and we have therefore made specific plans to enable us to join in common witness in our country'. To all of you who preach Christ to the unbelieving and to all who manifest the Spirit of Christ to their neighbours, we offer our encouragement and fellowship, and assure you of our prayers.

The contrast between the light of Christ and the darkness of our present-day world has been deeply on our minds and consciences. Fear of war, injustice and the suffering of people have challenged our obedience to the Servant of the Lord. Racial strife is a world problem, and we stand behind the convictions on this matter expressed by the Evanston Assembly in 1954. Christians everywhere are involved in the struggle for the elimination of segregation or discrimination on the grounds of race or colour.

We know that in the name of Christ, many in South Africa are engaged in this struggle. May all who thus serve, and all who suffer be strengthened. May dignity and unity among men be established through the righteousness of God, in your land as well as in those from which we come. We pray that as the peoples of Africa move into their new day the Church of Christ will play an ever-increasing creative role in promoting understanding, justice, faith, hope and love.

May we share with you our dominant conviction? It is simply stated in the theme of our meeting. Jesus Christ is the Light of the World!

In his name, we send you this message of greetings.

D. EXTRACTS FROM REPORTS
received by the Third Assembly and submitted to the churches

(These reports were prepared in the three Assembly-Sections on Unity, Witness and Service.)

(i) Unity

The love of the Father and the Son in the unity of the Holy Spirit is the source and goal of the unity which the Triune God wills for all men and creation. We believe that we share in this unity in the Church of Jesus Christ, who is before all things and in whom all things hold together. In him alone, given by the Father to be Head of the Body, the Church has its true unity. The reality of this unity was manifest at Pentecost in the gift of the Holy Spirit, through whom we know in this present age the first fruits of that perfect union of the Son with his Father, which will be known in its fullness only when all things are consummated by Christ in his glory. The Lord who is bringing all things into full unity at the last is he who constrains us to seek the unity which he wills for his Church on earth here and now.

We believe that the unity which is both God's will and his gift to his Church is being made visible as all in each place who are baptised into Jesus Christ and confess him as Lord and Saviour are brought by the Holy Spirit into one fully committed fellowship, holding the one apostolic faith, preaching the one Gospel, breaking the one bread, joining in common prayer, and having a corporate life reaching out in witness and service to all and who at the same time are united with the whole Christian fellowship in all places and all ages in such wise that ministry and members are accepted by all, and that all can act and speak together as occasion requires for the tasks to which God calls his people.

It is for such unity that we believe we must pray and work.

This brief description of our objective leaves many questions unanswered. We are not yet of a common mind on the interpretation and the means of achieving the goal we have described. We are clear that unity does not imply simple uniformity of organization, rite or expression. We all confess that sinful self-will operates to keep us separated and that in our human ignorance we cannot discern clearly the lines of God's design for the future. But it is our firm hope that through the Holy Spirit God's will as it is witnessed to in Holy Scripture will be more and more disclosed to us and in us. The achievement of unity will involve nothing less than a death and rebirth of many forms of church life as we have known them. We believe that nothing less costly can finally suffice.

The foregoing paragraph must be understood as brief description of the sort of unity which would correspond to God's gift and our task. It is not intended as a definition of the Church and it does not presuppose any one particular doctrine of the Church. . . . The 'Toronto Statement'[1] was a landmark in the World Council's thinking about itself and its relation to work for unity. Here we seek to carry that thought a stage further, not by dictating to the churches their conception of unity but by suggesting for further study an attempt to express more clearly the nature of our common goal. . . . We present this statement in the hope that the churches both inside and outside the World Council of Churches will study it with care, and, should it be found inadequate, will formulate alternative statements, which more fully comprehend 'both God's will and his gift'.

(ii) *Witness*

It is not because of the desperate nature of the problems of our age that the task of Witness to the Gospel of Christ is urgent today. The urgency of the Church's evangelistic task arises from the Gospel itself, because it is the Gospel of Jesus Christ. Christ loves the world, which he died to save. He is already the light of the world, of which he is Lord, and his light has preceded the bearers of the good news into the darkest places. The task of Christian witness is to point to him as the true light, which is already shining. . . .

Nevertheless the urgency of the predicament in which our age finds itself should underline for Christians their duty and their opportunity. The whole world has become for the first time in history an interdependent world, in which the peoples of all lands either must solve their problems of living together in peace or must perish together. . . . Christians know that God is the Lord of history and that therefore the critical issues of our times have not arisen outside his loving purpose and are not beyond his control. Hence for them times of crisis will become opportunities for witnessing to the Lord. . . .

God is his own witness; that is to say, God has been and is at work authenticating his own message to men. When we speak of witness we mean testimony to the whole activity of God in the creation and preservation of the world, but especially in his mighty acts in Israel's history and in the redemption of the world by Jesus Christ. To this testimony the Holy Spirit in the Church bears witness.

[1] See pp. 140–1.

God continues to bear witness to the Son, as the only Lord and Saviour of all men. In the apostolic witness, coming to us in Scripture in the Spirit-filled Church, God gives us the foundation of all subsequent witness. In the sacraments of baptism and the eucharist, God down the ages has drawn near to men in Jesus Christ and borne witness to his own faithfulness. In the faithful preaching of his Word, God himself bears testimony to the truth. In the very existence of the church, there is a constant witness—in silence as it were—to the reality of God's dealing with men in Jesus Christ.

We stand today in this long tradition of the Church's witness, having its origin in God Himself, repeating itself constantly in the life of the church. Therefore, we have confidence and enter with joy into the task of witness which has been laid upon us. We can speak as those who know in our own lives that 'he who believes in the Son of God has this testimony in his own heart'. We are convinced that Jesus is the risen, living Lord, victorious over sin and death. Of him and of the restored fellowship with God which he has worked, for us and for all men, we would speak to our brethren for whom Christ died.

Today men fear death, not so much as formerly because of the sanctions of judgement and hell, but because it brings a total end to their enjoyment of this world, apart from which they know of no other life. The Church in preaching Christ's death proclaims victory over the power of death itself and the reality of a further and richer life than this world knows. Baptism signifies passing through the waters of death and entering here and now upon the life of the age to come. . . .

The good news about Christ is relevant to all ages, but, since every age differs from other ages, so must its ways and forms of communicating the Gospel. In every age the Holy Spirit makes possible the communication of the truth, but often the new ways in which he seeks to lead Christ's witnesses seem strange and dangerous to those who are accustomed to traditional methods. Nevertheless, if some kind of break-through is to be made, the surmounting of obstacles and the seizing of opportunities must be attempted, so that we may confront the real situation of today and thus discover that through the power of the Spirit many apparent impossi-

bilities have become possibilities and that the word of proclamation has still its ancient power. . . .

To communicate the Gospel involves the willingness and
the ability of the evangelist to identify himself with those
whom he addresses. To get alongside our hearer, to sit where
he sits, is the essential condition upon which alone we may
claim the right to be heard. . . . We must search for a
common language in which we and our hearers may understand each other. The truth of the Bible can be conveyed in
twentieth century words and idioms. This does not imply
'popularizing' the Gospel but rather flexibility in translating
our familiar words and images into a new medium. Since we
cannot expect men to understand the vocabulary of the Bible
until they have learned its language, we must mould our
own speech into the vernacular of everyday language.

Christian witnesses must be prepared to be tested by the
Gospel which they proclaim. Communication involves much
more than speaking, and our message will have to be embodied in our life. We must be ready to be judged by the
aweful standard of the Christ whom we preach. If we are
affluent in the midst of poverty or indifferent amidst injustice
or suffering, our speaking will avail less than our silence.
The Church as manifested by the local congregation will
exhibit or obscure the presence of Christ, and onlookers will
judge by what they see. . . .

As Christians we believe that God is at work in all the
great changes which are taking place in our age. Christian
communication has to be effected within the orbit of these
changes. It is not enough to detect the judgement of God
upon the *status quo*, which is being destroyed in an age of
revolution. Times of revolution are precisely times when, if
opportunities are seized, the judgements of God can be made
plain and his purpose proclaimed to a world which will be
shaken out of its complacency by the events of the day.
Though we must resist the temptation to see the hand of
God in the particular movements of history of which we
personally approve, or to claim his blessing for every cause
which seems righteous at the moment, we may nevertheless
proclaim in such situations the Lordship of Christ over the
whole process which is changing the aspect of our world.
But we must firmly reject all those revolutionary movements

in all parts of the world which claim a half-religious sanction for a political or nationalistic end, and which pretend to a 'Messianic' significance that justifies even their excesses. No earthly kingdom can set itself up as the Kingdom of God on earth, and no political ambition is wholly conformed to the divine purpose. We must not be blind to the truth that our hope is in God alone, and we must read the signs of the times in the light of his historical dealings with men and with nations as we have learned about them in the Bible.

In all these areas of concern there is both danger and opportunity. We believe that in our present moment of history Christ still stands at the door and knocks. Our communication of the Gospel is, we believe, Christ's own knocking at the door. A door may be a point of entry or of exclusion. We must continue to knock in the name of Jesus at the very doors which are shut against him and against the claims of humanity. To our fellow-Christians we would speak this word of encouragement: the opportunities for witnessing patiently and faithfully to the deed of God in Christ are as many and as great as the difficulties which we face. We must grasp the opportunities, knowing that in them the Holy Spirit of God witnesses with us.

(iii) *Service*

Christian service, as distinct from the world's concept of philanthropy, springs from and is nourished by God's costly love as revealed by Jesus Christ. Any ethic of service must have its roots there. Briefly, the relevant Creed of the Church through the ages may be stated thus:

God the Father loves all his creatures, irrespective of their colour of social status; God the Son redeemed them at the cost of his life; God the Holy Spirit enables men to be holy (whole), and find their fulfilment in likeness to Christ and in joyful and creative living in community.

The measure of God's love for men is to be seen in the fact that his Son was willing to die for them.

Such is the God we worship and whose creatures we are called to love and serve for Christ's sake. All our service is a response to the God who first loved us. Justice is the expression of this love in society.

In serving him and them, we follow the Christ who

deliberately refused the way of force and chose the role of a servant. As the Father sent him, so he sends us to sacrifice ourselves in his service. As Christ took the form of a servant and gave himself for the redemption and reconciliation of the whole man and the whole world, Christians are called to take their part in his suffering and victorious ministry as servants of the Servant-Lord. The power for service is given by the Holy Spirit who uses the Church as his instrument in manifesting the Kingdom of God and Lordship of Jesus Christ in all human relations and all social structures. Service thus is a part of adoration of God and witnesses to His love for us and all men.

Reaffirming our common Christian faith, the Third Assembly of the World Council of Churches commends to its member churches and Christians all around the world the aspirations and needs, the sufferings and hope of all mankind, 'waiting for the manifestation of the Sons of God'. . . .

Ours is a world of many cultures. The assumption that Western culture is *the* culture, and that therefore 'Christian culture' is necessarily identified with the customs and traditions of Western civilization, is a hindrance to the spread of the Gospel and a stumbling block to those of other traditions.

No culture has been wholly static but some have changed very slowly. Inner tensions keep them flexible and capable of development, and gradually they change. But, because a culture is an integrated whole, the introduction of alien and unassimilable elements too strong to be resisted leads to its collapse. So, for example, the introduction of labour for wages, or the concept of individuality have sapped the foundations of ancient cultures. Some of the conflicts of culture of our time were unnecessary, brought about by the unconscious, or by the well-intentioned but unthinking, imposition of Western customs and traditions. Others were the inevitable results of scientific and technological developments. The great missionary movement of the Church, however sympathetic and understanding of other cultural values, could not but lead to deep-rooted clashes of loyalty.

The cost of cultural conflict is high. We are not concerned with a cold appraisement of sociological trends. We are concerned with men and women, with the shattering of tribal loyalties and community customs, with the dissolution of age-old family patterns, with the aged, lost and bewildered in unfamiliar ways. The price is paid in loneliness and uprootedness. The tragedy is in the conflict between opposing ways of life, each of which is felt to be good.

Man cannot live as true man in a rootless world. He needs the structure of a society. Taking the word back to its original meaning: Can a culture be cultivated? The manipulators of public opinion, the advertisers and the politicians, are attempting the task; but the fact is that a culture cannot be imposed. It grows. Nevertheless, when a culture is rapidly disintegrating one firm and stable sector may become the nucleus around which a new culture crystallizes. Historically, it may be a determined and disciplined political party. Or it may be a vigorous and vital religious faith. But it may also be that secularism is an essential element of culture in nations which have many religious communities.

All the constituents of a culture come within the realm of the dominion and intention of God, and his servants must claim them for him. 'Can the Christian Church be the nucleus around which will crystallize the culture of tomorrow?' is a question about the present response of man's faith, not a question about the ability of God.

Because Christ is the Light of the World he is not alien to any culture. A faith that is fixed in him, a company of Christian men and women rooted and grounded in him, serving him, in and through him loving God and neighbour, will be perhaps not so much a crystallizing nucleus—which is a cold and inorganic process—as the leaven in the lump which lives and grows and gives life. . . .

The churches are involved with all men in a common historical destiny. As servants of their Servant-Lord Jesus Christ they bring to the nations their obedience to Christ who is the Lord of the nations. They form a society that by its nature transcends political and ideological barriers; but through its members it is also deeply rooted in the life of nations with their political and ideological conflicts. In this situation the Church is called to a ministry of reconciliation, prayer and intercession. The nature of its task will vary according to the degree to which a church can influence the policy of the government of the country. In many places only renewal within the church will make constructive involvement in world affairs possible. Only a profound dedication to responsible world order in the heart of all churches and Christians will be adequate. . . .

We are forced to re-examine Christian service anew when we face world-wide and rapid social change. Some of our Christian forms of service are so dated as to be unfitted for contemporary society. Some are divided according to confessional and institutional lines. Some are too dependent on external help. Some are deficient in the distinctive Christian meaning of service. With humble repentance, accepting the judgement and the forgiveness of God in Christ, we must obey the Holy Spirit as he leads us to renew or extend our present forms of service, and search for new ways of expressing our obedience as the servant Church in the contemporary world. . . .

In a mass society of impersonal relationships, loneliness and frustration and conflict, the individual Christian must surely participate in the ministry of reconciliation. Precisely because government discharges an increasing number of services, we recognize the immense significance of each individual Christian who shares in secular service agencies and in government work by turning what might be impersonal service into truly personal service through a consciousness of the saving presence of Christ. Today qualified laymen have many opportunities to participate in the work of inter-governmental, governmental and private agencies in the less developed areas of the world such as malaria eradication and the Freedom from Hunger Campaign. The churches should encourage this. Moreover, the churches themselves in such areas have many undertakings requiring technically qualified workers, and the churches should seek wherever possible to use such Christian technicians as are available.

All this requires deeper understanding of stewardship in the Church. It should not be narrowly confined but should be seen in the light of total dedication of one's gifts to the glory of God in all spheres of life. More than ever, the churches must help laymen to realize that their responsibility to serve lies in their daily work and to train them accordingly. Signs of renewal can be seen here and there, but there is still much to be done. A Christian does not serve in the world as an isolated individual. He must be supported, guided, and strengthened by the corporate groups. . . .

Natural and social disasters create acute human needs which should be met immediately by the churches acting together. There are also widespread endemic needs, such as poverty, mental and physical diseases, hunger, illiteracy, unemployment and the plight of refugees which demand a maximum response in Christian service. In our time racial discrimination looms large and dangerous, defies the Christian faith, and needs immediate action by all the churches.

In these areas ecumenical demonstrations of inter-church aid are needed and they should be shared by all churches regardless of denominational allegiances. The static distinction of 'receiving church' and 'giving church' must go so that all will share spiritual, material and personal gifts in the light of the total economy of the household of God. . . .

In all this, it must be remembered that the Christian is not a 'philanthropist' and the Church is not a 'benevolent association'. The mark of the serving church is expressed through joy and suffering in Jesus Christ. The Christian Church is a community in which to rejoice with those who rejoice and weep with those who weep in the solidarity given in Jesus Christ. It is a community which is always open for service in and to the world as a living parable of the Kingdom 'until He come'.

APPENDIX III

MEMBER CHURCHES OF THE WORLD COUNCIL OF CHURCHES

(A) *Churches which became members at the inaugural Assembly of the Council in 1948*

AUSTRALASIA
Methodist Church of Australasia

AUSTRALIA
Church of England in Australia and Tasmania
Congregational Union of Australia
Federal Conference of Churches of Christ in Australia
Presbyterian Church of Australia

AUSTRIA
Evangelische Kirche A.u.H.B. in Österreich (Evangelical Church of the Augsburgian and Helvetic Confession)

BELGIUM
Église Chrétienne missionaire belge (Belgian Christian Missionary Church)
Église evangélique protestante de Belgique (Protestant Evangelical Church of Belgium)

BRAZIL
Igreja Metodista do Brasil (Methodist Church of Brazil)

BURMA
Church of India, Burma, and Ceylon[1]
Burma Baptist Convention

CANADA
The Anglican Church of Canada
Churches of Christ (Disciples)
Presbyterian Church in Canada
United Church of Canada
Yearly Meeting of the Society of Friends

CEYLON
Church of India, Burma, and Ceylon[1]

[1] Subsequently named the Church of India, Pakistan, Burma, and Ceylon.

CHINA

China Baptist Council
Chung Hua Chi-Tu Chiao-hui (Church of Christ in China)
Chung Hua Sheng Kung Hui (Anglican)
Hua Pei Kung Li Hui (North China Congregational
    Church)

CZECHOSLOVAKIA

Ceskobratska Cirkev Evangelicka (Evangelical Church of
    Czech Brethren)
Evangelicka Cirkev A.V. na Slovensku (Evangelical
    Church in Slovakia, Augsburgian Confession)
Ref. Cirkev na Slovensku (Reformed Church in Slovakia)

DENMARK

Den Evangelislutherske Folkekirke i Danmark (Church of
    Denmark)

EGYPT

Coptic Orthodox Church
Greek Orthodox Patriarchate of Alexandria

ESTHONIA

Evangelical Church in Esthonia

ETHIOPIA

Ethiopian Orthodox Church

FINLAND

Suomen   Evankelis-Luterilainen   Kirkko   (Evangelical
    Lutheran Church of Finland)

FRANCE

Église de la confession d'Augsbourg d'Alsace et de
    Lorraine (Evangelical Church of the Augsburgian
    Confession in Alsace and Lorraine)
Église evangélique lutherienne de France (Evangelical
    Lutheran Church of France)
Église reformée d'Alsace et de Lorraine (Reformed
    Church of Alsace and Lorraine)
Église reformée de France (Reformed Church of France)

GERMANY

Altkatholische Kirche in Deutschland (Old Catholic
    Church in Germany)
Evangelische Brüder-Unität (Moravian Church)
Evangelische Kirche in Deutschland (Evangelical Church in
    Germany)

(It was agreed by Central Committee that the constituent churches of the Evangelische Kirche be listed as under:

Evangelische Kirche in Berlin-Brandenburg
Pommersche Evangelische Kirche
Evangelische Kirche von Schlesien
Evangelische Kirche der Kirchenprovinz Sachsen
Evangelische Kirche von Westfalen
Evangelische Kirche im Rheinland
Evangelisch-Lutherische Landeskirche Sachsens[1]
Evangelisch-Lutherische Landeskirche Hannovers[1]
Evangelisch-Lutherische Kirche in Bayern[1]
Evangelisch-Lutherische Kirche in Thüringen[1]
Evangelisch-Lutherische Landeskirche Schleswig-Holsteins[1]
Evangelisch-Lutherische Landeskirche im Hamburgischen Staate[1]
Evangelisch-Lutherische Landeskirche Mecklenburgs[1]
Braunschweigische Evangelisch-Lutherische Landeskirche[1]
Evangelisch-Lutherische Kirche in Lübeck[1]
Evangelisch-Lutherische Landeskirche in Schaumburg-Lippe[1]
Evangelisch-Lutherische Landeskirche in Württenberg
Evangelisch-Lutherische Kirche in Oldenburg
Evangelisch-Lutherische Landeskirche Eutin
Evangelische Kirche in Hessen und Nassau
Evangelische Landeskirche in Kurhessen-Waldeck
Evangelische Landeskirche in Baden
Vereinigte Protestantische Kirche der Pfalz
Evangelische Landeskirche Anhalts
Bremische Evangelische Kirche
Evangelisch-Reformierte Kirche in Nordwestdeutschland)
Lippische Landeskirche

[1]This Church is directly a member of the World Council of Churches in accordance with the resolution of the General Synod of the United Evangelical Lutheran Church of Germany, dated 27 January 1949, which recommended that the member churches of the United Evangelical Lutheran Church should make the following declaration to the Council of the Evangelical Church in Germany concerning their relation to the World Council of Churches:

'The Evangelical Church in Germany has made it clear through its constitution that it is a federation (*Bund*) of confessionally determined churches. Moreover, the conditions of membership of the World Council of Churches have been determined at the Assembly at Amsterdam. Therefore, this Evangelical Lutheran Church declares concerning its membership in the World Council of Churches:

(i)   It is represented in the World Council as a church of the Evangelical Lutheran Confession.

(ii) Representatives which it sends to the World Council are to be identified as Evangelical Lutherans.

(iii) Within the limits of the competence of the Evangelical Church of Germany it is represented in the World Council through the intermediary of the Council of the Evangelical Church of Germany.'

Vereinigung der Deutschen Mennonitengemeinden
(Mennonite Church)

GREECE
Ekklesia tes Ellados (Church of Greece)
Greek Evangelical Church

HUNGARY
A Magyarorszagi Evangelikus Egyhaz (Lutheran Church
   of Hungary)
A Magyarorszagi Reformatus Egyhaz (Reformed Church
   of Hungary)

ICELAND
Evangelical Lutheran Church of Iceland

INDIA
Church of India, Burma, and Ceylon[1]
Church of South India
Federation of Evangelical Lutheran Churches in India
Mar Thoma Syrian Church of Malabar
Orthodox Syrian Church of the East
United Church of Northern India[2]

INDONESIA
Geredja Kristen Djawa Wetan (Christian Church in East
   Java)
Geredja Masehi Indjili di Minahasa (Christian Evangelical
   Church in the Minahassa)
Geredja Masehi Indjili Timor (Christian Evangelical
   Church in Timor)
Geredja Protestan Maluku (Protestant Church in the
   Moluccas)
Geredja Protestan di Indonesia (Protestant Church in
   Indonesia)
Huria Kristen Batak Protestant (Protestant Christian
   Batak Church)

ITALY
Chiesa Evangelica Metodista d'Italia (Evangelical
   Methodist Church of Italy)
Chiesa Evangelica Valdese (Waldensian Church)

[1] Subsequently named the Church of India, Pakistan, Burma and Ceylon.
[2] Subsequently named the United Church of Northern India and
Pakistan.

JAPAN
Nippon Kirisuto Kyodan (United Church of Christ in Japan)
Nippon Sei Ko Kwai (Anglican Church in Japan)

JORDAN
Greek Orthodox Patriarchate of Jerusalem

KOREA
Korean Methodist Church
Presbyterian Church of Korea

LEBANON (*see also* SYRIA)
Evangelical Synod of Syria and Lebanon
Union of the Armenian Evangelical Churches in the Near East

LITHUANIA
Reformed Church of Lithuania

MEXICO
Iglesia Metodista de Mejico (Methodist Church of Mexico)

NETHERLANDS
Algemene Doopsgezinde Societeit (General Mennonite Society)
Bond van Vrije Evangelische Gemeenten in Nederland (Union of Free Evangelical Congregations)
Evangelisch Lutherse Kerk (Evangelical Lutheran Church)
Nederlands Hervormde Kerk (Dutch Reformed Church)
Oud-Katholieke Kerk (Old Catholic Church)
Remonstrantse Broederschap (Arminian Church)
Unie van Baptisten Gemeenten in Nederland (Union of Baptist Congregations)

NEW ZEALAND
Associated Churches of Christ in New Zealand
Baptist Union of New Zealand
Church of the Province of New Zealand
Congregational Union of New Zealand
Methodist Church of New Zealand
Presbyterian Church of New Zealand

NORWAY
Norske Kirke (Church of Norway)

PAKISTAN
Church of India, Pakistan, Burma and Ceylon (formerly Church of India, Burma and Ceylon)

PHILIPPINE ISLANDS
United Church of Christ in the Philippines

POLAND
Kosciol Ewangelicko-Augsburski w Polsce (Evangelical
Church of the Augsburgian Confession)
Polski Narodoway Kosciol Katolicki (Catholic Church of
Poland)

RUMANIA
Biserica Lutherana Ungara din Romania (Hungarian
Lutheran Church in Rumania)
Biserica Protestanta Evangelica din Romania dupa
Confesiunea dela Augsburg (Protestant Evangelical
Church Augsburgian Confession)
Biserica Reformata din Romania (Transylvanian Reformed
Church)

SIAM (THAILAND)
Church of Christ in Siam (Thailand)

SOUTH AFRICA
Church of the Province of South Africa
Congregational Union of South Africa
Methodist Church of South Africa
Nederduits Gereformeerde Kerk van Transvaal (Dutch
Reformed Church of Transvaal)[1]
Nerderduits Hervormde Kerk van Afrika (Dutch Reformed
Church of Africa)[1]
Presbyterian Church of South Africa

SPAIN
Iglesia Evangelica Española (Spanish Evangelical Church)

SWEDEN
Svenska Kyrkan (Church of Sweden)
Svenska Missionsförbundet (Mission Covenant Church
of Sweden)

SWITZERLAND
Christkatholische Kirche der Schweiz (Old Catholic
Church)
Schweizerischer Evangelischer Kirchenbund–Federation
des Églises protestantes de la Suisse (Swiss Protestant
Church Federation)

SYRIA (see also LEBANON)
Greek Orthodox Patriarchate of Antioch
Evangelical Synod of Syria and Lebanon

[1]These churches withdrew from the World Council, 1961.

TURKEY
Ecumenical Patriarchate of Constantinople

UNITED KINGDOM AND EIRE
Baptist Union of Great Britian and Ireland
Churches of Christ in Great Britain and Ireland
Church of England
Church of Ireland
Church of Scotland
Church in Wales
Congregational Union of England and Wales
Congregational Union of Scotland
Episcopal Church in Scotland
Methodist Church
Methodist Church in Ireland
Presbyterian Church of England
Presbyterian Church in Ireland
Presbyterian Church of Wales
Salvation Army
United Free Church of Scotland

UNITED STATES OF AMERICA
African Methodist Episcopal Church
African Methodist Episcopal Zion Church
American Lutheran Church
Augustana Evangelical Lutheran Church[1]
Church of the Brethren
Coloured Methodist Episcopal Church (now Christian
    Methodist Episcopal Church)
Congregational Christian Churches of the United States
    of America[2]
Danish Evangelical Lutheran Church[3]
Evangelical and Reformed Church[2]
Evangelical United Brethren Church
International Convention of Christian Churches (Disciples
    of Christ)
Methodist Church
Moravian Church in America (Northern Province)
National Baptist Convention, U.S.A., Inc.
Northern Baptist Convention[4]

[1]Now part of Lutheran Church in America.
[2]Now part of the United Church of Christ.
[3]Now part of United Evangelical Lutheran Church.
[4]Now American Baptist Convention.

Polish National Catholic Church of America
Presbyterian Church in the U.S.
Presbyterian Church in the United States of America[1]
Protestant Episcopal Church
Reformed Church in America
Religious Society of Friends
    Five Years' Meeting of Friends
    General Conference of the Society of Friends
Romanian Orthodox Episcopate of America
Seventh Day Baptist General Conference
Syrian Antiochian Orthodox Archdiocese
United Evangelical Lutheran Church[2]
United Lutheran Church in America[3]
United Presbyterian Church[1]

WEST INDIES
Church of the Province of the West Indies

YUGOSLAVIA
Reformed Christian Church of Yugoslavia

(B) *Churches which became members 1948-60*

ARGENTINA
Sinodo Evangelico Aleman del Rio de la Plata

BRAZIL
Federacao Sinodal, Igréja Evangélica de Confisão Lutherana do Brasil (Synodal Federation, Evangelical Church of Lutheran Confession in Brazil)

CAMEROUN
Église Évangelique du Cameroun

CENTRAL AFRICA
Church of the Province of Central Africa

CEYLON
Methodist Church in Ceylon

CYPRUS
Church of Cyprus

CZECHOSLOVAKIA
Slezska Cirkev Evangelicka A.V. (Evangelical Church of the Augsburgian Confession in Silesia)

[1]Now United Presbyterian Church in the U.S.A.
[2]Now part of American Lutheran Church.
[3]Now part of Lutheran Church in America.

DENMARK
Baptist Union of Denmark

EAST AFRICA
Church of the Province of East Africa
Presbyterian Church of East Africa

FORMOSA
Tai-oan Ki-tok Tiu-lo Kau-hoe (Presbyterian Church in Formosa)

GHANA
Methodist Church
Presbyterian Church of Ghana

HUNGARY
Baptist Church of Hungary

INDONESIA
Geredja Kalimantan Evangelis (Evangelical Church in Kalimantan)
Geredja Kristen Sulawesi Tengah (Christian Church in Mid-Sulawesi)
Geredja Geredja Kristen di Djawa Tengah (Christian Churches in Mid-Java)
Geredja Kristen Pasundan (Sundanese Christian Church of West Java)
Geredja Gereformeerd di Indonesia (Reformed Church in Indonesia)

IRAN
Synod of the Evangelical Churches of North Iran

JAMAICA
Presbyterian Church of Jamaica

KOREA
Presbyterian Church in the Republic of Korea

MADAGASCAR
Église Evangélique de Madagascar
Church of Christ in Madagascar (formerly London Missionary Society Synod)

PHILIPPINE ISLANDS
Iglesia Catolica Filipino Independiente (Philippine Independent Church)

SOUTH AFRICA
Bantu Presbyterian Church of South Africa

Ned. Gereformeerde Kerk van de Kaap Provinsie (Dutch
  Reformed Church of South Africa of the Cape Province)[1]

SYRIA
Syrian Orthodox Patriarchate of Antioch and all the East

TOGO
Église Evangélique de Togo

UNITED KINGDOM AND EIRE
Moravian Church in Great Britain and Ireland

UNITED STATES OF AMERICA
American Evangelical Lutheran Church[2]
Evangelical Lutheran Church, U.S.A.[3]
Church of the East (Assyrian)
Hungarian Reformed Church in America
Moravian Church in America (Southern Province)
National Baptist Convention of America
Russian Orthodox Greek Catholic Church of North
  America

WEST AFRICA
Church of the Province of West Africa

(C) *Churches admitted to membership at the Third Assembly, New Delhi, 1961*

BULGARIA
Église Orthodoxe de Bulgarie (Bulgarian Orthodox
  Church)

CAMEROONS
Presbyterian Church in West Cameroon

CAMEROUN
Union des Églises Baptistes du Cameroun (Union of
  Baptist Churches of Cameroun)

CHILE
Iglesia Pentecostal de Chile (Pentecostal Church of Chile)
Mision Iglesia Pentecostal (Chile)

CONGO
Église Évangélique Manianga Matadi (Manianga Matadi
  Evangelical Church)

GABON
Église Évangélique du Gabon (Evangelical Church of
  Gabon)

[1] This church withdrew from the W.C.C. in 1961.
[2] Now part of Lutheran Church in America.
[3] Now part of American Lutheran Church.

NEW CALEDONIA
Église Évangélique en Nouvelle-Calédonie et aux Iles Loyauté (Evangelical Church in New Caledonia and the Loyalty Islands)

NEW HEBRIDES
Presbyterian Church of the New Hebrides

NIGERIA
Presbyterian Church of Nigeria

PAKISTAN
United Presbyterian Church of Pakistan

POLAND
Église Autocéphale Orthodoxe en Pologne (Orthodox Church of Poland)

RHODESIA
The United Church of Central Africa in Rhodesia

RUMANIA
Biserica Ortodoxa Romane (Rumanian Orthodox Church)

SAMOA
Congregational Christian Church in Samoa (Samoan Church, London Missionary Society)

SOUTH AFRICA
Bantu Congregational Church in South Africa
Moravian Church in the Western Cape Province

TANGANYIKA
Evangelical Church of North Western Tanganyika
Usambara-Digo Lutheran Church

TRINIDAD
Presbyterian Church in Trinidad

UGANDA AND RUANDA URUNDI
Church of the Province of Uganda and Ruanda Urundi

UNITED STATES
Suomi Synod—Finnish Evangelical Lutheran Church of America[1]

U.S.S.R.
Orthodox Church of Russia, Patriarchate of Moscow

[1]Now part of the Lutheran Church in America

(D) *Churches admitted to membership in August 1962*

Union of Evangelical Christian Baptists of USSR
Georgian Orthodox Church, USSR
Estonian Lutheran Church
Evangelical Lutheran Church of Latvia

Armenian Apostolic Church—Catholicosate of Etchmiadzin
Armenian Apostolic Church—Catholicosate of Cilicia
Evangelical Lutheran Church in Southern Africa—South East
    Region

APPENDIX IV

(A) *Former Member Councils of the International Missionary Council*

With the exception of the Norsk Misjonsrad, all these councils are now affiliated to the Commission on World Mission and Evangelism.

AUSTRALIA
National Missionary Council of Australia

BELGIUM
Société Belge de Missions Protestantes au Congo

BRAZIL
Confederação Evangélica do Brasil

CANADA
Canadian Council of Churches, Department of Overseas Missions

CEYLON
National Christian Council of Ceylon

CHINA
National Christian Council of China

CUBA
Council of Evangelical Churches

DENMARK
Dansk Missionsraad

FINLAND
Suomen Lähetysneuvosto

FRANCE
Société des Missions Evangéliques de Paris

GERMANY
Deutscher Evangelischer Missionsrat

GHANA
Christian Council of Ghana

GREAT BRITAIN
Conference of Missionary Societies in Great Britain and Ireland

HONG KONG
Hong Kong Christian Council

INDIA
   National Christian Council of India

INDONESIA
   National Council of Churches in Indonesia

JAMAICA
   Jamaica Christian Council

JAPAN
   National Christian Council of Japan

KOREA
   National Christian Council of Korea

MADAGASCAR
   Conseil des Églises

MALAYA
   Malaya Christian Council

MEXICO
   Concilio Evangélico de Mexico

NEAR EAST
   Near East Christian Council

NETHERLANDS
   Nederlandsche Zendings-Raad

NEW ZEALAND
   Commission on Overseas Missions and Inter-Church Aid
      of the National Council of Churches in New Zealand

NORTHERN RHODESIA
   Christian Council of Northern Rhodesia

NORWAY
   Norsk Misjonsråd

PAKISTAN
   All-Pakistan Christian Council

PHILIPPINES
   Philippine Federation of Christian Churches

PUERTO RICO
   Concilio Evangélico de Puerto Rico

RIVER PLATE
   Confederación de Iglesias Evangélicas del Rio de la Plata
      (Argentina, Paraguay, Uruguay)

SIERRA LEONE
   United Christian Council of Sierra Leone

SOUTH AFRICA
Christian Council of South Africa

SOUTHERN RHODESIA
Southern Rhodesia Christian Conference

SWEDEN
Svenska Missionsrådet

SWITZERLAND
{ Schweizerischer Evangelischer Missionsrat
{ Conseil Suisse des Missions Evangéliques

THAILAND
National Christian Council of Thailand

UNITED STATES
Division of Foreign Missions, National Council of the
Churches of Christ in the U.S.A.

(B) *National Councils associated with the World Council of Churches*

Australian Council for the World Council of Churches
Ecumenical Council of Churches in Austria
British Council of Churches
Burma Christian Council
Canadian Council of Churches
Ecumenical Council of Churches in Czechoslovakia
Danish Ecumenical Council
Ecumenical Council of Finland
Arbeitsgemeinschaft christlicher Kirchen in Deutschland
Hungarian Ecumenical Council
National Christian Council of India
National Council of Churches in Indonesia
National Christian Council of Japan
Ecumenical Council of Churches in the Netherlands
National Council of Churches in New Zealand
Philippine Federation of Christian Churches
Ecumenical Council of the Churches of Poland
Swedish Ecumenical Council
National Council of the Churches of Christ in the U.S.A.

APPENDIX V

SOME ILLUSTRATIVE STATISTICS

Precise statistics of the Christian movement on the world scale are hard to find. It is not only that there are significant areas in which there is no regular compilation of figures. Even where these are maintained, the bases of computation vary. The term 'church member', for example, may be applied to all baptized members or it may be used only of baptized communicant members. The phrase 'Christian community' may also be used with various shades of meaning, though it *generally* covers baptized children and adults, with 'adherents'. A careful attempt to secure accuracy in this field is made by the Editors of the *World Christian Handbook* (published by the World Dominion Press), a new edition of which is in course of preparation. Other source books are the *Statesman's Year Book*, *The Encyclopaedia Britannica Book of the Year*, and other standard annuals such as *Whitaker's Almanack* and the New York Telegram's *World Almanack*. The following samples, while subject to all the usual contingencies, may serve as a reasonably reliable set of illustrations:

Communicant Members

United Kingdom:

Church of England	c. 3,000,000
Church of Scotland	1,400,000
Methodist Church	750,000
Baptist Union	250,000
Congregational Union	220,000
Presbyterian Church of England	70,000
Evangelical Church in Germany	8,000,000
Reformed Church of France	195,000
Evangelical Church of the Greek Brethren	87,000
Reformed Church of Hungary	1,000,000
Presbyterian Church of Ghana	37,000
Church of South India	350,000
Kyodan, Japan	170,000

United States of America:
National Baptist Convention	4,500,000
Southern Baptist Convention	9,000,000
Methodist Church	9,500,000
Presbyterian Church in the U.S.A.	2,600,000
United Lutheran Church in America	2,000,000

World Estimates

Total Population—2,600,000,000

Christians:
Roman Catholic	500,000,000
Eastern Orthodox	130,000,000
Protestant	210,000,000
	840,000,000

Jews	12,000,000
Moslems	420,000,000
Buddhists	150,000,000
Hindus	300,000,000

INDEX